How to
WRITE YOUR OWN
PSION SERIES 3a PROGRAMS

The Complete Beginner's Guide

Other Psion Series 3a books published by Capall Bann:

Useful Programs for the Psion Series 3a. *Mike Shaw*
Using the Psion Series 3a. *Bill Aitken*

More titles covering the Psion Series 3a are in preparation.
Contact Capall Bann for the latest information

How to

WRITE YOUR OWN PSION SERIES 3A PROGRAMS

The Complete Beginner's Guide

Mike Shaw

"The power is in your hands..."

PUBLISHED BY
Capall Bann Publishing

First Published 1995

Capall Bann Publishing
Freshfields, Chieveley,
Berks, RG16 8TF

Wecome to the world of programming

I f you have never tried your hand at programming it's probably because you consider the task too difficult and beyond your capabilities. Which is a pity, because it isn't. Being able to program means you can create an infinite variety of additional facilities for your Psion Series 3a, from simply calculating the number of days between any two dates, to managing Club accounts and membership lists, from calculating how much wallpaper is needed to paper a room (given its dimensions) to stock control ... facilities to help do exactly what *you* want.

Writing simple programs is neither difficult nor beyond the capabilities of the majority - particularly where the Psion Series 3a is concerned, since it has a very 'English' programming language built in. It is far easier to learn the Series 3a programming language than it is to learn a foreign language - there are far fewer 'strange' words to assimilate (only about 250 altogether, of which only a handful are needed to get started), and the 'rules' are strict with virtually no exceptions to remember.

The Psion Series 3a is, of course, an extremely powerful and versatile computer, capable of tackling a myriad of tasks - far more than those already built in or can be bought 'off the shelf'.

This book gently leads complete beginners through the process of creating programs, from how to type them in through to writing comprehensive applications that can be installed on the system menu. Numerous example programs are provided to demonstrate the use of the language and techniques under discussion. *If you are an absolute beginner, it is recommended that you start at Chapter 1 and work your way through the book: by the end, you will be writing programs to meet your personal needs, confidently and competently.*

If you already have some programming experience in other 'high level' languages - such as Basic or Pascal - this book will introduce you to the structures and techniques of the Series 3a's programming language, OPL, and will be an invaluable source of reference for tapping into the very powerful graphics capabilities, which include menus, dialogs and windows.

For experienced programmers, this book will serve as an introduction to the high level aspects of the programming language.

A companion book to this one, "Useful Utilities for the Psion Series 3a" (also published by Capall Bann) provides listings for ten programs together with explanations of how they 'work'. The programs range from a biorhythm plotter to a bank account management system, and include an icon drawing program for those who wish to create system screen icons for their own applications. Entering programs that others have written is a useful way of extending programming knowledge.

Writing your own routines is an enjoyable and satisfying experience, rewarded by the addition of personalised facilities that make your Psion Series 3a even more useful.

By buying this book, that experience has already started...

Get to it!

Mike Shaw
September 1995

Contents

PART 3   Files and data handling

PART 4   Advanced topics

Appendices

PART 1

The Basics

In this Part of the book, you will be introduced to the principles of programming, and how to use the basic elements of the OPL language to create your own utilities and applications.

The Basics

CHAPTER 1
How it works

*This Chapter introduces you to the concept of computers
and how they work. It will give you a broad understanding
of*

- *A computer's structure*
- *How information is stored*
- *The binary system*
- *How Series 3a operates*

Why do you need to know?

When writing your own utilities and applications (programs) for a
computer, it is helpful to have a broad understanding of how the
machine works. Insight into what goes on when the applications are run
helps to explain in part why some things have to be done in a certain
way. Consequently, a brief description is given here as the first step in
learning to program your Series 3a: this description is presented in
general terms rather than the actual technicalities, to make it easier to
follow. If you have an understanding of the way computers work and
handle information, you may skip this Chapter completely. Otherwise, a
few minutes reading through it will be time well spent...

The core of the computer

The nerve centre of any computer is complex piece of circuitry known
as the Central Processing Unit, or CPU for short. Practically everything
that happens in the computer is under its control.   Unlike most
computers, the CPU inside the Series 3a is active as long as power is
available - even when the machine is 'switched off'.   It needs to be
active to maintain the internal clock, for example, and to check for
things like an alarm that you may have set.   The CPU works very fast
indeed - performing thousands of actions every second, and it is capable
of managing a variety of operations effectively at the same time. This
process is called 'multi-tasking'. The only time the CPU stops work is
when there is no power supply at all (i.e. when both the AA batteries

and the back-up lithium cell are removed from the Series 3a, and there is no mains power connected).

Computers must remember

The second most important part of any computer is its memory: all the instructions to make it work, and all the information you wish to keep and use must be stored so that it is available to the CPU for action. The memory can be likened to a 'warehouse' full of boxes - thousands upon thousands of them. Each box has an individual 'address', rather like the houses in a street. This address enables the CPU to locate the contents of a box as and when the need arises.

The memory boxes are used to store the instructions and information for the running of the computer, and to store all the data you wish to keep.

Two slots on the Series 3a cater for additional storage space to be 'plugged in', using Solid State Disks. These storage areas can be changed at will, whereas the storage space *inside* the Series 3a is always available. There are two distinct types of storage box within the Series 3a: these will be explained later.

Keeping in touch

A computer would be absolutely useless if you had no way to communicate with it, or if it had no way to communicate with you.

Broadly speaking, your instructions are communicated to the CPU through the keyboard. The CPU always keeps a close watch on what happens at the keyboard. Tap one of the 'icon' keys for a specific application - such as the Word processor - and all the instructions associated with that application are then 'lined up', ready for the CPU to take further action.

In the main, the CPU communicates with you through the screen. If you ever get stuck over what to do when using your Psion Series 3a, pressing the HELP key will have the CPU jumping into action to provide useful hints and guidance on the screen.

If the Series 3a is 'switched off' - so that the screen is not active, the CPU can attract your attention by making noises on the loudspeaker. For example, you may have requested an alarm call to remind yourself about an impending appointment: at the appropriate time the CPU will attract your attention through the loudspeaker. Switching on, the appropriate message is then displayed on the screen.

To achieve these and similar activities, the CPU has to keep in constant touch with other components in the computer - a master counting system or 'clock', for example. However, these other components need not concern you. It is sufficient to know that when you communicate with the CPU, it must understand your requirement. It doesn't have human intelligence, and so can only understand the precise instructions built into it. Fortunately, you don't need any knowledge of those instructions ... until you wish to create some of your own instructions (*programming*), and even then, an 'intermediate' stage enables you to write the instructions in a language both you and the computer can understand.

How the memory stores information

Let's now take a closer look at the computer's memory boxes, because it is quite important when programming that you appreciate just how information is stored.

Essentially, there are two types of memory box in a computer: the first type can be examined to see what's there, and it can be 'read' or a copy taken of the information it contains, but the information cannot be changed. It's rather like the information on a printed page: you can read it, and copy it, but you can't change it. This type of box is called *Read Only Memory*, or ROM. The instructions and information for running your Series 3a are contained inside boxes of this type. They *don't* need any power supply to retain the information they contain, and since you cannot change anything, your Series 3a will always be able to run the programs or 'software' that has been built into it by 'looking at' the information in these boxes. Even if it has been without batteries for a long time, when batteries are refitted, the Series 3a will be once again ready with all of its built in applications.

The second type of box is far more interesting to us, because the information it contains *can* be changed. It is rather like a blackboard: you can chalk things on it for reading or copying, and you can rub the information out and replace it with new information. Our programs and data are held in boxes of this type: we can 'write' information into a box, we can look at it or 'read' it, and we can change it or clear it out altogether. Collectively, boxes of this type go by the name *Random Access Memory*, or RAM for short.

This type of box needs a power supply to keep it active. No power supply, no information. It's as simple as that. That's why the Series 3a has a back-up lithium cell: if ever the main batteries fail, or you're changing them, the lithium cell keeps all the RAM boxes 'alive' until the batteries are re-installed. Providing you don't take longer than a few months...

The way these boxes operate is in many respects similar to the cassette tape in your recorder. Each time you record ('write') new information to the tape, you first erase what was there before. The same is true in these boxes - when new information goes in, the old information is lost. But this is no more of a problem than re-using a cassette tape: in fact in a computer there's less likelihood of making a mistake and recording over wanted information.

What's in the memory boxes?

It is fairly important to understand the way information is stored inside the boxes, particularly those that we can change. It would be rather nice to think that a box contains a specific 'chunk' of information, such as a complete address, or a shopping list.

Unfortunately, it doesn't. It doesn't even contain one word. In fact all that the box can contain is a number from 0 to 255 inclusive. That's 256 numbers in all, if you count zero. What's more, the number in the box can represent an instruction or part of an instruction, it can represent a *character*, such as the letter 'A' or the figure '2', or it can represent an actual *value* in real terms, that is, a number that can be used for mathematical operations such as adding or multiplying.

Here's the first important thing to note: as far as the computer is concerned a character '2' is quite different from a value '2'. To the computer, characters are just shapes that we humans use to communicate with each other. So a character '2' is just a shape. Values on the other hand are bits of information the computer can use for any mathematical operation you care to throw at it.

On the face of it, things are starting to look very complicated indeed - here we have a box that can contain a number from 0 to 255, and that number can represent an instruction, a character or a value: how on earth are you supposed to know which it is? The answer is, you don't have to know, most of the time, because the computer sorts it out for you. The only time you need to be concerned about what's going into the boxes is when you use 'variables' when writing programs, and at this point in time, you don't even have to worry about what a variable is.

The other question that has probably crossed your mind is 'if a box can only store a value up to 255, how are larger values stored?' The simple answer is that boxes are used in combination.

The more complicated answer starts with the fact that numbers are stored in computers using the *binary* system - that's a numbering system which has just two digits - a zero and a 'one'. Many people are unnecessarily frightened by the thought of a system that doesn't have any numbers in it other than a '0' and a '1'. You don't have to know anything at all about the binary system unless or until you want to get really deep into programming, so you can skip this next bit if you wish: on the other hand, why not dip in and see how easy it is?

Counting the binary way

In our normal, every day life, we use the *decimal* system of counting. The decimal system has ten different digits - '0' through to '9'. Yes, in this context, '0' is a digit. If you start counting from zero, when you get to '9' you'll have run out of different digits - the *symbols* that represent values. So you add '1' to the column to the left - increasing it from '0' to '1', and start again. You can now count from 10 to 19. And so the process goes on until you get to 99 - then you move to the next column to the left, and so on.

Each *column* in the decimal counting system has ten values - from 0 to 9. You're so used to it, you probably don't even think about how it works. But given a number such as '352', for example, you'll know immediately that this means '3 hundreds, plus 5 tens, plus 2 units'. That's because the right column represents units, the middle column represents tens, and left column represents hundreds.

Now, what happens if there's only '0' and a '1' to play around with? The highest you can count up to is '1', *unless* you use the same technique as when counting in the decimal system - add 'one' to the column to the left. So, counting this way in binary, you get

	0	(0 in the decimal system)
	1	(1 in the decimal system)
(add one to left)	**10**	(**2** in the decimal system)
	11	(3 in the decimal system)
(add one to left)	**100**	(**4** in the decimal system)
	101	(5 in the decimal system)
	110	(6 in the decimal system)
	111	(7 in the decimal system)
(add one to left)	**1000**	(**8** in the decimal system)

7

You can see that it works just the same as the decimal system - add one to the next left column when you've run out of numbers, then start counting up again from 0. Trouble is, these binary numbers look gibberish to us mortals who are more used to the decimal system. But there is an easy way to work out what the binary number is in decimal terms.

Take a look at the *binary* equivalents of the decimal numbers 1, 2, 4 and 8. They are 1, 10, 100, and 1000 respectively. And you can be assured that 16 is 10000 in binary and 32 is 100000. In other words, whereas in the decimal system each column to the left is another multiple of *ten* (10, 100, 1000, 10000), in the binary system each column to the left represents another multiple of *2* (2, 4, 8, 16, 32). Take for example the binary number '100001'. This has a '1' in both the '32' position and in the units position, so the decimal equivalent is '32+1', or 33. Similarly, the binary number '110010' is '32+16+2', or 50 in decimal.

Basically, that's all there is to the binary system. The reason it is used in computers is that it is very easy to have devices with two states (on or off, magnetised or not magnetised), but not so easy to have devices with more states. Inside each of our storage boxes, there are, in effect, eight 'switches' which can be either 'on' or 'off'. If 'on' they represent a '1', and if 'off' they represent a '0'. With eight switches, to represent eight 'columns' of binary numbers, you can count all the way up to 11111111 - which in decimal, is '128+64+32+16+8+4+2+1', or the number 255. Voila!

By taking *two* boxes at a time, you can count all the way up to 1111111111111111 in binary, which is 65535 in decimal. What about numbers that are even larger, or negative, or maybe have a decimal point in them somewhere (such as 56.7)? They're stored using a different technique: you don't need to know!

Just to finish off this little discussion, each of the eight 'switches' inside a memory box is known as a *bit* (short for *B*inary dig*IT*), and eight *bits* together- one 'box-full' - are known as a *byte*. And just so that you are aware of it, whereas 'k' in the decimal system stands for '1000', in the world of computers, 'k' stands for 1024. So a memory of 1kbyte actually means 1024 memory boxes.

How characters are stored

If a box can only store a number from 0 to 255, how on earth does it hold a *character* like the letter 'A'? That's where another department inside the computer comes in, which is rather like a *picture gallery*. Most of the time, the CPU is clever enough to know (or to be able to work out) when the contents of a box are meant to be a character. The picture gallery has a collection of shapes - character patterns - and each shape is numbered for reference.

So when a number in a memory box is meant to be a *character* the CPU looks up the associated pattern in the 'picture gallery'. For example, the character 'A' has the 'reference number' of 65. If the Psion Series 3a finds the value '65' in a memory box, which it knows is meant to be a *character*, it pops along to the picture gallery, and 'looks up' the shape that corresponds to '65'. When displayed on the screen, you'll recognise this pattern as the character 'A'. Later on, you will be able to write a little program that will let you see the character patterns associated with most of the 255 numbers a box can hold: some numbers are actually used as very special 'instructions', like 'start a new line on the screen or printer', or 'bleep the loudspeaker'.

How values are stored

If you read the paragraphs on the binary system, you'll know that two boxes together can save numbers up to 65 thousand odd. In practice, the range goes from -32768 to +32767 (one of the 'bits' is used to indicate minus or plus). These are all whole numbers, called *integers*: they have no decimal point. By using two more boxes (four in all), larger *integer* values in the range -2147483648 to +2147483647 can be stored. Later on, you'll see how to tell the computer when you want the boxes to be used for these larger values (called *long integers*) instead of ordinary integers.

Of course, these values are fine as far as they go, but what about values with a decimal point in them, such as 4.5? Well, these are stored quite differently, using more boxes and a system that you don't have to worry about (sighs of relief): all you *do* have to remember when programming is to tell the computer when you want the boxes to store a number with a decimal point in it, and as you'll see, that is very easy indeed. So don't panic.

As a matter of interest, values with a decimal point in them are called *floating point* numbers, the 'floating' bit meaning that the decimal point can be anywhere you like. The range of floating point values that can be stored is truly astronomical - far larger than you'll ever need.

How instructions are obeyed

At the CPU level, computer instructions are really just a series of numbers: each number, or rather series of numbers, is an instruction to perform some task or other. To program a computer using just these numbers is a very difficult task - so much so that, even for professional programmers, alternative ways are devised to convert what's wanted into the numbers that the computer CPU can understand. These 'ways' are the *programming languages.* Fortunately for us, OPL, the language built into Series 3a to allow you to create your own programs, is very 'English', and, once you get the hang of it, very easy to understand and use.

But, given that the CPU only accepts 'numbers' as instructions, how does it work? First of all, it must be stated that each group of numbers represents the simplest of instructions. One instruction, for example, would be *'Go to a memory box, and copy whatever number you find there into another box'*, with the addresses of the boxes concerned forming part of the instruction group of numbers.

All the instructions for running the Series 3a's built in applications are contained in memory boxes of the 'read-only' type (ROM). There's hundreds of thousands of them - the Series 3a is capable of doing quite a lot!

Inside the CPU, there is a 'meter' which is called 'The Program Counter'. It is set to the address of the box containing the start of the next instruction to be dealt with. When Series 3a is powered up for the very first time, the CPU jumps into action, looks at the Program Counter meter, sees a '0' (it resets to zero when there is no power at all), and immediately has a look at the first instruction which starts at Box '0'. The CPU examines the instruction, obeys it, and re-adjusts the Program Counter to the *address* of the start of the next instruction. It then examines and obeys that instruction, and so on. It is capable of obeying thousands of instructions every second.

Once a power supply is installed, the CPU is continually active, even though nothing may be appearing on the screen. Much of what it does goes on in the background, or behind the scenes. For example, tucked away in the computer is a counting device, like a clock, which counts hundreds of thousands of times a second at a very precise rate. The CPU keeps a close watch on this device, and every time a particular value is reached, it jumps into action to perform its 'background' duties. These could include things like checking to see whether it's time to ring an alarm to let you know about an appointment, or more simply to add another second to the clock display, or to check whether anything has happened at the keyboard recently and, if not, to save power by closing down the display - automatically 'switching off'. The CPU is, in fact, capable sharing its time between a number of specific duties - including the tasks we give it as well as those that go on in the background.

As you will see when you come to program your Series 3a, instructions can run around in loops. For example, when Series 3a is switched off, the instructions will be saying to the CPU something like '*Go and see whether the* ON *key has been pressed*'. The next instruction will be saying '*If it has, go do what's necessary to switch-on* (jump to instruction so-and-so - achieved by setting the Program Counter to a new value). *But if it hasn't, then go back to the last instruction, which says Go and see if the* ON *key ...*'. Loops, and the ability to branch off according to the results of a test, are very common in programming.

And that's all you really need to know about the way a computer works.

A CPU, where all the action takes place

11

CHAPTER 2
Let's get started!

At the end of this Chapter you will know how to
* *Start and name a new program.*
* *Enter a program.*
* *Handle syntax errors.*
* *Run a program.*
* *Load a program file for editing.*
* *Copy and rename files and programs.*
* *Delete a source or program file.*

The mechanics of programming

Let's get those itchy fingers working to show that learning to program is really quite an easy process. We'll start by looking at how programs are put together, then we'll enter a very simple program, run it, and see how it works. We will then discuss how to run it from the main System screen, how to edit it, and how to delete it.

The main objective of this Chapter is the actual *mechanics* of using Series 3a to write and edit programs. Follow the discussion and instructions given carefully, so that you become familiar with the processes involved.

How a program is constructed

The first thing to understand is the way that a program is put together on the Series 3a.

A complete program is made up of one or more *procedures*. A procedure is a programming unit that performs a distinct action. It may be the entire program, or just a part of a program, that is to say, one of a series of procedures that together perform the overall requirement. Every procedure *always* starts with the word PROC, and *always* ends with the word ENDP.

A number of procedures can be written, one after the other, and saved as one *file*. All the procedures in one file could, together, form one complete program. However, a program need not be completely contained in one file: there are occasions when it is more convenient to use several files, one of which contains a 'library' of often used routines.

Each *procedure* must have a name, and each *file* must have a name. Generally speaking, you'll use the same name for the file and for the *first* procedure in that file, though this is not necessary. The *file* name is the one that will appear under the first OPL icon, so you will usually give it a name that reflects the overall function of the program. *Procedure* names, on the other hand, should reflect the operation of that particular piece of the program. Consequently you will name *procedures* and *files* according to what they do, so that you will be able to remember them.

To summarise:

1. A *file* can contain one or more *procedures*.
2. A *program* can consist of one or more procedures, and could comprise one or more *files*.

We will start with *single* procedure (and hence, *single* file) programs, so that you become familiar with the concept. Later on in the book, we will deal with programs that consist of two or more procedures contained in one module. We will then deal with multi-procedure Modules.

Starting a new program
First, here are the steps you'll take every time you want to start a new program.

1. Select the first OPL icon on the screen (shown here) using the arrow keys.
2. Press the MENU button.
3. Select the 'File' option from the list at the top of the screen, and then select the **New file** option from the list that 'drops down' (use the arrow keys to highlight an option, and press ENTER to 'select' it).

A *'Dialog'* box will appear. You now have to name the program file. **The name must always start with a letter, can include numbers after that, if you want, must never be more than eight characters long, and must not include a space.**

We'll call this first program 'MYFIRST', so type in MYFIRST as the File Name. You'll see another option in this Dialog box - 'Disk'. Unless you have a RAM SSD fitted, make sure that 'Disk' is set to 'Internal': programs should be developed using RAM memory (which can be overwritten), since they get changed frequently during

13

development and you will want to recoup the memory. Use the up and down arrow keys to select the Disk option, and the left and right arrow keys to change it to 'Internal' if necessary. Then press the ENTER button.

The screen will clear, and you will see 'PROC :' on the top line, and spaced below it, the word ENDP. Our program (a single procedure) will be written between these two lines.

Note: You are now in the Program Editor, which is similar to the Series 3a's Word processor. For ease of reading your programs, set the character widths to 'Monospaced': you'll find this option by pressing the MENU key, selecting Special, then Set Preferences. Monospacing makes all characters, including spaces, the same width and easier to check against the listings in this book. You may also wish to set Tabs, Spaces and Carriage returns to 'Yes' so that they can be seen. The *Indentation* option on the *Prog* menu item allows you to set the number of spaces indented when the tab key is pressed. Having *Auto-indent* set to *Yes* will help to make programs easier to read. Remember, too, you can 'zoom' in and out using the PSION and Z keys to show more or less text at a time.

You must now name the *procedure*, and this is done by entering the name *after* the word PROC and *before* the colon (the cursor - that flashing line - should be in position ready for you). We will give this procedure the same name as the module, so type in 'MYFIRST' **but *don't* press** ENTER: instead, press the down arrow key. Pressing ENTER will cause the colon to go down to the next line - which is not what is wanted. Your screen should now look something like this

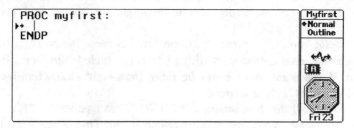

with the *cursor* flashing after the tab symbol on the second line. Remember that every procedure must have the word PROC (which stands for PROCedure) followed by the procedure's name and a colon as the first line, and must end with the word ENDP, (which stands for END Procedure). This is so that both you and the Series 3a know what the procedure is called, and where it begins and ends.

> **Note:** Refer to the Word processing part of your User's Manual for details on how to use the various keys on the keyboard to enter and edit text.

You are now ready to start entering the program. Type in, paying particular attention to the quote marks:

```
PRINT "Hey look! I can program!"
```

followed by the ENTER key. The line you have just entered is a program *statement*, or an instruction to Series 3a to do something. To help you identify the OPL language words when entering programs, they are written in monospaced CAPITAL letters. In practice, these can be entered as small letters if you wish, but it won't be so easy to distinguish the OPL words when examining your programs.

The cursor should be on the next line down and indented, so now enter each of the following lines the same way, remembering to press the ENTER key after each line. Pressing ENTER tells Series 3a that one statement has been completed - and it will also position the cursor on the next line for you, already indented. (*From now on, it will be assumed that you press the* ENTER *key at the end of each program line*).

```
PAUSE 40
BEEP 16,400
PRINT "Heck, It ain't so hard!"
PRINT "Press any key to finish"
GET
```

Your complete program should now look like this on the screen:

```
PROC MYFIRST:
+ PRINT "Hey look!  I can program!"
+ PAUSE 40
+ BEEP 16,400
+ PRINT "Heck, It ain't so hard!"
+ PRINT
+ PRINT "Press any key to finish"
▸+ GET
  ENDP
```

15

That's it. Not the most exciting program in the world, but you have to start somewhere. At the moment, your program is written in a way that *we* understand (you will!), but it is not quite in the form that the Series 3a can use. So, the next step is to get Series 3a to *translate* it for you - and at the same time, a check will be made for the things you may have done wrong when entering the program - such as spelling mistakes or *syntax* errors.

Press the MENU key, select the *Prog* option at the top of the screen, and then select *Translate* from the drop-down list. Note the alternative 'short-cut' keypress combination - PSION key and ⊤ key pressed at the same time. You'll soon get into the habit of using this combination, as it is quicker and easier than using the MENU key and selecting the options you require. The *S3 Translate* option on this menu is for translating programs written for the Psion Series *3*, which is unable to make use of the larger screen available to the Series *3a*.

If you made any mistakes when entering the program, now is the time they'll show up, because a message such as '**Syntax Error**' will be displayed on the screen. If this has happened to you, the flashing cursor will jump to the point where Series 3a had a problem, usually just after the error. The ball's now in your court: check that you have spelt the words correctly, that you have spaces in the correct places (between the key word that starts each line and the 'instruction' that follows it), and check that you have used numbers for the '40' - and not the letter 'O'. Computers know the difference between the letter 'O' and the number '0'. Be careful. If you did have an error, correct it, and translate it again as before.

If you get a '**Memory full**' message, refer to your User's Guide on how to free up some memory before you try to translate the program again. Series 3a needs room to translate and run your programs.

When there are no mistakes in your program after it has been translated, Series 3a will display a message asking you if you want to run it. Usually you will want to test it out straight away, so press the ⓨ key ... and there it is! The screen will display

```
Hey look! I can program!
```

followed soon after by a 'bleep', and the two lines:

```
Heck, It ain't so hard!
Press any key to finish
```

Press any key on the keyboard, and you will be returned to the Program Editor screen, with everything just as you left it.

There shouldn't be any problems running this program, but you ought to be aware that sometimes, even when a program *translates* satisfactorily, it doesn't always *run* properly because of other types of error. These are called 'run-time' errors, and usually relate to things that the Series 3a hasn't been properly informed about. We'll discuss this type of problem later on.

Re-running your program

Before we see how this little program works, you'll no doubt like to run it all again: otherwise it would have been a lot of effort for such short lived glory.

To run a program whilst you're in the Program Editor of the Series 3a:

1. Select '*Prog*' from the menu at the top (MENU key first, remember), and select '*Run*' from the list of options, *or* press the PSION and ⊡ keys at the same time. This is the *short-cut* method.
2. A dialog box will appear, asking you for the name of the program *file* you wish to run: when you have a lot of translated programs, you can choose the name of any of them by using the left or right arrow keys. You'll also be able to choose where the file was saved (if you have SSDs fitted). When the file you want is on display (which it should be now), press ENTER.

Note that only *translated* programs can run, so if you make changes to a procedure or program but don't translate it, it is the unchanged *translated* version that will run. Always translate a program after you have made changes to it!

One of the things that happens when a file is successfully translated is its name appears under a special 'OPL' icon on the main 'System' screen display .

To run the MYFIRST program from the System screen press the 'SYSTEM' button to bring up the System screen display. Use the arrow keys on the keyboard to move the 'highlight' until it's at the right OPL icon and over 'MYFIRST', then press ENTER. (When you have more files translated, they'll all be listed. You select the one you want with the up and down arrow keys).

What does it all mean?

You have entered your first program. But what does it all mean? First of all, each line is a separate instruction or *statement* to the Series 3a to do something. The first word on each line in the program is generally either a *command*, a *function,* or a *variable* being assigned a value.

Series 3a understands well over 200 different *commands* and *functions:* you have just met a few of them. A *command* is generally an order to do something, while a *function* is generally an instruction to get or evaluate and 'return' some information. Most of the time, a *function* is not the first thing that will appear on a line, but we'll worry about that later on. Let's have a brief look at what the words in this particular program mean (we'll cover most of them again in greater detail).

The word PRINT in the first line is a command. It tells Series 3a that something must be 'printed' or displayed on the screen. What is to be printed forms the second part of the statement: "Hey look! I can program!". So that Series 3a can differentiate between actual words that are to be displayed and other things like *variables*, the words are placed between quotation marks. The format is

```
PRINT "what we want printed on the screen"
```

Whenever you want to spell out what will appear on the screen, that's the format to use. What happens if you just have PRINT, without anything following it? You get a blank line on the screen. We'll deal with PRINT in more detail in a later Chapter. The next program line

```
PAUSE 40
```

is another command.

PAUSE tells Series 3a to spin its wheels for a while - the time it spends spinning its wheels being given by the number after the word PAUSE (known as a *parameter*). This number tells Series 3a how many *twentieths* of a second to wait. So the '40' in our program will cause Series 3a to wait for 2 seconds. (40 twentieths). This number can also be negative - we could have written, for example PAUSE −40: this tells Series 3a to wait for 2 seconds *or* until a key is pressed, whichever comes first. We could also have written a '0' as the number.

This is a special instruction: it doesn't mean don't wait, it means wait until a key is pressed.

The next line is another command. BEEP tells Series 3a to make a noise at the loudspeaker. The length of the beep is given by the first number, which is a measure of *thirty-seconds* of a second. So 16 here means half a second. The second number gives the frequency by a rather wondrous formula - which we'll discuss in another Chapter.

There follows two more PRINT command lines, and then the line which simply says

```
GET
```

This is an instruction to Series 3a to wait until a key is pressed. It can also be used to 'save' the *character code* for the pressed key. The character code is the value that Series 3a uses to determine what character pattern to put on the screen. We didn't need to know which key had been pressed in this program, so we haven't bothered to save the information.

Why use GET instead of 'PAUSE 0'? To show you that, when programming, there is invariably more than one way to do something! Why use GET at all? Because without it, the program would end and vanish from the screen before you'd had a chance to read anything! You have to tell Series 3a to 'hang on', before it obeys the next instruction - which is to end running the program - and return to the previous screen display.

Starting a new program file from the Program Editor

If you are already using the Program Editor, you can start a new program file by simply

1. Pressing the MENU key
2. Selecting '*File*' from the options at the top (press ENTER), then '*New File*' (press ENTER), and then type in the new file's name.

If you aren't already in the Program Editor, then you start a new program file in the same way we started MYFIRST.

Note that, on the System display, the file that is currently being edited is in bold letters.

Editing an existing file

From the System screen, cursor along to the left OPL icon, then cursor down to the name of the file you wish to edit, and press ENTER.

From the Program Editor, either

• Press the MENU key, select the *'File'* option, then select the *'Open file'* option, *or*

• Press the PSION and '🔲' keys simultaneously.

Either way, a Dialog box will open, and you can use the left and right arrow keys to select the file you wish to edit (if there's more than one). Make your selection and press ENTER.

Deleting a file

The procedure for deleting an OPL file from your Series 3a is the same as that for deleting any file.

Note that, once you have written and translated a program file, its name will appear under both of the OPL icons in the system screen display. The file under the left icon is known as the *source* code: that's the file you wrote. The file under the right icon is the *translated* code - and is the program that you actually run.

If you delete the *source* code file, you will have no way to make changes to the program, unless you type it in all over again. If you have Solid State Disks, or have a link to a PC, it is recommended that you save the file before deleting it, unless you are absolutely sure you will not want to use it again.

If you delete the translated code file, you will not be able to run it until you have translated the source code again.

Remember too that every time you make changes to the source code, it must be translated before those changes take effect.

To delete a source code file:

1. Press the 'SYSTEM' button to bring up the System screen display. Use the arrow keys on the keyboard to move the highlight until it's at the left OPL icon, then use the arrow keys if necessary to select the program file you wish to delete.

2. If the file you have selected is in bold lettering, it means that it is 'active'. You must make it *inactive* before you can delete it. So Press the DELETE key. A Dialog box will appear, asking you if you want to 'quit' the selected file (i.e. make it inactive). Press the '🔲' key.

3. Press the MENU key, to display the option list at the top of the screen, select *'File'*, and press ENTER, then select *'Delete File'*: (the short-cut is the PSION and '🅳' keys pressed simultaneously). Now when you press ENTER the selected file will be displayed: as before, you can select another file to delete, if any are present, using the left and right arrow keys.

4. Press ENTER to continue, (or ESC to abort the deletion). Another Dialog box will appear asking you to confirm the deletion by pressing the '🆈' or '🅽' key. If you press '🆈', the file will be deleted. If you press '🅽', you will be returned to the previous Dialog box: press ESC to abandon the deletion.

Remember that when you delete a source code file, you delete it for ever. Consequently you should be absolutely sure you have no further use for the file before deleting it! Having said that, many of the procedures in this book are of a trivial nature, written purely to help you understand a particular process. They do take up valuable space, so when you feel happy about it, delete them to free up memory.

Deleting a translated program

The procedure for deleting a translated program is exactly the same as that for deleting a source code file. The only difference is, you will select the program from the list under the right OPL icon.

Duplicating a source code file

There may be times when you want to make changes to a source code file, but don't want to lose the 'original'. You can do this two ways: by first saving the file again under a different name, and by copying it.

To save the file again under a different name:

1. From the System display, or from the Program Editor, first select the file concerned and press ENTER to make that file 'active'. Then, from the Program Editor, either press the MENU button and select *'File'* and *'Save as'*, *or* use the short-cut combination PSION and '🅰' keys. (Don't use PSION and '🅰' from the System display - that does something else!)

2. A Dialog box will appear, prompting you for the new name for the file: make your entry (remembering the rules for file names) and press ENTER. Don't worry about the *'Use new file'* option: that's for the styles in Word. The Program Editor has its own style.

21

To copy a file:

1. Press the System button. Examine the name of the file you wish to copy: if it is in bold letters, it is 'active', so press the DELETE key to make it inactive. Make sure the highlight is at the left OPL icon, then *either* press MENU, select '*File*' and then '*Copy file*', *or* press the PSION and '[C]' keys at the same time.

2. Press ENTER, and a Dialog box will appear. At '*From file: Name*' select the file you wish to copy using the left or right arrow keys. Then cursor down to the '*To file: Name*', and type in the name for your new file, and press ENTER. You can also opt to save your file on a Solid State Disk, if fitted, or on a remotely connected computer, by selecting the '*Disk*' option.

Having saved your file under a new name, remember that it will need to be translated before it can be run under the *new* name.

You can now select the original or the newly named file for further editing.

Renaming source or translated program files

On the System display, set the highlight over the name of the program file name you wish to rename. Make sure it is 'inactive', pressing the DELETE key if necessary, and *either* press MENU, select '*File*' and '*Rename file*' and press ENTER, *or* press PSION and '[R]' together.

A Dialog box will appear. If the file you wish to rename isn't the one selected in the '*From: Name*' option, select it using the left or right arrow keys. Then cursor down to the '*To: Name*' option and enter the new name, finishing by pressing the ENTER key.

The selected source or translated program will be renamed.

Your first taste

You have now written your first program, translated it, and run it. You should now have a good idea how to handle your files for editing, and so on. And you should have a general, though perhaps sketchy idea of what it's all about. Let's summarise it all.

1. A program is made up of one or more *procedures*. The program in this Chapter has just one procedure. A procedure starts with the word PROC followed by its name and a colon, and ends with the word ENDP. The procedure name must never be more than eight

characters (and that includes an *identifier*, which will be discussed later), and must start with a letter.

2. Each line of a procedure is an instruction or *statement* telling the Series 3a to do something. These statements use a key word which is either a *command* (an instruction to do something), or a *function* (an instruction to get some information and, usually, save it somewhere). You are advised to type in the key words in capital letters, so that they're easy to spot.

A few final points that haven't been mentioned yet, and you're ready to take the next step.

1. You *can* have more than one statement on a line, provided that each of the statements is separated by a space and a colon. Thus

   ```
   PAUSE 40 :BEEP 16,400
   ```

   However, this can sometimes make programs harder to read and 'debug'.

2. A procedure in one file can 'call' or use procedures in *other* files, by *loading* those files first. More about this at the right time...

3. When a file contains more than one procedure, it is the *first* procedure that is first executed when the file is run. The other procedures in the file are, in effect, 'sub-procedures', which must be 'called' in order to be executed. This, too, we'll deal with later on.

4. The name of a program that is *running* is shown in bold under the right OPL icon on the System screen display. The name of a file being *edited* in the Program Editor is also shown in bold, under the left OPL icon on the System display.

5. When you are 'in' a program that is *running*, you can stop it by pressing the PSION and the ESC key at the same time. **This is extremely useful for those occasions when a program seems to 'hang' - or 'lock up'.**

   To pause a program that is running, press the CONTROL key and the '⑤' key at the same time. You can resume running the program by pressing CONTROL and '⑤' again.

Finally, from now on only when appropriate will a *file name* be suggested to you (that's the name the procedure or procedures will be saved as, remember, and the name that will appear under the right OPL icon). While working through this book, each single program should be saved as a separate file: if you try to tack other programs to an existing file, those procedures won't run unless specifically called by the first procedure in the file. You can give the file any name you choose, but is recommended that you give it the same name as the first procedure.

```
+    Disk Internal, 138K free    →
                 \OPL\*
Easter.opl          720    12:08am    19/12/94 +
Exchrate.opl       2523     6:38pm    19/03/95
Fonts.opl           216     8:12pm    27/04/95
Mpg.opl             762     2:22pm    02/01/95
Music.opl           658     3:10pm    22/04/95
Qrytest.opl         205     9:07pm    02/05/95
Sounds.opl          186     2:46pm    22/04/95 +
```

Pressing the TAB key whilst on any file name shows all the files in the same directory. You can use the cursor keys to move around the files, and if you pressed the TAB key whilst in a Dialog, then pressing ENTER on a file name will select that file.

CHAPTER 3
Planning the program

This Chapter gives you an idea of how to plan your program, a process often ignored by would-be programmers ... at their peril.

The way it was...

Not too many years ago, newcomers to the world of programming used a language called 'BASIC'. It was (and still is) an easy language to learn, but in the early days, it had no 'structure': programs written in BASIC tended to be one long, ghastly string of statements.

Invariably a program needs to 'branch off' under certain conditions, and these 'branches' were just tacked in among the rest of the program lines. The result was that at the end of the day, such programs were very difficult to add to, or change, because they were so convoluted and involved.

To give an example of why a program may need to branch, consider a routine for making a hot drink (if only the Series 3a could be so programmed!). The program may start by asking "Tea or coffee?", and according to your choice, it will branch off to perform the necessary operations. All branches could well come back to one 'end' point - where the computer proudly announces "*Your* (whatever the choice was) *is made, oh master!*"

Now such a program *could* be written in one long listing, but what a mess it could look, especially after you later decided to add a few more drinks, and options (*with or without milk? do you want sugar?*).

The solution is what has become known as *structured* programming: breaking the program up into little blocks, as separate routines or procedures, and then having just one, short(ish) main or master procedure that calls the others as and when they're needed.

The way it is

The Series 3a is designed to let you structure your programs. It makes life much easier, and means that you can, eventually, design 'blocks' which can be used in a number of different programs, so you don't have to keep re-inventing the wheel. Once you have designed a neat procedure to perform a particular task, you can use it over and over again in *other* programs by *loading* it into those programs. Apart from making life easier, it also saves computer space, since the particular piece of program code is written only once.

Structuring a program means you have to think about it a bit before you actually start writing the code. You have to ask yourself what exactly do you want the program to achieve, how will the user interact with it, and so on. A very large program can in many respects be like building a house. To simply start digging foundations and then plod away tacking on a bit here and a bit there without any planning is a recipe for a pretty grim looking house, which may or may not, at the end of the day, serve its purpose. And when it comes to adding another room, or a service such as central heating ... the mind boggles.

The problem is nowhere near as pronounced for short, simple programs: these can be, and in most instances are, written in one 'chunk'. But as soon as there is a routine or a set of instructions that needs to be repeated, then the program should be broken up into sections or *procedures*.

Let us take an example. Let us suppose you wish to write a game program that requires a dice throw. If you had to write the dice-throw routine at every point it is needed, you'd have the routine repeated a number of times unnecessarily. If, on the other hand, the dice-throw routine is written as one discrete procedure, that procedure can be 'called' whenever it is needed. The dice-throw routine becomes one of the 'blocks' in your program. Later on, should you wish to make changes to the dice-throw routine - to simulate the throw of *two* dice, perhaps, it is a simple matter to make the change. Once. The method of calling one procedure from another will be discussed at the appropriate time.

Right way or wrong way?

One of the interesting facts about programming is that, if you were to give each of 100 programmers the task of writing a program to perform a particular task on a particular type of computer, you'd end up with 100 different solutions. They may perform the same task, but if you were to examine the actual instructions, they'd almost certainly be different.

Some of the programs will require a lot of memory while others will use very little memory. Some will operate very fast, and some will be comparatively slow. Some will be easy to understand, and others look extremely complex. Some will be 'user-friendly' - that is, have lots of prompts to guide the user through what is required, while others will leave the user wondering what he is supposed to do next.

The reason why each solution will be different is that everyone has their own idea of how to tackle the requirement. The truth of the matter is there is no *right* or *wrong* way to write a program: only *good* ways and *bad* ways. If it works and does the job expected of it, it is 'right'. If it doesn't - then it's wrong.

Later on, when more experienced, you'll be able to look back over a program and think "I could have written that better - to run faster or take up less room, or to be more user-friendly". And if you used the structured approach, you'll be able to make your improvements fairly easily.

So, when you first start to write your own programs, don't worry about whether they're right or wrong: worry about whether or not they're going to work!

Define your requirement

As previously mentioned, the first thing to do when writing a program is to define what you want it to do as clearly as possible. Not in your head. On paper. Make sure that you cover everything, including how you will want to use the program.

Once you have a little knowledge of the programming language, you can start the task by writing 'pseudo' code: this isn't the exact instructions, but an outline of the instructions that you want performed. For example, let us suppose that you're in the carpet business, and you want to write a program that will quickly tell you how many square yards of carpet are needed for a particular sized room, and what the cost is going to be given the price of the carpet per square yard. In broad terms, the program needs to do the following:

1) Get the size of the room.
2) Work out the area in square yards.
3) Round *up* to the next nearest square yard, and possibly display the answer.
4) Get the cost of the carpet per square yard.
5) Work out the carpeting cost, and display the answer.

We have defined the basic requirement. But the program can go further: we can provide a 'loop', allowing the user to specify another room size, or another carpet cost, or both, without having to re-run the program each time.

Getting the room size and working out the square yards of carpet needed is one entire action. Provided that the area is known, getting the cost of the carpet per square yard and calculating the carpeting cost is another complete action. We could therefore create two 'blocks' or procedures to do the donkey work:

Procedure a: Get room size and work out square yardage of carpet needed.

Procedure b: Get cost of carpet and work out cost of carpeting room.

Procedure *a* we shall call AREA, and procedure *b* we shall call COST. Now we can have another main procedure, which we will call CARPET, to do the following:

1) Get *area* ('call' the AREA procedure)
2) Get *cost* ('call' the COST procedure)
3) Another cost?   *Yes*   Repeat from (2) again
                             No   Go on to (4)
4) Another area?   *Yes*   Repeat from (1) again
                             No   End the program

If you follow this last routine through step by step, you will see that it starts off the same way as before, but having worked out the cost of a carpet for a particular room, it will allow us to change the cost of the carpet and come up with the new answer, or go right back and get a whole new room size entirely.

The illustration (shown opposite) setting out the requirements diagrammatically is known as a *flow chart*. This one is fairly straightforward, but nevertheless, as you can see, a flow chart helps in understanding the requirement. It also makes programming easier, because each box can be taken as a separate unit, and the program written accordingly. (In a later Chapter, we'll write the code for this program).

The "CALL" in the top two boxes is a way of saying 'go and do the separate procedure, and then come back here'. You will see that there are various ways of making 'calls' to other procedures - and as it happens, the actual OPL word 'CALL' is *not* one that we will be using in this book: it is one of the words that is used for writing code at the 'machine's own level' and as such is beyond the scope of this book. Be assured, you won't need to use it yet!

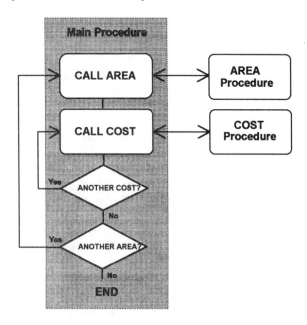

Fig. 3.1 Flow Chart for the Carpet Program

The calculations

Having worked out what you want your program to do, and defined a structure for it in the form of a flow chart, the next stage before settling down to write and test the code is to make a note of any calculations the program may need to make, and write them down. This step may not always be necessary: for the program under discussion, the calculations are fairly trivial, and could easily wait until you're actually preparing the code. However, as we shall be concentrating on other matters in later Chapters, we'll deal with the mathematics of this program now.

Floor area is given by the very simple formula, *length x breadth*. We want the answer in square yards, but will most likely want to input the measurements in feet. Thus we can say

$$\text{area in sq. yds} = \frac{\text{length x breadth in feet}}{9}$$

Whatever the area is, it needs to be rounded up to the next whole number (because carpets are bought in square yards). So if the answer works out to be 11.2 square yards, we need to round that up to be 12 square yards. There are a number of ways this can be done. One is to check whether there is any 'decimal' value to the answer, and if so, add one to the 'whole number' or *integer* part. Any decimal values will be dropped, of course.

Having obtained an area in square yards, the next thing we need is simply the cost of the carpet required. This is given by

Carpet cost   =   area in sq. yards x cost per sq. yard

It can sometimes happen, when making the calculations required for a program, that another routine may be called for. A particular calculation may appear in several different places throughout the program: if this is the case, then a procedure - or *function* - can be prepared to handle that calculation. And it is at the planning stage you need to know whether such a procedure will be necessary so that you can write the program accordingly.

Planning a program properly before it is started is a stage that many would-be programmers tend to ignore. A small proportion of programmers can afford to ignore in depth planning for their programs - they can call upon previous experience and skills, particularly for short programs. Unfortunately, the rest believe they belong to that small proportion, then find they waste a considerable amount of time trying to 'debug' their programs. So the game plan is, first state what the program must do in 'English' and in clear steps, breaking each part down to its smallest requirement. Then prepare a 'flow chart': this will help to determine whether the logic of the program is correct and makes sense: if it doesn't work for you, it definitely won't work for the computer!

CHAPTER 4
The Variables

This Chapter discusses
- *What variables are, and the different types used by OPL.*
- *How to name variables, and to tell Series 3a about them.*
- *The difference between LOCAL and GLOBAL variables.*
- *The scope of GLOBAL variables.*
- *How to pass values to other procedures.*
- *How to return a value from a function to the calling routine.*
- *About variables that don't need declaring*
- *How to use constants wisely.*

The unknown quantities

It's now time to get started on the language itself, and the first step in this direction is to look at the various ways there are of saving information that is likely to change or be different each time the program is run ... the *variable* information.

Whenever you write a program or procedure, you will almost always need to work with different sets of figures or data each time the program is run. Taking the 'Carpet' program outlined in Chapter 3 as a typical example, each time the program is run you will want to enter the room's measurements and the cost of the carpet at the keyboard. This information has to be stored somewhere for subsequent action: the alternative is to actually re-write the program with the relevant figures each time it is used, and that, obviously, is an utter waste of time and programming effort.

What we do is to tell Series 3a that we have unknown quantities to be stored - quantities that could be different each time the program is run. We do this by telling Series 3a to set aside memory boxes specially for these quantities and, to make it easy for ourselves and the Series 3a, we give those memory boxes *names*. *We* identify the storage boxes by names of our choosing; Series 3a converts those names into *addresses* which point to the relevant storage boxes. Think of it as a row of houses: we give our houses names, but the postman prefers to use the house numbers - it's easier for him to find the address with numbers.

The unknown quantities are called *variables*, and it is much easier for *us* to remember what information the variable will be holding if we

31

give it an appropriate *name*. The Psion Series 3a will work out the actual addresses of the memory boxes it allocates to the variables ... all you have to do is to tell it the names of the variables you're going to use. But before we discuss how you tell Series 3a to set aside the appropriate memory boxes for each variable, let us look at the nature of the variables themselves.

Types of variable

There are two fundamental *categories* of variable. First there are those that hold real *numbers* of one kind or another - that is, values that are going to be used for mathematical operations of some sort: these are called *numeric* variables. Then there are the variables that hold text or *characters*, which can be letters or numbers or any other symbol that can be entered from the keyboard. These are called *string* variables and cannot be used *directly* in mathematical operations, although as we shall see later, it is possible to convert them into numeric values if they contain numbers. Characters, remember, are just 'shapes' as far as the computer is concerned, and they are stored, in effect, as 'reference numbers' to a library of shapes. It can seem strange, at first, that a number held in a *string variable* is different from a number held in a *numeric variable*. Remember, though, that the string variable in effect holds the *shape* of the number (or rather a reference to the shape in a library of shapes), not its actual value.

The two categories of variable are discussed separately.

Numeric variables

You may recall, from Chapter 1, that numbers for mathematical operations can be stored in memory boxes in various ways. For example, we can use two boxes to store whole numbers in the range -32768 to +32767, and four boxes to store whole numbers in the range -2147483648 to +2147483647. These two types are called *integers* and *long integers* respectively.

Numbers that have a decimal point in them are called *floating point* numbers, and have to be stored in a different way, using more boxes. *Integers* and *long integers* can never have a decimal point in them, and it is important that you understand this when you use integer variables - and integer *constants* - in program calculations. A *constant* is a value which never changes when the program is run. It might be, for example, a conversion factor - such as may be used to convert inches to centimetres. Such a value would never change.

String variables

String variables require as many boxes as there are *characters* to be saved or stored, plus a few more that you needn't worry about. If you want to use a *string* variable, you have to know when you start programming how many boxes you want Series 3a to set aside (ignoring those extra ones just mentioned - Series 3a sees to those on your behalf): your program must allow for the maximum number likely to be stored.

Arrays

The numeric and string variables described above are just *single* variables: that is to say, they hold just one value. But there are many occasions when you'll want a group of variables of the same type - to which you will want to give the same basic name. For example, you may wish to store up to the first seven letters of people's names - Peter, Michael, Karen, Edwina, and so on. You could put these into their own individual memory boxes, but it is often more convenient to create an *array* of boxes. An array is a series of boxes, all with the same basic name, but with a numeric *sub-address* contained in brackets immediately after the name to identify the individual element. Thus, people's names could be held in an array variable with the basic name 'name$' (don't worry about the '$' symbol yet), and with individual array elements of name$(1), name$(2) and so on.

With such an array, it is easy to get at any of the individual elements very quickly. For example, once the program had been initiated and set up, 'Peter' could be stored in name$(1), 'Michael' in name$(2), and so on. It is very easy for a program to automatically or sequentially access the names, by using the *sub address*. The storage of the first three elements would look like this:

Array element	Memory boxes						
Name$(1)	P	E	T	E	R		
Name$(2)	M	I	C	H	A	E	L
Name$(3)	K	A	R	E	N		

Note that some of the allocated boxes have nothing in them: but *could* have if the names were longer: we have allowed for the first seven letters, remember.

In a similar way, *numeric* values of like types and of the same grouping can be placed into arrays for easy access during the running of the program. 'Like types' means integers, or long integers, or floating point numbers. And 'like groupings' means being able to share the same basic variable name, such as 'Items ( )'.

Naming variables

We now come to the rules that *must* be obeyed when you name a variable. First, you must know the variable's *type*, so that you can *identify* it for the Series 3a: Series 3a needs to know how many boxes to allocate for that variable, remember.

Variable names are effectively in two parts: the *name* part which enables you - and Series 3a - to know which individual set of memory boxes we're talking about. This is followed by an *identifier* part, which tells Series 3a the *kind* of variable being stored - and hence how many individual memory boxes will be required for the storage.

The name part

- Can be up to eight characters long, *including* the identifier.
- Must *always* start with a letter, but after that, can be any combination of letters and numbers.
- Must *not* be one of the OPL function or command words - that is, words that are part of the OPL language itself.
- *Must* end with the identifier symbol which describes the type of variable, with the sole exception of *floating point* variables - which have no identifying character.

The identifying symbols are as follows:

%	Integers
&	Long Integers
$	Strings
	Floating point

Finally, it doesn't matter whether you use capital or lower case letters: Series 3a takes them both to be the same. Thus CARpet%, carPET%, CARPET% and carpet% all have the same meaning to Series 3a.

When naming variables, it is useful for your later understanding of the program to give meaningful names. Where memory space is at an absolute premium, it is equally wise to keep the names as short as possible. Fortunately the days when only one or two lettered variables were permissible have long gone. So, if a variable is going to be used to store the length of a room, it makes sense to call it 'LENGTH'. If space is important, you may choose to call it simply 'L', but be warned, you may later wonder what the variable is being used for!

To help distinguish variable names from OPL words in this book, variables are written as *lower* case and OPL words as *upper* case: you will find it useful to do the same when entering programs, since it helps when locating and correcting errors.

Let us now look at some *valid* variable names.

Cost	Floating point type
Cost$	String type
COST$	String type, exactly the same as that above.
Cost%	Integer type
Astro1&	Long integer type
P234R678	Floating point type
OutCome&	Long Integer type
Week%(52)	52 integer variables, Week%(1) to Week%(52)

Remember that each variable can store only the kind of information specified by its identifier. Now here are some variable names that are *not* valid:

Week	Its an OPL word (but week% is OK!)
4tune	It starts with a number
b2345678%	It's too long
wow*	Incorrect identifier (*)
doll/ar$	Invalid character (/)

Using OPL words for variable names is a common error, particularly since OPL covers quite a few words that are in common usage!

Declaring variables

Having decided what variable names you want to use in your program, and what types of variable they are going to be, you now have to let Series 3a know. This is done at the very beginning of a program or procedure, by a process called 'declaring the variables'. There are two ways you can declare variables - as LOCALs, and as GLOBALs.

LOCAL variables are used *only* in the procedure in which they are declared. So if every procedure in a program has a variable called

35

'junk', then each one will be quite separate and distinct from the others, and unaffected by any changes made to the others.

GLOBAL variables on the other hand can be used in any and every procedure 'called' by the procedure they're declared in, and also in the procedures that *they* call. When a GLOBAL variable has its value changed by a procedure, the new value will be used throughout all of the subsequently called procedures in program, until it is changed again. GLOBAL variables are, therefore, a useful way of 'passing information' between procedures. However, it is not the only way. When we examine methods of calling other procedures, we shall see that there is another way to pass information back and forth between procedures.

Variables are declared by using the OPL word LOCAL or GLOBAL, followed by the list of variable names, each separated by a comma. Generally speaking, every variable must be declared: Series 3a *must* be informed in order to set aside memory boxes accordingly.

For *string* variables (variables that hold a series or string of characters), it is also essential to inform Series 3a how many memory boxes must be reserved for storing the characters. So if you want to store eight characters in a LOCAL string variable called student$, it would have to be declared as

```
LOCAL student$(8)
```

Yes, this *looks* like an 'array': if you want an array of five string variables with the common, basic name student$, each of which is eight characters long (they must all be the same length), then the *array* dimension comes first in the bracket, and is separated from the number of characters dimension by a comma, thus

```
LOCAL student$(5,8)
```

The '5' says there are five elements in the array, and the '8' says that each element can store up to 8 characters.

Arrays of other variables simply have the number of elements in the array enclosed in brackets. Thus

```
LOCAL price(5),item%(10)
```

will declare an array of five floating point variables with the common name 'price', and an array of ten integer variables with the common name 'item%'.

Here is an example of what the first lines of a procedure will look like, with the variables declared:

```
PROC test:
    GLOBAL allover%,lots$(16)
    LOCAL junk,women&(5),t%
    ...
    ENDP
```

This declares two GLOBAL variables: the integer 'allover%', and the string 'lots$' which can be used to store up to 16 characters. The three LOCAL variables declared are 'junk' (floating point), women&(5) (an array of 5 long integers), and t% (an integer). All the procedures that this one calls can make use of - and change - the values in the GLOBAL variables 'allover%' and 'lots$', but the values of 'junk', 'women&()' and 't%' can be used and changed only by this procedure called 'test'.

Note that if a procedure called by 'test' has a LOCAL variable *also* named 'allover%' declared, then *that* 'allover%' will be unique to that procedure, and any changes made to its value will *not* affect the globally declared 'allover%' in the main 'test' procedure. So be careful not to duplicate the names of globally declared variables.

The following test procedure demonstrates this, and will also show you how one procedure 'calls' another. Enter the first procedure (test) as explained in Chapter 2, then press ENTER to move down to a clear line, and enter the second procedure: note that for this procedure, you must enter the PROC and ENDP procedure start and finish words yourself: they are automatically inserted for you only for the *first* procedure in a file.

```
PROC test:
GLOBAL allover%
allover%=1
PRINT "Test procedure allover%=",allover%
subs:
PRINT "But on return, allover$=";allover%
```

```
    GET
    ENDP

    PROC subs:
    LOCAL allover%
    PRINT "On entering subs, allover%=",allover%
    allover%=5
    PRINT "subs changed allover% to",allover%
    ENDP
```

Don't worry about how this program works: its operation will become apparent in later Chapters. But note how the procedure subs is called by simply naming it with a following colon. Translate and run this program, and the following information should be displayed (this is just the top left of the screen):

```
Test procedure allover%= 1
On entering subs, allover%= 0
subs changed allover% to 5
But on return, allover%= 1
```

As you can see, the allover% declared as a GLOBAL in the test procedure *hasn't been used or affected by the change made in the* subs *routine*, because this procedure also has allover% declared as a LOCAL variable. If, after establishing that, you type REM at the beginning of the declaration line in the subs procedure so that it reads

```
            REM LOCAL allover%
```

then translate and run the program again, you will see that this time allover% *is* used and changed by the subs procedure.

```
Test procedure allover%= 1
On entering subs, allover%= 1
subs changed allover% to 5
But on return, allover%= 5
```

The REM prevents the declaration line from being translated: this OPL word is discussed later.

Scope of GLOBAL variables

The scope or hierarchy of GLOBAL variables is indicated by the following diagram. In this diagram - which is *not* a flow chart - procedures are assumed to be *calling* only those procedures to their immediate right. It shows how procedures can use the GLOBAL variables of those procedures that call it, but not the GLOBAL variables of those that *they* call. Note that GLOBAL variables don't have to be re-declared in subsequent procedures.

Note how 'PROC One' calls *all* of the other procedures, but has access only to GLOBAL variable a. 'PROC Four' on the other hand, because it is called by 'PROC One' or 'PROC Two', also has access to *their* variables, a and b respectively, as well as its own GLOBAL variable '*d*'.

This kind of hierarchy can occur when you start preparing 'libraries' of routines for use in a number of programs, where a library procedure itself calls other routines.

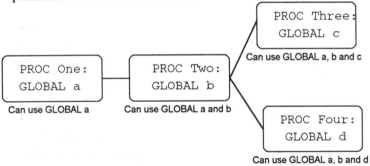

Non-declared variables

Strictly speaking, there's no such thing as a 'non-declared' variable: Series 3a needs to know all about *any* variables you may want to store. However, not all variables have to be declared by LOCAL or GLOBAL statements. There are three basic types of such variable. There are values that have been passed as *parameters*. There are variables, or parameters, that are used when creating or opening files. And there are the Series 3a Calculator memories.

Values passed as parameters

It has already been stated that GLOBAL variables are one way of making variables available to other procedures. It isn't the only way, and it isn't always the neatest way. In fact, for many very short procedures and *functions* which always act on specific information that's passed to them, GLOBAL variables represent a very clumsy approach.

To explain this, and to demonstrate how values can be passed as *parameters*, here is a short procedure that gives the remainder left after one number has been divided by another. This is a very handy routine, found in several other programming languages under the name Mod, but not in OPL.

We will call the procedure 'mod'. It will need two values to work on: the number to be divided, which we will call 'n', and the divisor, which we will call 'd'. Both will be floating point values. Now, whenever we call this procedure, we want to be able to pass to it values for 'n' and 'd', and we want the answer to be 'returned' to the calling routine.

Incidentally, a procedure which 'returns' a value is known as a *function*. There are numerous *functions* in the OPL language itself: SIN() and UPPER$() are two examples.

Passing values *to* the procedure is done by naming the variables, not as LOCAL or GLOBAL, but as *parameters* in the called procedure's name. As shown in bold here:

```
PROC mod: (n,d)
```

What we are saying, in effect, is that whenever the procedure 'mod' is called, the two values that need to be worked on must be *included* in the *calling* statement. Series 3a knows that information is being passed from one place to another, by the way the procedure is named - with parameters in brackets, after the colon. Note how the parameters are separated by a comma, and of course, it is important to include the type *identifier* with the variable name. In this instance, both variables are of the floating point type.

The call is made, remember, by simply naming the procedure, as if it were an OPL word, but followed by a colon. Where parameters have to be passed to the procedure, they are included in brackets, *in the correct order* and *of the correct variable type*. So a typical call to our 'mod' procedure could look like this:

mod:(yr,4)

'yr' is a floating point variable, which could typically contain a year like 1991 (not a floating point value, but it is important that the variable *is* floating point). Strictly speaking, the 4 should be written as 4.0, the floating point form, but as it is 'declared' in the mod procedure as floating point parameter, Series 3a will force the real value 4 into a floating point variable format. However, if instead of the 4 we had used an integer variable, such as 'v%', then Series 3a would have been very confused, because we've stated we want to pass an *integer* variable (two storage boxes) into a floating point variable (four storage boxes): the result would be a TYPE MISMATCH error message when the program is translated.

Another thing to notice is that the *names* of the variables in the mod procedure need *not* be the same as those passed to it: only the *types* must tally. It's a very important point.

Also you should note that the values of variables passed to a function *cannot be changed by the function*. For example, in the function procedure 'mod:(n,d)', you can *use* the values of 'n' and 'd' to make calculations or whatever, but you cannot *change* their values.

In the 'mod' procedure, to calculate the remainder when 'n' is divided by 'd', we can use the following assignment

rmndr = n-(INT(n/d)*d)

INT is an OPL key word, which means 'take the integer of whatever value or expression is in the brackets that immediately follow' (in other words, forget the decimal point and anything that follows it). In this case, the expression 'n/d'. The '/' and '*' symbols mean 'divide' and 'multiply' respectively.

Briefly, it works is like this (skip this paragraph if you don't care how it works). The number 'n' is divided by the divisor 'd', then the decimal part is eliminated completely - by taking the integer. This gives us the *whole* number of times 'd' divides into 'n'. That whole number is then multiplied by the divisor again, and that gives the nearest whole number below the original number, that is exactly divisible by the divisor. This is then deducted from the original number, and that's the

41

remainder. Try it for yourself using any two numbers. (The next Chapter deals with the way Series 3a handles arithmetic).

In this expression, it looks like we need to store the answer somewhere - in a variable called 'rmndr', perhaps. But there is no need, because now we come to a way of passing a variable or a result of a calculation *back* to the routine that called it. And that's with the OPL key word RETURN. The format for this word is

RETURN *the value of a variable or result of an expression*

In other words, we can 'return' a variable (which means Series 3a will pass back to the calling routine the *value* held in the variable's memory boxes), or we can return the *result* of an expression. So you don't need to waste space by declaring a local variable to hold the answer. You can 'return' it to the calling routine with the line

```
RETURN n-(INT(n/d)*d)
```

And that's it. The complete procedure looks like this:

```
PROC MOD:(n,d)
  RETURN n-(INT(n/d)*d)
ENDP
```

The calling procedure will have a line such as

```
rmndr=mod:(1994,4)
```

The result of the mod:() function's calculation will be passed back and stored in the variable rmndr. This should demonstrate how to pass values to a *function* procedure, and how to return a *single* value back to the calling routine.

Note that, as mod is a *function*, you won't be able to run it directly after it has been translated: it needs to be *called* by another procedure (or used in the Calculator). We'll do this in a later Chapter.

There are a few things about functions you should note:
1. Only *one* value can be *returned* to a calling routine. To return more, you'll have to use GLOBAL variables.
2. Where a value is being returned, the procedure name must be followed by the correct identifier for the type of value being

returned. So if the procedure is to return a *string* variable, its *name* must reflect this by being called something like 'answer$:(quest$,part%)'. Note the identifying $ sign to show that, whatever else this function does, it returns a string. Note too that the name, including the identifier, must not be more than eight characters.

3. You use the functions you write just like OPL functions. That means assigning them to a variable, or using them as part of an another expression.

Variables used when opening files

This is not the ideal place to deal with the data file handling capabilities of Series 3a. However, you should be aware that, when data files are created or opened, certain *field-names* have to be specified amongst other information, and this is *not* done by use of the words LOCAL or GLOBAL. Data files, incidentally, are groups of records and so on, that you decide to store in memory, so that you can call them back for perusal/work at a later time. The Diary, Database and Word Processor in your Series 3a all produce files that you can recall. With OPL, you can also create files to do what you want the way you want.

Using the calculator memories

You will no doubt be aware that the calculator in Series 3a has ten memories. These are designated 'M0' to 'M9', and are all of the floating point type. Series 3a knows about them (there's a surprise!), and so if you want to use them, you can without having to declare them first. You simply use their 'name'.

Any information you store in any of the ten calculator memories *remains in that memory* even after the program has finished running. This makes the calculator memories a useful way to store values between programs, or for the next time the program is used, and for passing data to the calculator for the calculator's use. You may know that you can run OPL *functions* from the calculator. However, you must be aware that the calculator memories could be changed by other programs you may write, or from within the calculator itself. Their use should not be a substitute for creating your own variables.

Constants (real values)

Before leaving the subject of variables, real values or *constants* should be mentioned. Constants are those values that actually get written into your program and consequently never change, rather than those entered whilst it is running.

For example, you may write a routine that converts degrees Celsius (or Centigrade) to degrees Fahrenheit, which will probably contain a line something like this:

```
fahr=32+(c*9/5)
```

In this, 32, 9 and 5 are constants. Trouble is, the way they're written, they have no decimal point - and Series 3a will take them to be *integers* and store them accordingly. Integers, remember, can *never* have a decimal point, and the result of dividing an integer by an integer (as in 9/5 in the example line) will be an integer: which will give you the wrong result. As an integer, 9/5 is '1' not the expected '1.8'.

Consequently it is particularly important when using constants to make sure that they are entered in the correct form. Entering 9.0/5 or 9/5.0 will force *one* of the values into a floating point format, and that, in turn, will force the division result into floating point format. So you'll get the correct answer. Be careful with constants!

CHAPTER 5
The maths of programming

In this Chapter you'll learn about
* *Series 3a's basic mathematical operators*
* *The order in which calculations are made*
* *Mixing different types of variable in calculations*
* *Making calculations whilst programming*

Don't panic!

You don't have to know any more maths to write a computer program than you need to make a simple calculation using pencil and paper. For those who have never seen a computer program, and who can vaguely remember something about 'algebra' at school, some lines in a program can look downright stupid.

Here's an example:

```
x = x+1
```

Now common sense tells you that x (which we take here to mean 'any number') cannot be equal to the *same* number *plus one*. No, and this line doesn't mean that: which is why we need to spend just a few moments looking at the way maths works in a computer program.

The line '$x=x+1$', and lines similar to it, are really *instructions* or *statements* to the Series 3a, and not equations. In an equation, what's on the left hand side of the equals sign is said to equal what's on the right hand side. In a computer statement, the *result* of what's on the right hand side is *stored* in the variable name listed on the left hand side. The 'equals' sign represents an *assignment*.

So the line '$x=x+1$' is an instruction to Series 3a. It takes the right-hand side first, looks into the memory boxes labelled or addressed as 'x', adds one to the number found there, then *puts the answer into the boxes labelled* 'x': which, as it happens, are also the boxes Series 3a looked into on the right hand side.

If you could sit there watching the boxes addressed as 'x' while this is going on, you'd see that Series 3a comes along with its strict instructions, looks in the x boxes, adds one to the number it finds there, then, looking at the next part of the instruction, discovers that the answer has to be dropped back into the same boxes.

The value of x has been *incremented*.

In computer statements, the left hand side of an equals sign denotes *where* any calculation or value that's on the right hand side is to be stored.

So you can 'assign' a value to a variable in a program, with a line something like

```
x=42.5
```

The maths operators

Series 3a can be programmed to perform all of the operations an ordinary calculator offers, and many that a calculator doesn't offer. What can confuse is that there are no apparent multiplication or division symbols. They're there, however, but under a different guise. Here's the list of symbols used for the different mathematical operations:

+	Add
-	Subtract
-	Unary minus (that means 'change the sign')
*	Multiply
/	Divide
**	Raise to a power
%	Percentages

The percentages operator '%' is used in conjunction with any of the four basic mathematical operators, to produce different kinds of result.

These are summed up as follows:

240*2%	Says 'What is 2% of 240?': the answer is 4.8
240+2%	Says 'Add 2% of 240 to 240': the answer is 244.8 (*240+4.8*)
240-2%	Says 'Deduct 2% of 240 from 240': the answer is 235.2 (*240-4.8*)
240/2%	Says 'What is 240 two percent of?': the answer is 12000

Note that if a *variable* were to be used instead of a real or constant value, the '%' would have to be separated from it by a space - otherwise Series 3a would think it was looking at an *integer* variable! Thus

100+vat %   Says 'Get the value in the *vat* boxes, take *that percentage* of 100, and add it to 100'

whereas

100+vat%   Says 'add 100 to the value stored in the integer variable box designated vat%'

There are two other ways the percentage operator can be used mathematically, and that's with two of the *logical* operators '>' and '<'. We'll be meeting these in some detail when we discuss decision making in a later Chapter, but essentially they usually mean *'greater than'* and *'less than'* respectively. With the percentage operator, they mean

102>2%   Says 'What number, when increased by 2%, becomes 102%?': the answer is 100

102<2%   Says 'What amount of 102 does a 2% increase represent?': the answer is 2.

These operators are very useful for VAT operations. For example, to find out what a price was *before* VAT has been added the format would be:

VATprice **>** *VATrate* **%**

The '*VATprice*' and '*VATrate*' are replaced by actual values or variables. Similarly, to find out how much of a total price the VAT part is:

VATprice **<** *VATrate* **%**

The order of calculation

When Series 3a sees it has something to work out (an 'expression'), it doesn't necessarily work from left to right, but gives priority to certain operators. It looks through the calculation that has to be made, and tackles the operators in this order:

47

First	**	(*powers*)
	-	(*unary minus or 'sign change*)
	* /	(*multiplication and division*)
	+ -	(*adding and subtraction*)
Last	< >	(*logical operators*)

There are in fact other *logical* operators as well, which will be dealt with later.

Where an expression has operators of equal precedence, they are worked out from left to right, except for powers, which are worked out from right to left. It is important that you realise this, otherwise you'll get unexpected results.

You can *force* Series 3a to ignore its precedence and perform parts of a calculation in a different order, by enclosing those parts within brackets. Series 3a will look for brackets, and work out what's inside them first following the rules given above. This all looks very complicated, but in fact it is more complicated to explain. Let us look at some examples.

2+3*4	evaluates as 3 times 4, *then* plus 2 = 14
(2+3)*4	evaluates as 2 plus 3, *then* times 4 = 20
2+3*4/6	evaluates as 3 times 4, divided by 6, plus 2 = 4
4*(2+3)/5	evaluates as 2 plus 3, times 4, divided by 5 = 4

When in doubt, enclose the parts you want calculated first within brackets.

Mixing variables and constant types

Series 3a follows specific rules when performing calculations on different types of variable and constant. Remember that an integer (or long integer) number doesn't have a decimal point, and an integer variable *can't* have a decimal point.

As a general comment, Series 3a tries to perform the simplest arithmetic possible on an expression. Thus, if all values in the expression are integers, it performs integer arithmetic. This can, however, cause problems. Integer variables have a limited range (-32768 to +32767). If an integer expression produces a result outside this range, you will get an error ('**Integer Overflow**'). Thus

```
x&=400*400
```

seems legitimate enough: both integer values to be multiplied are within the acceptable range. The result - 160000 - however, is *not* within the range. Even though the variable that's going to store the result, x&, is a *long* integer, Series 3a will attempt *integer* arithmetic. The solution is to convert one of the values to a floating point variable, or better, to a long integer. Thus, either of the next two example lines will produce a correct result (the INT function returns a long integer of the value immediately following it in brackets:

```
x&=400.0*400
x&=INT(400)*400
```

If an integer value is to be added, subtracted, multiplied or divided by a floating point value, Series 3a first converts the integer to a floating point value. The result is stored in a variable according to the *type* declared for that variable. For example:

```
cost%=30+0.175*30
```

First, the 30 is converted to a floating point value (30.0) and is then multiplied by 0.175. The result, 5.25, is then added to 30.0 to give 35.25. Series 3a then looks at where this answer is to be saved, and discovers that it has to go into the *integer* memory boxes, 'cost%'. So it saves 35.25 as an integer, which is 35.

Series 3a obeys its rules implicitly: it is up to you to make sure that the correct instructions are given: in the above example, if you didn't want to lose the decimal part of the answer, cost% would have to be a floating point variable, such as cost.

Note that when Series 3a converts a floating point value to an integer value, it simply loses everything after the decimal point.

One final point: if the result of a calculation is larger than the variable that's going to hold it is capable of handling, then you will get an error. To give an example:

```
x%=100.5*1000.2
```

would produce an error, because the result of the calculation is outside the range permitted for integer variables.

Making calculations whilst programming

You will probably be aware that the Program Editor is, in fact, a specially adapted form of the word processor built into Series 3a. *'Evaluate'*, one of the options available under the *'Edit'* menu, can be an extremely useful tool whilst you are programming to make calculations during the editing process.

'Evaluate' (the short-cut keys are PSION and '[E]') works only on real values, not variables. The procedure is straightforward. You either highlight the calculation you want evaluated by holding down the SHIFT key and the left or right arrow keys, or use the arrow keys to position the cursor after the calculation, and then either select *'Evaluate'* from the *'Edit'* menu, or press the short-cut key combination. It is often quicker to make a calculation by entering it as a line on its own, rather than going to the calculator section of Series 3a - particularly if you want the result of the calculation as a value in your program. When the calculation is evaluated, the calculation part remains highlighted - so that you can quickly delete it if you wish (using the DELETE key), whilst the answer is not highlighted.

You can use any of the mathematical functions available in the Calculator. Try this:

1)   Load any program file.
2)   On a line on its own, enter `sin(45)`
3)   Highlight it (SHIFT and arrow keys), or place the cursor at the end of the line.
4)   Press the PSION and [E] keys simultaneously.

The answer will be displayed at the end of the line you have entered.

You can set the format for the *'Evaluate'* option, from the System screen:

1)   Press the 'SYSTEM' button to get to the System display, then press the MENU key.
2)   Select *Control*, then *Evaluate format*.

You can now set the format for the displayed answer to 'General' (*floating point*), 'Fixed' and hexadecimal. If you select 'Fixed' you will also be able to set the number of decimal places. You can also set whether trigonometric functions act on degrees or radians for evaluations.

The ability to set the format enables you to convert hexadecimal numbers to decimal numbers and vice versa. With *'Evaluate'* set to the 'General' format, enter $A2 on its own line in the Program Editor, highlight it, and press the PSION and [E] keys: the decimal equivalent, '162' will be displayed. Now set the *Evaluate* format to hexadecimal, highlight the '162' and evaluate it by pressing the PSION and [E] keys, and the hexadecimal equivalent of 162 (&A2) will be displayed.

NOTE: Hexadecimal numbers are represented by prefixing them with a '$' (integers) or '&' (long integers). Evaluate converts decimal values to *long* integers.

CHAPTER 6
From keyboard to screen

This Chapter introduces you to the basic methods of
* *Entering information at the keyboard for the text screen*
* *Controlling the text screen display.*
The keyboard *words covered are:*
    INPUT, EDIT, GET, GET$, KEY, KEY$, KMOD.
The text screen *words covered are:*
    PRINT, FONT, STYLE, SCREEN, AT, CLS, CURSOR
    ON/OFF, SCREENINFO, OFF

Getting data into and out of a program

Armed with the essential components of a program, you're now in a position to start learning about the basic words in the OPL language, and perhaps the most important of these are the words associated with getting information from the keyboard into the program, and for displaying information on the screen. This Chapter deals with the basic OPL words involved for the *text* screen: they simply produce 'words' on the screen, with none of the menus or dialog displays used for the built-in applications. Later Chapters will deal with these *graphic* methods of requesting and displaying information, which, while more 'picturesque' and will undoubtedly be used more often, are also slightly more complex.

Inputs from the keyboard

Almost without exception, the programs you write will need to have information in one form or another entered from the keyboard. The 'Carpet' program, planned earlier, is a typical example: in this program, each time it is run you will want to enter the relevant measurements and cost from the keyboard.

OPL has a number of words which allow you to input information from the keyboard. Those related to the *text* screen are now described.

INPUT   This command instructs the Series 3a to get an input of key presses from the keyboard until the ENTER key is pressed, displaying the characters on the screen as they are entered.

The entered information obviously has to be stored by Series 3a for use in the program. There are two ways to use INPUT: the first is

INPUT *variable*

The *variable* must have been previously declared, of course, and can be any of the basic variable types - integer, long integer, floating point or string. The type you use will depend on the kind of information you want entered from the keyboard.

If you want only *whole numbers* to be entered from the keyboard, then you'll use an integer or long integer variable (depending on the maximum value the entered number will be allowed to have). If you want to allow for a decimal entry or for very large numbers outside the range of integer variable, use a floating point variable. If you want *characters* (which can include numbers) to be entered from the keyboard, then use a *string* variable: this must have been declared with sufficient 'space' to allow for the maximum number of characters you're going to allow to be entered. Thus, typical instructions could look like this

INPUT v%   Input an integer value and store it in v%
INPUT v&   Input a long integer and store it in v&
INPUT v   Input a floating point value and store it in v
INPUT v$ Input a character string and store it in v$

If an incorrect key is pressed for the type of data being entered, then Series 3a will reject it and give the user the chance to re-enter the input: the cursor is moved to the next line, and Series 3a shows it didn't accept the previous input by displaying a question mark. You can avoid this happening by the use of 'error trapping', but we're not ready for that yet.

The second way to use INPUT is:
INPUT *LogicalFile.field*

53

Here, instead of using a GLOBAL or LOCAL declared variable, a *file field* variable is used. Files and their fields are discussed in a later Chapter.

EDIT This is a rather special word enabling the user to 'edit' a 'string of characters' from the keyboard. In some respects it's like INPUT when used for a string. With INPUT, everything that has to be stored is entered at the keyboard. With EDIT, a *previously stored* string can be changed, or 'edited'. Hence the name (!). The format for the instruction is

EDIT a$

where *a$* is any string variable, and holds the string of characters to be edited. The characters are displayed on the screen. So if *a$* held the string "Edit me now", then "Edit me now" would be displayed on the screen.

You can use all the usual editing keys - the arrow or cursor keys to move along the line, the DELETE key, and so on. The ESC key will completely clear the line. You can continue editing the string until the ENTER key is pressed. At that point, the newly edited information is stored back in the variable *a$*. Of course, as with all string variables, *a$* must have been declared with sufficient 'boxes' or spaces for the characters: you won't be able to add more characters to the string than have been allowed for in your declaration (using the LOCAL or GLOBAL instruction).

GET This function was introduced earlier, in Chapter 2. It waits for a key to be pressed, and 'returns' the *character code* for that key. The character code, remember, is the number which Series 3a uses to determine the actual character shape. In this instance, however, it returns the *number* and not the shape or character itself.

Series 3a needs to know what to do with the character code, so the general format for using GET is:

g%=GET

where g% is an *integer* variable that has been previously declared. You can of course use any integer variable - it doesn't have to be g%: GET will always return an integer though, so don't use any other type of variable.

> **Note:** OPL words that are functions - such as GET - all return a value or a character string which can be assigned to a variable. Sometimes, the value is not required, and so the assignment isn't necessary. This is the case with GET, for example, when it is used simply to stop the program continuing until a key is pressed.

For all of the keyboard characters, the character number obtained by GET is the ASCII code number, which is generally the same for all computers.

GET returns special codes or numbers for some of the keys on your keyboard. These are:

DELETE	Returns the value 8
TAB	Returns the value 9
ENTER	Returns the value 13
ESC	Returns the value 27
UP ARROW	Returns the value 256
DOWN ARROW	Returns the value 257
RIGHT ARROW	Returns the value 258
LEFT ARROW	Returns the value 259
PAGEUP	Returns the value 260
PAGEDOWN	Returns the value 261
HOME	Returns the value 262
END	Returns the value 263
MENU	Returns the value 290
HELP	Returns the value 291
◆	Returns the value 292

If the PSION key is pressed simultaneously with any other key, then 512 is added to the value normally returned by that key. Thus pressing the PSION and HELP keys together will return a value of 803 (*291+512*).

You can use these values to test whether one of the 'function' keys has been pressed during your program. The numbers returned by the alphabetic and numeric keys of your keyboard are listed in your Operating Manual.

GET$ This function is similar to GET - Series 3a waits for a key on the keyboard to be pressed. The difference is, in this instance, the actual *character* is saved. The format for using GET$ is

$$g\$=GET\$$$

Notice that this time a *string* variable must be used which should, of course, be declared to hold at least one character.

KEY This too is similar to GET, but in this case, Series 3a *doesn't wait* until a key has been pressed. Instead, it reports the character code of any key that has been pressed since the *last time the keyboard was 'polled'* or checked for a keypress using one of the OPL keyboard input words such as INPUT or GET. You'd use this instruction to find out whether a key had been pressed whilst 'other things' had been going on - in a game program, for example. As with GET, KEY returns an integer, and it is necessary to tell Series 3a where to store it. Thus the general format is:

$$k\%=KEY$$

If no key has been pressed, then KEY returns a zero - so the value held by *k%* would be '0'. The codes returned by the special keys are the same as for GET.

KEY$ This function is the same as KEY, except that it returns the *character* rather than the character code of any key pressed since the last time the keyboard was 'polled'. The format for the instruction is

$$k\$=KEY\$$$

If no key has been pressed, then a *null* string is returned. That means the 'string' holds no characters at all: in computer terms, $k\$$ is said to be equal to "" (two quote marks with nothing between them).

KMOD   This function returns a code number to indicate which *modifier* key was pressed at the time of the last access to the keyboard. There are four modifier keys - SHIFT, CONTROL, PSION and CAPS ON. The value returned by KMOD (always an integer) is such that you can tell which of the keys were pressed. It works on the binary system discussed in Chapter 1. First, here are the codes for the keys:

SHIFT	returns 2	(10 in binary)
CONTROL	returns 4	(100 in binary)
PSION	returns 8	(1000 in binary)
CAPS ON	returns 16	(10000 in binary)

Note that the modifier for the CAPS key is *not* the keypress - which would be the ◆ (Diamond) key, but whether the CAPS 'lock' had been turned on previously (PSION and CAPS keys).

As before, Series 3a needs to know where to store the information, so the format for the KMOD instruction is

km%=KMOD

Now let us look at the values that can be returned. First of all, if no modifier key has be pressed, then KMOD returns a zero (km%=0). If any *one* of the modifier keys has been pressed, then the value shown will be returned. So if, for example, the PSION key had been pressed, then KMOD would return 8 (1000 in binary). If more than one key has been pressed, then the value returned is the *sum* of the values shown above. Thus, if both the SHIFT key and the CONTROL key had been pressed simultaneously, then KMOD returns 6 (2+4): *km%* will hold the value 6, or 110 in binary.

Note how each key has a single unique binary digit reference: this is known as a 'flag'. Later on you will see that there are ways to 'pick out' the information regarding which keys have been pressed, by using 'logical' operators to determine whether the 'flag' has been set.

Before we put some of these words to use, let us take a look at the instructions available for *displaying* text on the screen.

Basic screen display instructions

Achieving a neat and orderly display on the screen of Series 3a helps to give a program a professional look. At this stage, we're going to look at the most common instructions available for controlling the *text* screen's appearance and display.

PRINT This (with its graphic relatives) is probably one of the most important words in OPL, for it enables your 'work' to be displayed in the screen window. The general format is

```
PRINT variable or expression list
```

A number of *variables* and/or *expressions* can be included on the same line by separating each of them with a semi-colon or a comma. The rules are:
A semi-colon between two *variables* and/or *expressions* will result in them being displayed without any spaces between them.
A comma between two variables and/or expressions will cause a space to be printed between them.
After the PRINT statement has been performed, the cursor is place at the start of the *next* line *unless* the statement *ends* (a) with a semi-colon, in which case it is placed at the next character position on the same line, or (b) a comma, in which case the cursor is positioned one space further along on the same line.
Where it is required to display a message or a string of characters, then that message or string must be enclosed between quotation marks.
A PRINT statement without any variables simply positions the cursor (flashing bar) on the next line: the cursor position marks where the next print-out will occur.

Those are the rules. Now let us have a look at some typical PRINT statements, and examine what the results of them will be. We'll assume some variables have certain values:

```
a$    =      "Hello"
b%    =      1994
c     =      3.147
```

Here are some examples of PRINT statements:

```
PRINT a$;b%      display = Hello1994
PRINT a$,b%      display = Hello 1994
PRINT b%;c       display = 19943.147
PRINT b%,c       display =1994 3.147
```

Notice how a comma causes a space to be introduced between the variable displays. Here are some more examples using 'strings' and 'string variables':

```
PRINT a$;a$           display = HelloHello
PRINT a$,a$           display = Hello Hello
PRINT a$;" all"       display = Hello all
PRINT a$,"all"        display = Hello all
PRINT "Hallo","all"   display = Hello all
```

PRINT can also be used to display the result of *functions* or *expressions*. For example, to display the result of the 'mod' function developed in Chapter 4, you'd have a statement line something like this

```
PRINT mod:(1991,4)      display = 3
```

What happens here is that Series 3a sees the PRINT statement, then looks at the next bit to see what it has to display. It finds the 'mod' function (which must, of course, have been written as a part of the same program file, or *loaded* in with another file). It performs the necessary calculation and displays the result - in this case, 3. One more example:

PRINT "2 x 3 =",2*3   *display* = 2 x 3 = 6

Remember that, if a semi-colon is included at the *end* of a
PRINT statement line, then the cursor isn't positioned at the
beginning of the next line after the PRINT statement has
been executed, but is instead left at the end of the displayed
line. So the following two lines in a procedure:

PRINT "Hi there";
PRINT " everyone!"

would result in a display on the screen of

Hi there everyone!

When the screen is filled up and there's no more room at the
bottom to display anything else, the screen display *scrolls*
upwards, that is to say, every line moves up one, and the top
line is lost. The new line to display then appears on the
bottom. This can be avoided, if desired, with the OPL word
AT, discussed later.

Finally, PRINT always *overwrites* any text that is *already*
on the text screen where the new display is to appear.

The appearance of the text can be controlled with the FONT command:

FONT   This command determines the *font* and the *style* to be used
for the entire text screen display. The format is

FONT *id%,style%*

where *id%* determines which of a range of fonts is to be
used, and *style%* determines how the font will appear
(bold, underlined and so on). A wide range of fonts is built
into the ROM of your Series 3a, and these have identification
values (*id%*) as follows:

Font id	Description	Size[1] (pixels)
1	Series 3, Normal[2]	8
2	Series 3, Bold[2]	8
3	Series 3, Digits[2]	6x6
4	Monospaced	8x8
5	Roman (Serif), proportional spacing	8
6	Roman (Serif), proportional spacing	11
7	Roman (Serif), proportional spacing	13
8	Roman (Serif), proportional spacing	16
9	Swiss (Sans Serif), proportional spacing	8
10	Swiss (Sans Serif), proportional spacing	11
11	Swiss (Sans Serif), proportional spacing	13
12	Swiss (Sans Serif), proportional spacing	16
13	Monospaced	6x6

1. For proportional fonts, the width in pixels: varies according to the letter. Monospaced font characters all have an equal width, as specified.
2. These three fonts are provided to give compatibility with the Series 3 machine, which doesn't have the screen capabilities or font range of the Series 3a.

Note: After a FONT command, the *text* screen is cleared, so you cannot use this command to *mix* fonts on the text screen. It is possible, however, to make minor changes to the style, using the STYLE command.

There is also an identification value of $9A in hexadecimal, which loads the machine's default font. This is machine dependent and is font 11 for the Series 3a, and font 1 for the Series 3. Note that, although font 5 is, technically, a serif font, in practice the serif is too small to be seen at this size.

The styles available with the FONT command are as follows:

STYLE	Decimal Value	Binary Value
Bold	1	1
Underlined	2	10
Inverse	4	100
Double Height	8	1000
Monospacing	16	10000
Italic	32	100000

The styles can be used in any combination by simply adding the values. For example, if you wanted the selected font to be Bold and Double-Height, you would set `style%` to 9 (1+8). It would of course be pointless to set the style of a normally monospaced face to monospacing. As you can see, the range of type sizes and styles available to you is quite extensive. Notice too how each style has a unique, single binary value.

You don't have to specify the font each time you wish to change the style of its display. You can use the OPL word STYLE.

STYLE   This command can be used to modify the display of any new text input. Unlike the FONT command, STYLE does *not* clear the screen, and so enables you to mix a few styles of the same font in one text display. The format is

STYLE `style%`

where `style%` is a constant or integer variable with values as in the table above, except that Bold (1), Double Height (8) and Monospacing (16) are not available.

You will probably be aware that your Series 3a produces its displays in 'windows'. When you run a program that involves only text, Series 3a will assume you want the whole screen to be used as the window area. However, you can define a specific area of the screen for text print-outs with the OPL word SCREEN. (You can, in addition, define up to eight screen areas or windows for graphics displays).

SCREEN   This command allows you to specify an area of the whole text screen for the text displays. There are two ways to use the SCREEN instruction. The first has the format

SCREEN `width%,height%`

where `width%` is the number of characters wide you want the window to be, and `height%` is the number of rows deep, *based on the character size of the selected font and style* (FONT command). Whatever your choice, with *this* format the 'window' is positioned centrally in the display area. Characters are displayed within the screen in the same way that they are displayed on the default 'overall' screen. They will 'wrap' to the next line if they extend beyond the right edge, and will cause the text in the screen to scroll if there are more lines than allowed for by the height. If you specify a screen size which is too great for the Series 3a screen, because of the size of the font selected, then you will get an error when the program is run. For example, setting `height%` to 5 when using font 8 with double height style will produce an error, since the characters are too large to fit in five lines on the screen.

You may not want the text window to appear in the centre of the screen, but instead in a particular area of the display, in which case the second form of the instruction would be used:

> SCREEN `width%,height%,cols%,rows%`

where `width%` and `height%` are the width and height of the window, as before, and `cols%` and `rows%` determine the top left corner of the window in terms of character positions. `Cols%` is the number of characters in from the left, and `rows%` is the number of rows down from the top. Note that whichever format is used, the specified screen area does not have a border, nor is the entire screen area 'cleared': *new* text is limited to display *only* within the specified area, until a new area is specified.

Normally, the first time you PRINT to a any screen, the displayed data appears at the top left. Thereafter, the cursor is positioned according to the way you have used the PRINT command. This may not be what you want - you may wish to have your data displayed at a specific location on the screen. You can achieve this by using the AT command:

AT   AT allows you to position the *text* cursor at a specific character location within the text screen. The format is

> AT `column%,row%`

where `column%` represents the number of characters across the screen, from the left, and `row%` represents the number of rows down the screen, from the top. Thus

```
AT 5,3
```

would position the cursor 5 characters from the left and 3 rows down, and that's where the next item to be displayed on the screen will occur. AT can also be used before an INPUT statement: in this case, the data entered at the keyboard will be positioned at the location determined by the AT statement.

CLS   This OPL command, which stands for CLear Screen, completely clears the contents of the text window. It is very useful for keeping the display nice and tidy between different kinds of operation, and to prevent the display from scrolling all the time. For example, in the Carpet program discussed earlier, once one set of information has been displayed and is finished with, a CLS can be used to clear the screen ready for the next display of information. The alternative would be for the text on the screen to scroll up as new information is added, which is unsightly.

CURSOR OFF/ON   There may be times when your program is running that you don't want the cursor to be seen flashing away merrily on the screen. You can switch it 'off' with the instruction line

```
CURSOR OFF
```

The cursor is still positioned where specified in the screen window - by the AT command, for example - but you won't be able to see it. To turn the cursor display on again, use the instruction:

```
CURSOR ON
```

OFF   This instruction switches off the Psion Series 3a. It can be used in a program to provide, for example, a welcome message for the next time your machine is switched on. When switched on again, the program continues with the instruction following the OFF command. Here is a very simple example:

```
PROC swoff:
  OFF
  PRINT "Welcome back!"
  GET
ENDP
```

You can use OFF x%, where x% is a value between 8 and 16383, to have automatic switch on after x% seconds: you can also switch on in the normal manner during the 'off' period. Be careful not to include this command in a loop - otherwise you may have to reset your machine!

Information about the text screen display

When programs involve the use of both the text window and graphics windows, it is sometimes useful to have information about the text screen. The text screen size is slightly smaller than the *actual* screen of the Series 3a, with a few pixels gap all round. (A pixel is the smallest 'point' on the screen). This gap depends on the font selected for the screen size when the SCREEN command is executed, and is referred to as the top and left margins. If your program needs this information about the text screen, it can be obtained by use of the OPL function SCREENINFO.

SCREENINFO This instruction provides complete details about the *current* text screen, and has the format:

```
                SCREENINFO info%()
```

where info%() is any integer array variable that must have been declared (as a LOCAL or GLOBAL) with at least *10* elements. After the instruction has been executed, the contents of each element in the array are as follows:

info%(1)	Size of the left margin, in pixels
info%(2)	Size of the top margin, in pixels
info%(3)	Text screen width, as number of characters in the current font.
info%(4)	Text screen height, as number of characters in current font.
info%(6)	Identification number of the currently selected font.
info%(7)	Pixel width of the currently selected font.

info%(8)   Pixel height of a text line in the currently
              selected font.
info%(5), info%(9),and info%(10) are reserved
              for later use.

Example programs

The example programs which complete this Chapter demonstrate the use of some the OPL words just discussed. There is nothing like 'hands on' experience to get the feel of programming your Series 3a, so it will be well worth while entering the examples, experimenting with them as suggested in the accompanying text, then deleting them when you are satisfied you understand the principles involved.

Getting an Input

Here is a simple program that will accept an input of data from the keyboard. You are asked to enter your name and age, and then a message is displayed. In this procedure, the CLS command is used to clear the screen between the input and displayed results. Enter the program carefully (it uses a *function* not yet discussed - YEAR - which returns the current year as determined by the Psion Series 3a's built in clock), then translate and run it.

```
PROC intest:
     LOCAL name$(24),age%
     PRINT "What's your name?",
     INPUT name$
     PRINT " How old are you?",
     INPUT age%
     CLS
     PRINT "Hello, ";name$
     PRINT "You were born in",YEAR-age%
     GET
ENDP
```

When you're satisfied that this routine works, edit it by entering semi-colons instead of commas at the end of the first two **PRINT** statement lines. See what happens too, if you declare name$() to have only, say, 5 characters (name$(5)) - and try to input *more* than five characters.

Calling another procedure

In Chapter 4 we developed a *function*, called mod: (), which returns the remainder after one number is divided by another. You'll remember that we couldn't run it directly, since it needs to be *called* by another procedure. Here's a program to do just that. Enter *both* the calling procedure *and* the mod: () procedure in the *one* program file. Both of them must be entered before you translate and run the program, otherwise you'll get an error message when you try to run it.

Notice that the parameters used in the *calling routine*, 'num' and 'den', are not the same as those in the mod: () routine itself. They don't have to be. However, the variable *types* must be the same, otherwise you'll get a '**Type violation**' error when the program is run. To demonstrate this point, after you have tested the program as it is written, edit it by entering two integer values, say '12' and '5', in place of 'num' and 'den' respectively in the line which reads 'PRINT ... mod:(num,den)'.

```
PROC modtest:
        LOCAL num,den
        PRINT "Enter a number:",
        INPUT num
        PRINT "Divide it by?",
        INPUT den
        PRINT "The remainder is",mod:(num,den)
        GET
ENDP

PROC mod:(n,d)
        RETURN n-(INT(n/d)*d)
ENDP
```

Incidentally, you'll notice when you're entering the *second* procedure in this program that Series 3a doesn't automatically display 'PROC' or 'ENDP' for you: you must enter these yourself. Also, you'll notice you have to enter the 'first' indent of this procedure yourself: Series 3a automatically indents thereafter to your *last* indented position.

> Note: There is also another, more sophisticated, construction for *calling* procedures, which enables the *program itself* to determine which procedure should be called, according to a test of some kind. This is dealt with in the Chapter on Creating Menus in Part 2.

Editing text

Here's a program to demonstrate the use of EDIT. You'll be prompted to enter a *string* of characters, and then you'll be asked to change them. Both the original and the changed inputs will be displayed.

```
PROC editest:
     LOCAL new$(32),old$(32)
     PRINT "Enter something now:"
     INPUT new$
     old$=new$
     CLS
     PRINT "Now change it"
     EDIT new$
     CLS
     AT 1,2
     PRINT "You started with"
     PRINT old$
     AT 1,4
     PRINT "...and changed it to"
     PRINT new$
     GET
ENDP
```

Pick a font and style

This program allows you to experiment with the various built in fonts and styles available on the Series 3a. Remember that after the use of the FONT command the screen is cleared, making the use of the CLS command unnecessary. The screen is not automatically cleared after STYLE, however. To save having to re-run the program after examining each font and style, this program uses a *loop* instruction (DO...UNTIL), which is discussed in detail in a later Chapter. When invited to enter a style reference number the first time, you can enter a value for a single style, or, to get a combination of styles, you simple add the associated style numbers. Thus, to get a style of Double Height (8) and Italic (32), you would enter 40 (8+32). When asked to *change* the style, remember that only Underlining (2), Inverse (4) or Italic (32) are available, singly or in combination (e.g. 6 for inverse underlining): any value entered which does not contain these values (e.g. - '0' or '1') will clear the corresponding style if it has previously been set. When translated and run, the program will continue to ask for your inputs until you press the ESC key when requested. (ESC 'returns' a value of '27' into the variable g%).

WARNING
Font 3 is the Series 3 *numeric* face - use it and you won't be able to read the display!

Note that there are several lines in this program which are too long to be entered as one line in this book, indicated by *same line continued*. *You must enter both parts in* one *line on your Series 3a, without any spaces between the two parts.*

```
PROC fonts:
 LOCAL fid%,sty%,g%
 DO
   STYLE 0
   PRINT "Font id (1 to 13)? ";
   INPUT fid%
   PRINT "Style (1,2,4,8,16,
same line continued      32 or combinations)?",
   INPUT sty%
   FONT fid%,sty%
   AT 1,2
   PRINT "Font",fid%,"and Style",
same line continued sty%,"looks like this"
   GET
   AT 1,3
   PRINT "Change style to (2,4,
same line continued      32 or combinations)?",
   INPUT sty%
   STYLE sty%
   AT 1,4
   PRINT "Same Font in style",sty%
   STYLE 4
   AT 1,1
   PRINT "Press ESC to finish"
   g%=GET
   CLS
 UNTIL g%=27
ENDP
```

CHAPTER 7
Making decisions

This Chapter introduces the techniques used in programs
for making decisions and acting accordingly.
OPL words covered are
  IF, ELSEIF, ELSE, ENDIF, AND, OR, NOT
and the logical operators
  < *and* >.

Putting things to the test

One of the most essential elements of most programs is an ability to
'test' or compare two values, and to act according to the result. For
example, you may have a situation in a program which demands a 'Yes'
or 'No' input from the user. The user's requirement can be obtained by
displaying the message "Yes or No?", and then testing the keyboard to
see whether the 'Y' or 'N' key has been pressed - using INPUT or
GET$, for example. You will want Series 3a to act according to the
result. How do you do this? With the extremely powerful little OPL
word, IF, and its associated words ELSEIF, ELSE and ENDIF.

The general structure or format is as follows:

IF   a comparison or condition test is <u>correct</u> ...
        perform *these* instructions, then go to the instruction after ENDIF
ELSEIF   a second comparison or condition test is <u>correct</u>
        perform *these* instructions then go to the instruction after ENDIF
ELSEIF   a third comparison or condition test is <u>correct</u>
        perform *these* instructions then go to the instruction after ENDIF
ELSE   if all other tests fail,
        perform these instructions then go to the instruction after ENDIF
ENDIF

Now let us look at these words in more detail.

IF   This tells the Series 3a to make the 'condition' test that
          immediately follows it on the same line. If the condition is
          correct or *true* then Series 3a will obey the *next*
          instruction(s), until it comes to an ELSEIF, an ELSE or an

ENDIF instruction, at which point it will jump to the instruction immediately following the ENDIF statement.

If the condition is *not true*, then Series 3a jumps to the next ELSEIF, ELSE or ENDIF instruction (whichever comes first). In other words, it doesn't obey any of the instructions that immediately follow the IF statement. We'll examine the condition tests you can use in detail later on, but so that you get the idea, here is an example. Say we want to know whether the value of a variable v% is equal to 100. The test line would look like this

IF v%=100

Normally, a line such as v%=100 would be an *assignment*: you will recall from an earlier Chapter that it would mean 'put the value 100 in the memory boxes labelled v%'. Following one of the condition testing words (IF, ELSEIF) however, it is in effect asking the question '*is this true?*'.

So, with the line IF v%=100, Series 3a sees the IF command, looks at what follows, and discovers that, in effect, it is being asked '*does v%=100?*'. It looks at v%, and if it finds it is in fact 100 (*true*), it obeys the instructions that immediately follow until - as mentioned earlier - it reaches ELSEIF, ELSE or ENDIF. It then jumps to the statement line immediately following the ENDIF statement.

If on the other hand it finds that v% is *not* equal to 100, then it ignores the following instructions, and jumps straightaway to the next ELSEIF, ELSE or the statement following ENDIF, to see what it should do instead.

ELSEIF Is very similar to IF, in that it needs to be followed by a condition test. ELSEIF is never the *first* in a series of tests, always one of the intermediate ones. The effect of an ELSEIF test is exactly the same as described for IF. You can have as many ELSEIF lines in a procedure as you need - or *none* at all. All you need to bear in mind is that Series 3a starts with an IF statement and continues down through the

ELSEIF statements (if any), making the tests until a *true* condition occurs.

ELSE   This instruction says to Series 3a *"If the previous IF and (if they exist) all the ELSEIF tests have proved to be not true then do this..."*. All the instructions that follow are then obeyed until ENDIF is reached, at which point Series 3a jumps to the instruction following ENDIF.

ELSE can appear only once in an IF...ENDIF series of tests, and it must *always* be the last one before ENDIF. If you think about it, it would be silly to follow an ELSE with an ELSEIF, since Series 3a obeys only *one block or set of instructions* in an IF...ENDIF series.

ENDIF   Series 3a needs to know where it has to get the *next* instruction once it has completed all of the tests and any instructions performed as a result of those tests. ENDIF is what it looks for: once the series of instructions has been completed, it looks for an ENDIF and then obeys the next instruction.

There's nothing like an example to make it all crystal clear. Here's a little procedure that should help: enter it carefully, then run it: it will help to demonstrate the way IF and its associated words work. Notice the indents on lines following IF statements: this is to help when writing and checking procedures, so you can see clearly which instructions are to be obeyed, and where a jump is to be made if a test proves to be not true.

```
PROC iftest1:
  IF 3=3
    PRINT "Three=three!"
  ELSEIF 4=4
    PRINT "Four=four!"
  ELSE
    PRINT "Nothing=anything!"
  ENDIF
  PRINT "Press a key"
  GET
ENDP
```

If entered properly, when you translate and run the procedure the screen will display "Three=three!". But "Four=four!" won't be displayed, nor will "Nothing=anything!". Having found the result of the first IF test to be *true*, Series 3a obeys the instruction immediately following - to print "Three=three!". The next instruction is an ELSEIF - so it has completed all the instructions it must do on a *true* result, and consequently jumps to the statement after ENDIF, which is PRINT. Remember, Psion Series 3a will perform *only* the instructions following the *first* true result of a test.

Now edit the program - make the first IF line read

```
IF 3=6
```

and translate and run the procedure again. This time, "Four=four!" should be displayed: the IF statement proved to be *not true*, so the ELSEIF test was made and found to be *true*. One more edit - this time change the ELSEIF line to read

```
ELSEIF 4=1
```

leaving the other changes alone, of course. Now on translating and running the procedure, the display will read "Nothing=anything!". Here, having found both the IF and the ELSEIF tests to be *untrue*, Series 3a sees the ELSE statement, and says to itself "I must obey the next instruction(s) then".

Supposing you didn't want anything to happen if the previous instructions proved to be *not true*? Simple: don't include the ELSE statement or its instruction set.

The only statement that *must* appear after an IF statement is an ENDIF.

Nested IF statements

Series 3a will allow you to include an IF...ENDIF structure *within* an IF...ENDIF structure. In fact, you can go on *nesting* IF structures quite a few times before Series 3a will complain. Go back to our previous example, and edit it again to read exactly as the following procedure (use the TAB key to indent lines).

When you run this procedure, you should get the message "N doesn't = Y". Notice how indenting the lines makes the program easier to read and to follow what is happening.

Notice too that *each* IF has an ENDIF at the end of its own little series of statements. This is very important, and is the cause of many a headache when debugging programs. Series 3a won't understand what to do if there's an ENDIF missing, or if there's one too many, or if it is in the wrong place. In fact it will give you a message that something is wrong when you try to translate the procedure prior to running it.

That's one very good reason for using indents. (If you're not already doing so, use the TAB key for indenting).

```
PROC iftest1:
    IF 3=3
        IF "N"="Y"
            PRINT "Oh dear!"
        ELSE
            PRINT "N doesn't = Y"
        ENDIF
    ELSEIF 4=4
        PRINT "Four=four!"
    ELSE
        PRINT "Nothing=anything!"
    ENDIF
    PRINT "Press a key"
    GET
ENDP
```

An IF ELSE ENDIF sequence nested within an IF ELSEIF sequence.

In this last example, we tested the equality of *strings*. It ought to be mentioned here that when strings are tested for equality, Series 3a looks for a *perfect* match: thus

$$IF \quad "A"="a"$$

would produce a *not true* result.

Now let us look at the condition tests that can be made following an IF or an ELSEIF statement.

The logic of it all

The first thing to understand, perhaps, is how Series 3a recognises or 'indicates' a *true* and a *not true* condition. With the lines IF $v\%=100$ or IF $3=3$ and so on, when Series 3a makes the condition test it needs to store the result away 'privately' so that it can then use that result for the next part of the instruction. It does this by storing away the value

'-1' if the result of a condition test is *true*, and '0' if the result is *not true*'.

However, when Series comes to analyse and act on the *result* of the test, it takes *any value* to be *true*, and '0' or zero to be *not true*. This is a valuable feature that we can use in our programs, because it means we can make a test for '0' without bothering to use the '=' sign.

For example, let us say that v% has a value of '0'. The line

```
IF v%
```

would result in *not true*, because Series 3a looks at v%, finds it has no *condition* to test, so takes the *value* of v% as the result. If v% had any value whatsoever - not just '-1' but 345 say, then it would come up with the answer *true*. This is often useful in programs when you wish to test whether a variable has any value at all. For string variables, such as v$, the *null* string or ' "" ' is the same as zero in numeric strings. So

```
IF v$
```

will be *not true* if v$ = "", and *true* if there are any characters in the string.

Series 3a will also make a condition test if the test 'expression' is enclosed in brackets. This is easily demonstrated by the following procedure (enter, translate and run it):

```
PROC iftest2:
     PRINT (4=4)
     GET
ENDP
```

The screen will display '-1' - showing that the result of the test is *true* (4 does in fact, equal 4 ... a great relief to us all). The result of a test with a *true* result is stored as '-1', and the instruction is to print that result. Now edit the procedure so that the part in brackets is (4=8) and run it again. This time, the screen will display '0', showing that the result of the test is *not true*.

The fact that Series 3a 'returns' or saves a value of -1 or zero according to the result of a test is useful in another way. This is best explained by an example. Suppose you want a variable v% to have a value of, say, 5 if a condition is *true*, and a value of zero if the condition is *not true*. You could write it like this:

```
...
IF  condition test is true
        v%=5
ELSE
        v%=0
ENDIF
```

There's nothing wrong with that - it will work fine. But as you have just seen, if the condition test is enclosed in brackets, Series 3a will return -1 or zero according to the result of the test. So you could write a line like this:

```
v%=-5*(condition test)
```

The value you want for v% is made *negative* in this line, so that if the condition test turns out to be *true*, it will be multiplied by '-1', and as you know, -5 times -1 gives +5. If on the other hand the result of the condition test is zero (*not true*), -5 will be multiplied by zero - and anything times zero is zero.

This is a slightly more advanced programming technique, but as you can see, it can save a few lines of code. On the 'down' side, it is not as easy to see clearly what the code is doing as the 'IF...ELSE...ENDIF' version.

Logical operators

Now you know how Series 3a makes its condition tests (and stores the result for itself), let us have a look at the various tests at your disposal. The '=' sign on its own is not adequate for all programming requirements: suppose, for example, you wanted to test whether a variable was *greater than* a certain value, or *less than* the value of another variable. This would difficult if we could only make the 'equals' test.

> This symbol asks the question "Is what's on the *left* of the symbol *greater than* what's on the right of it?". If it *is* greater, the answer is *true*. If it isn't, the answer is *not true*. Typical statements could be:

```
IF a>b
IF a%>b%
IF "A">"B"
```

If the value of left hand side is greater than the value of the right hand side, then the result is *true* (-1). Otherwise, the result is *not true*.

The last example IF "A">"B" would result in *not true*, because Series 3a looks at the *character codes* when comparing strings. The character code for "A" is less than the character code for "B". As it happens, it's also less than the character code for "a". It's worth looking at a few more examples of string comparisons, because they can be extremely useful in many types of program. Enter the following procedure and run it.

```
PROC iftest3:
  PRINT ("XYZ">"XYA")
  GET
ENDP
```

Notice the brackets round the part following the PRINT statement: that tells Series 3a it has to evaluate what's in the brackets and to display the result. You should get a display '-1', which indicates that Series 3a has tested along the line and found that "XYZ" is indeed 'greater' than "XYA": in other words, in an alphabetic listing, 'XYZ' would come *after* 'XYA', and so is considered to be 'greater'. Now go back to the procedure and edit "XYZ" to read just "XY", and run it again. This time, the result should be '0', meaning *not true*: in an alphabetic listing, "XY" would come *before* "XYA", and so would be less, and the test condition would not be true.

<   This is similar to the symbol above, except that the question this time is "Is what's on the left of the symbol *less than* what's on the right?". Thus

```
IF 4<6                    results in true (-1)
IF "B"<"A"                results in not true (0)
```

>= This combination of the '*greater than*' and '*equals*' tests produces a *true* result if what's on the left side is *equal to or greater than* what's on the right side, or, another way of saying the same thing, if the left side is *not* less than the right side (it may be equal, but not less). Thus

```
IF 10>=10        results in true (-1)
IF 10>=9         results in true (-1)
IF 10>=19        results in not true (0)
```

Note that the 'greater than' sign must come before the 'equals' sign.

<= This combination produces a *true* result if the left side is equal to *or* less than the right side, or rephrased, if the left side *is not* greater than the right side.

<> This combination produces a *true* result if the left side is either greater than or less than the right side, or, as is more commonly expressed, *if the left side is **not** equal to the right side*. Thus

```
IF 4<>6          results in true (-1)
IF 4<>4          results in not true (0)
```

AND This OPL word can be used in several different ways. Most commonly, it links two conditions in an IF test: if *both* conditions are *true*, then the overall result is *true*. But if either one is *not true*, then the overall result is *not true*.

Supposing, for example, you wish to find out whether the value of a variable $v\%$ is the *character code* for a numeral. Character codes, remember, are used by Series 3a to display a pattern on the screen. The numeric character codes run from 48, the code for '0', to 57, the code for '9'. You *could* do this with two IF tests, checking first that the value is 48 or more, then, if that's true, checking to see whether it is 57 or less.

```
IF v%>=48
 IF v%<=57
        Reaching here means v% is the character code
        for a numeral
```

```
ENDIF
ENDIF
```

With the AND operator, you can make the test in one line, as follows

```
IF (v%>=48) AND (v%<=57)
```
Reaching here means v% is the character code for a numeral
```
ENDIF
```

Notice how the two tests are enclosed within brackets: this is important, as without them, AND can act in a different way, as you shall see a little later on. Incidentally, the above little piece of program could also have been written in a slightly shorter way:

```
IF (v%>47) AND (v%<58)
```
Reaching here means v% is the character code for a numeral
```
ENDIF
```

The first method said "If v% is *equal to or greater than* 48 ..." and so on, whilst the second method said "If v% is *greater than 47* ...": for both methods, '48' is the lowest value to meet the test condition.

You can have as many condition tests on a line as you need - you are not restricted to just two as in the above examples. For example, if for some delightfully obscure reason you wanted to know whether v% is the character code for any numeral *except* '5' (code 53), then the line could read

```
IF (v%>47) AND (v%<58) AND (v%<>53)
```

Bearing in mind our earlier discussion on the way Series 3a determines the result of a test, AND can also be used with two values: thus you can write things like

```
(x AND y)
(a% AND b%)
```

However, the way AND works with integer (or long integer) values or variables is different to the way it works with floating point values or variables, although the general principle is the same.

With *floating point variables* (or values), AND works pretty much in the expected way: if both of the two variables are non-zero, then the result is -1. If either of the two variables is zero, then the result is zero (0). To demonstrate this, enter the following procedure:

```
PROC andtest1:
   LOCAL x,y
   x=1.2
   y=2.4
   IF x AND y
       PRINT "True: neither is zero"
   ELSE
       PRINT "Not true: one is zero"
   ENDIF
   GET
ENDP
```

When you run this, the screen should display

```
True: neither is zero
```

Now edit the procedure, changing the line x=1.2 to read x=0 (that's a zero), and run it again. This time, the display should read

```
Not true: one is zero.
```

With *integer* (or *long integer*) variables, AND compares the two values *bit by bit*, and sets a corresponding *bit* in the returned value to '1' if the two bits tested are '1', and to '0' if either bit is '0'. (Unfortunately, you need to understand a little bit about the binary system to appreciate all this - so if you missed it out in Chapter 1, now is the time to pop back there for a quick read).

The results of this can look pretty weird if you don't know what's going on. To demonstrate, enter the following procedure:

```
PROC andtest2:
  LOCAL x%,y%
  PRINT "Input x%:",
  INPUT x%
  PRINT "Input y%:",
  INPUT y%
  PRINT x%,"AND",y%,"=",(x% AND y%)
  GET
ENDP
```

Run it, and when prompted for x% enter 4 (and press
ENTER), and when prompted for y% enter 6 (and press
ENTER). The screen should display

$$4 \text{ AND } 6 = 4$$

Strange? Run the program again, and this time enter 3 for
x% and 6 for y%. This time, the screen should display

$$3 \text{ AND } 6 = 2$$

Not the kind of sums you're familiar with, no doubt. Let us
examine what is happening.

As previously mentioned, when used with integers, AND
looks at the binary digits of each value. So let us first look at
the binary equivalents for the decimal numbers '4' and '6'

```
4 =   00100
6 =   00110
```

Now, looking at each column in turn, starting from the right,
you'll see that there is a '0' in each value. So the rightmost
column of the result will be '0'.

```
Result = ...0
```

In the next column, one value has a '1', and the other a '0':
but AND will return a '1' only if *both* tested values are '1', so
again, the result for this column will be a '0':

```
Result = ..00
```

In the next column, the bits of both values are a '1', so the
result will have a '1' in that position:

```
Result = .100
```

That's as far as we need to go, since the rest of the bits are all 0's. So the result of ANDing 4 and 6 is, in binary, 100. And *that*, in decimal notation, is 4. Hence the first answer. Now let's look at the second example - '3 AND 6'. In binary, it would look like this

3	=	0011
6	=	0110
Result	=	0010

The result, '10' in binary, is '2' in decimal notation.

You are probably wondering what's the point of all this. Why do you need to perform such seemingly useless operations? Later on, in slightly more advanced programming, it is useful to be able to *mask out* a value, or to test whether a particular *bit* in a binary value is equal to '1'. We met such a typical case when we discussed the codes returned by KMOD (Chapter 6). To recap:

SHIFT	returns 2	(10 in binary)
CONTROL	returns 4	(100 in binary)
PSION	returns 8	(1000 in binary)
CAPS *on*	returns 16	(10000 in binary)

So if *km%* holds the value returned by KMOD, you can test whether the PSION key was pressed by a line

```
IF km% AND 8
```

This will return *true* if the bit representing '8' in *km%* is set - indicating that the PSION key has been pressed. If the result is 0 or *not true*, then the PSION key hasn't been pressed.

Why not simply use a statement such as IF km%=8? Because this will be true *only* when km%=8: whereas IF km% AND 8 will be true for *any value of* km% *that has the 'bit' representing 8 set*: in other words, for '10' (binary 1010), for 12 (binary 1100), for 28 (binary 11100), and so on.

The 'bits' set in the returned value from KMOD are called *flags*. There are many occasions when a returned set of flags will have more than one of the bits or flags 'set', and using the operator AND is the simplest way to make the test in such cases.

You will find it useful to experiment with the procedure andtest2, entering different values for x% and y%, and checking the results, as we have just done.

OR This is very similar to AND: however, instead of producing a *true* result if *both* conditions are *true*, OR produces a *true* result if *either* condition is *true*. Thus the line

```
IF (a%=4) OR (b%=6)
```

will produce a *true* result if *either* (or *both*) a%=4 *or* b%=6. This kind of test is useful if you want 'things to happen' if *either* of two particular conditions are met. Compare this kind of test with AND, where *all* conditions have to be met for 'things to happen'.

As with AND, OR can be used on individual values as well as to link two conditional tests. Also, all of the discussion on AND about how it works with integers (or long integers) and floating point variables applies to OR. The difference, remember, is that OR produces a *true* result, or sets a bit to '1', if *either* of the conditions is *true*, or in the case of integers, if *either* of the tested bits is '1'.

Edit the PROC andtest2 program by changing both of the ANDs (on the last PRINT line) to OR. Then run it a few times checking the results.

NOT This, as it sounds, *negates* a single conditional test. In other words, it switches the result of a test - if the result was *true*, NOT makes it *not true*. If the result was *not true*, NOT makes it *true*. Thus,

```
IF v%=4
```

would produce a *true* result if v% equalled 4, whereas

```
IF NOT(v%=4)
```

would produce a *true* result if v% equalled anything but 4. Notice the brackets round the `v%=4`: they're needed to keep the `v%=4` part as a separate test.

This example could have been written `IF v%<>4`. As you can see, when programming, there's usually more way than one to achieve what you want. Use of the word `NOT` can sometimes make the logic of a program easier to write or follow.

Unlike `AND` and `OR`, `NOT` cannot be used to link two floating point or integer variables or values: it can be used only on a *single* variable or value. Used with floating point variables, it returns *true* (-1) if the variable is zero, and *not true* if the variable is non-zero.

Used with integer or long integer variables, `NOT` returns what is called the *one's compliment*. Essentially what that means is it looks at the binary value of the integer, and turns all of the bits set to '1' to a zero, and all of the bits set to zero to a '1'. You won't need to use this feature for a long time, if ever.

Mixed condition tests

The `AND` and `OR` operators can be used in combination when testing for specific conditions, but it is important that you enclose the parts you want treated together within brackets. For example

    IF ((Condition 1) AND (Condition 2)) OR (Condition 3)

will result in *true* if *either*

a) *Both* Condition 1 *and* Condition 2 are *true*

or b) Condition 3 is *true.*

In this next example,

    IF (Condition 1) AND ((Condition 2) OR (Condition 3))

Condition 1 *must* be true, and *either* Condition 2 *or* Condition 3 (or *both*) must be true for the overall result to be true. As you can see, it is important to get the logic clear in your own mind to achieve the desired results.

CHAPTER 8
Going round in circles

This Chapter covers methods for
- *Jumping to other sets of instructions according to tested conditions.*
- *Repeating sequences of instructions in a loop until certain conditions are met.*
- *Breaking out of a loop or a program.*

The OPL words discussed are

```
GOTO, VECTOR, WHILE...ENDWH, DO...UNTIL,
REM, BREAK, CONTINUE, STOP.
```

Repeat performance

Most of the time, you will want to be able to repeat your programs without exiting and re-running them. There will also be many situations where you will want a series of instructions repeated until certain conditions are met: for example, you could accept and act upon inputs from the keyboard until a specific key is pressed. We met an example of this in Chapter 6, with the 'Fonts:' program.

Series 3a has a variety of words and structures that enable you to do this. A particular program could be written using virtually any of these structures - which structure you pick when writing your program is to some extent a matter of style and experience. Indeed, it is in this area that most programmers produce different sections of code to achieve the same result. As mentioned at the beginning of this book, no one way is necessarily right or wrong, but each has particular merits and benefits for the specific task in hand. Let us first look at the options available.

Jumping around

One of the simplest ways to repeat a series of instructions is to use the OPL word GOTO. It is also considered to be the crudest and most *unstructured* method of transferring the instruction sequence. GOTO is a relic from the very early days of computing, and its use can make code difficult to analyse and change at a later date. In all but a very, very few instances it can be avoided. Nevertheless, like most programming languages, Series 3a offers the option, and so we will discuss it.

85

GOTO This word usually follows a condition test of some kind, and is always followed by a *label*, that is, the name of a 'marker' placed at some point in the *same* procedure (i.e. between the same PROC and ENDP words as the GOTO appears). Labels are simply convenient names that you choose, and are always identified as a label to Series 3a by two colons immediately after the name, e.g. 'Start::', and 'Repeat::'.

Labels are just that: they appear between statement lines to mark the point where instructions are to jump to when directed by a GOTO (and similar commands).

> **Note**: Labels must be no longer than eight characters, and must always start with a letter.

When naming the label in a GOTO command, you can either include or omit the colons, although including them will help you to identify what them at a later date. Here is a procedure using GOTO. It multiplies an *integer* input by 2, until you've had enough.

```
PROC times2a:
  LOCAL y%,q$(1)
getnum::
  CLS
  PRINT "Enter a number:",
  INPUT y%
  PRINT y%,"times 2 =",y%*2
  PRINT "Another go? (Press Y or N)"
getans::
  q$=GET$
  IF (q$="Y") OR (q$="y")
    GOTO getnum::
  ELSEIF (q$="N") OR (q$="n")
    GOTO done::
  ELSE
    GOTO getans::
  ENDIF
done::
  PRINT "Bye now!"
  GET
ENDP
```

The indents in this procedure help you to identify the labels clearly. Notice how the program loops around according to the answer to the question "Another go? (Press Y or N)": if you enter "Y" or "y" at the keyboard, processing will jump back to getnum::. If you enter "N" or "n", then processing jumps to done::, and continues to the end of the procedure. Press any other key - and that's not good enough: the program is written to have a "Y" or "N" answer - so it loops round to getans:: to get another keypress. Notice that tests are made for both the upper or lower case letters (capitals or small letters): you must allow for the fact that the CAPS key may be on.

This is a pretty long procedure for what it does, and as we shall see, it can be shortened without loss of clarity by using the other structures available. Also, later on when we discuss *strings*, you'll find that you won't have to test for both upper and lower case inputs: you will be able to convert the input to one or the other and simply test for *that* condition.

As mentioned previously, GOTO is a very crude way of controlling program flow: an examination of the very short procedure on the preceding page shows how convoluted it can be to follow through. Larger programs become even worse to check through when using the GOTO command, and it should therefore be avoided as far as possible. There are, of course, far better techniques for controlling the flow. In fact all the alternatives are better.

Slightly better, for example, is the VECTOR command.

VECTOR This OPL word, similar to *ON...GOTO* structures in the BASIC language, allows you to jump to one of a number of labels, which can be located anywhere in the same procedure except *within* the VECTOR instruction set itself. The jump is made according to an integer parameter that follows the VECTOR command. The format is

```
VECTOR v%
    label1,label2,label3, ... labeln
ENDV
```

The list of labels in the VECTOR structure needn't all be on the same line, but can be spread over a few lines if you wish. However, you must *not* place a comma after a label at the *end* of a line: a comma is used only to separate two labels on the *same* line.

v% is a variable which must have its value set in another part of the program, and this value should be equal to or less than the number of labels in the list, otherwise processing jumps to the instruction *following* the ENDV statement.

When Series 3a meets the VECTOR command, it looks at the value of the integer variable following it, then picks the label in that position in the list, and jumps to the corresponding label in the procedure. The label names can be anything you choose (as long as they obey the 'rules' of course), and you can, if you wish, include the two colons after their names in the list. The labels marking positions in the procedure *must* have the two colons after them.

Unfortunately, having jumped to a label, *the program continues on without further jumps* (unlike the IF structure, which jumps to ENDIF once a sequence of instructions has been executed).. So if you have a sequence of five labels, and the jump is directed to the first label in the sequence, the code in *all* the subsequent labels will be executed, unless you add further specific jumps.

Here is the times2a procedure again, this time using the VECTOR command. Since the VECTOR command is not really designed for *string* values, this time we'll have the user input a '1' for 'more' and a '2' to 'end'. Notice the corresponding changes to the variables used (q% instead of q$).

```
PROC times2b:
    LOCAL y%,q%
    getnum::
        CLS
        PRINT "Enter a number:",
        INPUT y%
        PRINT y%,"times 2 =",y%*2
        PRINT "Another? (1=Yes, 2=No)"
    getans::
        q%=GET-48
        VECTOR q%
```

```
          getnum,done
     ENDV
     GOTO getans
done::
     PRINT "Bye now!"
     GET
ENDP
```

The input obtained from the keyboard has to be 'converted' to a *real* value of '1' or '2': the GET command, remember, gets the *character code* for the pressed key, and the character codes for the keys '1' and '2' are 49 and 50 respectively. Hence 48 is deducted from whatever was input in order to arrive at a real value of 1 or 2. If neither the '1' or '2' key was pressed, then processing jumps from the VECTOR command to the statement following ENDV, which instructs Series 3a to GOTO getans, to get another input from the keyboard. Perhaps this highlights the fact that VECTOR is not really suited to acting on keyboard inputs. Nevertheless it *is* useful where a consecutive series of integer values are available: as we shall see later on, selecting from a list or 'menu' of items produces an integer result from '1' to the number of items in the list. VECTOR is perfect for this kind of situation, since it can eliminate a whole series of IF tests.

Notice, too, that two of the labels in this procedure - getnum:: and getans:: - *precede* the VECTOR statement: care must be undertaken to ensure that there is a *programmed* way out of such loops. (The PSION and ESC keys pressed together will take you out of a running program, but this should not be your only 'escape route')

Looping around

As mentioned at the beginning of this Chapter, there are numerous occasions when you will want to repeat a series of instructions until a certain condition is met. We saw this with the two procedures times2a and times2b, where we wanted the instructions covering the input of a number and the 'times 2' calculation to be repeated until the user entered "n" or "N". This was just one example: a vast majority of programs that you write will require some instructions to be repeated one way or another. Series 3a provides two 'structures' for doing this: WHILE...ENDWH, and DO...UNTIL.

WHILE...ENDWH   The general format for this structure is

```
WHILE condition test is true
...do the necessary operations
ENDWH
```

The test for whether the instructions that follow should be obeyed is made at the *beginning* of the 'loop'. If the result of the test is *true,* then the instructions that immediately follow are obeyed. On reaching ENDWH, Series 3a 'loops' back to the WHILE statement line, *and performs the condition test again.*

It is *vitally* important, therefore, that during the instruction sequence something is 'done' to *change the possible outcome of the test,* otherwise the loop will go on for ever. (Or until you press the PSION and the ESC keys simultaneously)

If the result of the condition test following the WHILE statement is *not true,* then the instruction set is not performed at all: processing jumps immediately to the statement following the ENDWH statement. Notice that, like the IF...ENDIF structure, Series 3a needs to be told where the WHILE instruction set ends.

An important feature about WHILE...ENDWH is that, if the condition test proves to be *not true,* the intermediate instructions are not obeyed at all.

Let us now look at the 'times2' procedure again, this time written using the WHILE structure. Notice the indents between the WHILE and the ENDWH statements: as with the indents used with the IF...ENDIF structure, this helps to make the procedure easier to read, 'debug' and change, by keeping associated pieces of code in an identifiable 'chunk'. It also helps to ascertain that both parts of the structure - the WHILE and ENDWH statements - match up.   You will get an error when you translate the procedure if one of the words is missing.

```
PROC times2c:
    LOCAL y%,q$(1)
    q$="Y"
```

```
      WHILE (q$="Y") OR (q$="y")
         CLS
         PRINT "Enter a number:",
         INPUT y%
         PRINT y%,"times 2 =",y%*2
         PRINT "Another? (Y or N)"
         q$=GET$
      ENDWH
      PRINT "Bye now!"
      GET
ENDP
```

You will notice that all the IF tests and labels of the previous two versions of the 'times2' procedure have been eliminated, shortening the procedure. Admittedly, this time tests are made only for a 'Yes' input: *any* key other than 'Y' or 'y' will result in the procedure ending.

Notice the line q$="Y". When q$ is declared in the first line, it has no value - it is 'initiated' as a null string, or, put another way, it is made equal to "". If we didn't have the line q$="Y", therefore, the WHILE condition test would give a *not true* result - and the instructions within the loop would not be obeyed at all. Test this for yourself, if you wish, either by deleting the line, or amending it to read
REM q$="Y"

REM   stands for REMark, and it tells Series 3a to ignore the *rest* of the line or statement that follows it. You can place a REM statement *after* another statement on a line, *without* preceding it with a colon (as you must with all other statements on the same line as another). However, there must be at least one space between the end of a statement and the REM instruction.

REM is a useful word for adding explanatory notes to a procedure, or for temporarily knocking out an instruction line. Adding notes to a procedure - particularly during its development - can be vital to the understanding of the program at a later date. It is surprising how often a piece of code can look extremely obscure even a few days after it was written.

After you have checked that without the line q$="Y" the procedure simply ends, you can delete the REM word.

As with IF, although Series 3a determines a *true* condition as -1, it will recognise *any* value as being *true*. Consequently, one could have a segment of code that looks like this:

```
. . .
c%=4
WHILE c%
        do things
        c%=c%-1
ENDWH
. . .
```

In this example, each time the instructions in the loop are performed, the value of c% is decreased by 1 (it is said to be *decremented*). After four 'passes' through the loop, c% will be equal to zero: the WHILE condition test will then give a *not true* result - and processing jumps to the statement following ENDWH. This is one useful way of having a loop repeated a specific number of times. For example, suppose you wanted to produce the first five values in the 13 times multiplication table. Here's a procedure to do it:

```
PROC times13a:
        LOCAL c%
        c%=5
        WHILE c%
           PRINT "13 times",6-c%,"=",13*(6-c%)
           c%=c%-1
        ENDWH
        GET
ENDP
```

The value of c% is subtracted from 6 to give 1,2,3,4,5 on each successive pass through the loop, to get an ascending table.

Finally, you can use AND and OR in the condition test following WHILE. Now, here is another loop structure.

DO...UNTIL   The general format for this structure is

```
        DO
                . . .do the necessary operations
        UNTIL condition test becomes true
```

Notice that with this structure, the condition test is made at the *end* of the instruction set. If the condition test proves to be *true*, the instruction loop is *not* repeated. If on the other hand the condition test proves to be *not true*, then the instruction set *is* repeated. As with WHILE...ENDWH something must be 'done' within the loop to change the possible outcome of the test, or the loop will run for ever. Amen.

With the DO...UNTIL structure, the instruction set is *always* obeyed at least once. WHILE...ENDWH, remember, could miss the instructions set out if the initial condition test is *not true*.

This distinguishing factor should enable you to pick the appropriate structure for the task in hand: if you *definitely* want the instructions to be performed at least once, come what may, then choose the DO...UNTIL. If you want the instructions to be performed only under a certain condition (or conditions) then choose WHILE...ENDWH.

Here's the 'times2' procedure yet again, using DO...UNTIL.

```
PROC times2d:
     LOCAL y%,q$(1)
     DO
        CLS
        PRINT "Enter a number:",
        INPUT y%
        PRINT y%,"times 2 =",y%*2
        PRINT "Another? (Y or N)"
        q$=GET$
     UNTIL (q$="N") OR (q$="n")
     PRINT "Bye now!"
     GET
ENDP
```

Notice that, this time, the line q$="Y" (used in the WHILE...ENDWH version), isn't needed: the instructions within the loop will be obeyed once *whatever* the value of q$ the first time round. Compare PROC times2d with PROC times2a, which used a host of IF and GOTO statements: you will agree, it's shorter and neater!

As with IF and WHILE, the condition test following the UNTIL statement can incorporate the logic operators AND and OR. And equally, while Series 3a determines a *true* condition as -1, it will recognise *any* value as being *true*. The 'times13a' procedure could be re-written like this:

```
PROC times13b:
    LOCAL c%
    DO
        c%=c%+1
        PRINT "13 times",c%,"=",13*c%
    UNTIL c%=5
    GET
ENDP
```

This, too, is marginally shorter than its WHILE...ENDWH counterpart, since we have been able to lose a line (c%=5). It also highlights the fact that, if you want the instructions performed at least once, the DO...UNTIL structure is usually the best choice. Notice the different ordering of the instructions within the loop (as well as the line changes). The first time round, c% will have just been initiated, and will therefore be equal to zero. By making c%=c%+1 the first instruction in the loop (to *increment* it by one), we ensure that 13 won't be multiplied by zero. On the fifth pass through the loop, the instructions are obeyed with c%=5, but then the UNTIL condition will prove to be *true*, and the loop won't be repeated.

You will also notice that WHILE...ENDWH performs the intermediate instructions *while* the test condition *is* true, whereas the DO...UNTIL performs the intermediate instructions *until* the test condition *becomes* true.

Nesting loops

When discussing IF it was stated that IF structures can be 'nested' - that is, you can have IF structures within IF structures. The same is true of WHILE...ENDWH and DO...UNTIL structures. In fact, all of these structures can be 'nested' within each other almost at will (the limit is eight levels of nesting).

The important things to remember when nesting structures, mixed or otherwise, are

a)   Each individual structure must be terminated properly (with ENDIF, ENDWH or UNTIL, according to the structure).

b)   Each structure must be properly terminated at its own nested level.

b) You can have no more than *eight* nested structures, mixed or otherwise. That's Series 3a's limit: but it should be more than enough to cope with even the most complex of programs you're ever likely to devise.

Leaving a loop prematurely

You have seen that WHILE...ENDWH and DO...UNTIL loops run until a certain condition is met, as tested at the WHILE or UNTIL statement. There may be times, however, when you want an extra way to leave the loop - another condition that's quite different from that being tested in the normal run of events. Alternatively, you may wish to cancel the current trip through the instruction loop if a particular condition is met. Series 3a has ways of allowing you to do these things. The two OPL words concerned are BREAK and CONTINUE. There is also an instruction which will allow you to break out of the program completely - STOP.

BREAK   This statement, which usually follows a condition test of some kind, causes Series 3a to 'break' out of an instruction loop. Program execution continues with the statement following the loop terminator (ENDWH or UNTIL).

Here's the times13b procedure going up to 50 times 13, with a way to stop it before it reaches 50 by simply pressing any key.

```
PROC times13c:
    LOCAL c%
    DO
        IF KEY
            BREAK
        ENDIF
        c%=c%+1
        PRINT "13 times",c%,"=",13*c%
    UNTIL c%=50
    IF c%<>50
        PRINT "Shucks! You stopped me!"
    ELSE
        PRINT "I went all the way!"
    ENDIF
    GET
ENDP
```

When you run this procedure, press a key before it reaches '13 times 50', and you'll break out of the loop. You will recall that the KEY command looks to see if a key has been pressed since the last time the keyboard was 'polled'. If a key hasn't been pressed, it returns a zero - which the IF statement regards as being *not true*. As soon as a key is pressed the IF statement considers it to be *true*, and hence obeys the BREAK instruction.

CONTINUE   With BREAK, a 'jump' is made out of the loop to the instruction following the loop terminator. With CONTINUE, however, the 'jump' is made to the *condition testing line*, WHILE or UNTIL. This means the test is made again - and program execution will either continue round the loop again or not, according to the result of the condition test. It is probably true to say that CONTINUE will always follow its *own* condition test - an IF statement, for example. Let's look at an example, using the DO...UNTIL structure. This procedure will give the '13 times' table up to 12x13, but only if the user decides to see the result of each multiplication displayed. Enter this procedure *very* carefully - making sure that you have the UNTIL line correct!

```
PROC times13d:
    LOCAL c%,q$(1)
    DO
        c%=c%+1
        PRINT c%,"times 13? (Y or any key)",
        q$=GET$
        IF (q$="Y") OR (q$="y")
            PRINT c%*13
        ELSE
            PRINT
            CONTINUE
        ENDIF
    UNTIL c%>11
ENDP
```

For each pass through the loop, you will be asked if you want to see the result. Press any key except 'Y' and processing will jump down to UNTIL, where it will test for the value of c% to determine whether the loop should be repeated or not. Note that this time the test is made for c% being *greater than* 11: this is to prevent any possibility of c% becoming greater than 12 (that sounds a bit double Dutch, but remember that c% will have a value of 12 running through the instructions the last time round). Notice too that there is a plain PRINT statement before the CONTINUE command. This is to keep the display reasonably neat and understandable (try it without that PRINT statement - and say 'no' to one of the questions, to see the difference!)

STOP   This instruction, which usually follows a condition test of some kind, causes the program to stop running completely. Unlike BREAK and CONTINUE, which can be used only within DO...UNTIL or WHILE...ENDWH structures, STOP can be used *anywhere* in a program.

Here's the 'times13d' procedure, re-written to go up to 100 unless the user cries "Enough!". (It's also a good example of 'nested' statements!).

```
PROC times13e:
 LOCAL c%,q$(1),a$(1)
 DO
  c%=c%+1
  PRINT c%,"times 13? (Y or any key)",
  q$=GET$
   IF (q$="Y") OR (q$="y")
    PRINT c%*13
    PRINT "More? ('Y' or any key)"
    a$=GET$
    IF (a$="Y") OR (a$="y")
       CONTINUE
    ELSE
       STOP
    ENDIF
   ELSE
    PRINT
    CONTINUE
   ENDIF
 UNTIL c%>=100
ENDP
```

Loop structures play a very important role in all but a very few programs: it is well worth your while running the examples in this Chapter, and experimenting with them so that you are familiar with the way they work.

CHAPTER 9
Strings and things

This Chapter deals with the manipulation of 'string' types of variable. The OPL words covered are:
CHR$, ASC, UPPER$, LOWER$, LEN, LEFT$, RIGHT$, MID$, LOC, REPT$.

What's the character?

In Chapter 1, it was stated that *characters* are stored as *numbers*, and that Series 3a turns these numbers into the 'shapes' we recognise as characters, when it knows we want the shape and not the number displayed on the screen. We can also force Series 3a to 'convert' a number into its corresponding character shape by using the OPL function CHR$.

CHR$ (n%) This function 'returns' the character shape or pattern corresponding to the integer value or variable n%, which *must* be within the range 0 to 255. Some numbers below 32 do not produce character shapes (they are used as special 'instructions'), and 255 is the upper limit for a value that can be stored in a single memory box. Because a *character* is returned by CHR$ (), it must be stored in a *string* type of variable so that Series 3a knows what to do with it when called upon. (Any value stored in *string variable* memory boxes is regarded as being a number for translation into a character shape). The general format for the instruction is:

c$=CHR$ (n%)

However, since CHR$ () is a *function*, it can be used as part of another statement, such as PRINT. Thus,

PRINT CHR$ (n%)

is equally valid as an instruction. If you look at the complete Character Set, shown in your User Manual, you will notice that there are more characters than can be accessed direct from the keyboard. CHR$ ( ) gives you a way of accessing the characters that are *not* accessible from the keyboard, should you wish to display them.

The following simple procedure allows you to enter a number, for display of the corresponding character. Since it allows only for numbers to be entered - and since you will want to test a few numbers without having to re-run the program each time, the routine will continue running until '0' is entered.

Notice a little test is included in this procedure to 'trap' inputs that are too high. You will find when you run this program that some of the numbers below 32 don't display a character at all, while others display characters used by Series 3a for its own displays (a padlock, telephone symbol, and so on).

```
PROC characts:
 LOCAL c$(1),num%
 DO
  CLS
  PRINT "Enter 0 (zero) to finish"
  AT 1,3
  PRINT "Which character number?",
  INPUT num%
  IF num%>255
   CONTINUE
  ENDIF
  AT 1,4
  PRINT "Character",num%,"=",CHR$(num%)
  GET
 UNTIL num%=0
ENDP
```

The main non-displayable character codes are

7	This gives a beep sound
8	This performs a backspace.
9	This performs a tab operation.
10	This performs a line feed operation.
12	This clears the screen or, on printers, gives a form feed.
13	This performs a 'carriage return' (ENTER) operation.
27	As well as producing an 'arrow', this is also the code for the ESC key

These can be useful in your own programs when providing an output for a printer.

What's the character code?

Just as there's an OPL instruction to 'convert' a number into a character, so there's an instruction to convert a character into its equivalent code number.

ASC(*c$*) returns the integer number corresponding to the character *c$* (or the *first* character of the string *c$*), and the general format for the instruction is

$$v\%=ASC(c\$)$$

Alternatively, the actual *character* can be given within quotation marks, to show that it *is* a character, and not the name of a variable:

$$v\%=ASC("A")$$

As with CHR$() and other functions, ASC() can be used as part of another statement without saving the returned value.

Incidentally, if you are wondering why this function is called 'ASC', the reason is it is short for 'ASCII', which stands for 'American Standard Code for Information Interchange', and is the standard used by virtually *all* computers to define the numeric codes for characters. Thus, whatever computer you use, the letter 'A' is the character for the code value '65': '65' is said to be the ASCII code or ASCII value for the letter 'A'.

OPL also provides another method for determining the code for an individual character, and that's by using the '%' sign *before* the character concerned. Thus:

$$v\%=\%A$$

would return, and store in v%, the character *code* for the capital letter 'A' (which is 65). The method you use - ASC() or '%' - is really just a matter of choice. However, it must be said that although this method is shorter (and easier to program, since you don't have to worry about the code number), until you become familiar with programming, use of the '%' symbol *could* produce confusion. This is because the symbol is capable of being used in three different ways: as the 'terminator' of a variable (or procedure) name to denote an integer, as a 'percentage' operator, and as a way of saying *the code, not the character of what follows*.

When using ASC(a$), if a$ is a null string (i.e., it contains no characters, so is equal to ""), then the value returned is zero.

Joining strings (concatenation)

A *string*, you will recall, is a series of *characters*, all contained in the one string type of variable. There are many, many occasions when you will want to join two or more strings together (which is called *concatenating*). This is done very easily by simply using a '+' sign between the different strings you want to join. The string variable that will hold the concatenation must have been declared large enough to hold the entire string, of course.

You can join string *variables* and string *literals* in any combination. A string *literal* is where the actual characters are used, between quotation marks. Here are some examples to help make it clear: they all assume that

a$	holds the word "Lolly"
p$	holds "Pops"
r$	has been declared of sufficient length.

Concatenation produces the following results:

r$=a$+p$	r$ holds "LollyPops"
r$=a$+" "+p$	r$ holds "Lolly Pops"
r$="Green "+a$	r$ holds "Green Lolly"
r$=p$+a$	r$ holds "PopsLolly"

You don't need to concatenate strings just to print them out: you can use the PRINT statement for a whole series of variables, remember, by separating them with a semi-colon (no space) or a comma (one space). So to print out the above examples without saving the concatenated strings, you would have:

PRINT a$;p$	Displays "LollyPops"
PRINT a$,p$	Displays "Lolly Pops"
PRINT "Green ";a$	Displays "Green Lolly"
PRINT p$;a$	Displays "PopsLolly"

101

Changing the case

In one of the programs in Chapter 8, tests had to be made to see whether or not a particular key had been pressed at the keyboard. One of the lines in the procedure looked like this:

```
IF (q$="Y") OR (q$="y")
```

In other words, we had to test for the possibility that the SHIFT key was also pressed, or allow for the fact that the CAPS may be on. OPL allows you to avoid making such tests, by enabling you to convert a string to all upper case (capitals) or lower case characters. The two functions concerned are UPPER$ () and LOWER$ ().

UPPER$ (*str$***)** As you might imagine, this returns the string *str$* as *all* upper case characters. It only changes *alphabetic* characters of course - numeric characters are left as they are. So if *str$* holds the string "abC123", UPPER$ (*str$*) would return the string "ABC123". As with any function, UPPER$ () can be used as part of another statement. Thus

```
q$=UPPER$(GET$)
```

would return the *upper case* version of whatever alphabetic key had been pressed. So if 'y' had been pressed - irrespective of whether the SHIFT key is pressed or the CAPS set to on - then q$ would hold the character 'Y'. Similarly,

```
PRINT UPPER$("y")
```

would display 'Y', and if q$ held the characters "n123", then

```
PRINT UPPER$(q$)
```

would display 'N123'.

LOWER$ (*str$***)** This does the opposite to UPPER$ (): it changes all the capital letters in the string *str$* to lower case letters. Apart from that, its operations are the same.

How long is a string?

Even though you specify how many characters a particular string variable can hold as a maximum when you declare it, what you may not know is exactly how many characters the string *actually* holds at any time. This information is often required - when formatting a display, for example - and, fortunately, there is an OPL function to give us the answer.

LEN (*str$*)   This function returns the number of characters actually contained in the string variable represented by *str$*. (Not the number of characters that *str$* has been *declared* to be able to hold).

The format is

$$n\%=LEN(str\$)$$

LEN () can also be used as part of other statements. Thus, if *str$* holds the string "What a good idea", then

```
PRINT LEN(str$)
```

would display the number '16', which is the number of characters in the string, including the spaces.

Cutting strings

Just as there are times when you will want to join strings together, there will be many occasions when you'll find it useful to examine or snip out a part of a string variable. There are three ways OPL enables you to do this: you can take some characters from the start, some characters from the end, or some characters from the middle. Which just about covers every possibility!

**LEFT$** (*str$*, *n%*) This function returns the leftmost number of characters, as determined by *n%*, from the string *str$*. The format is

$$newstr\$=LEFT\$(str\$,n\%)$$

The function can also be used as part of another statement.

```
PRINT LEFT$(str$,n%)
```

As an example, if *str$* held the string "What a good idea", then after the statement

```
newstr$=LEFT$(str$,4)
```

newstr$ would hold the string "What".

RIGHT$ (*str$,n%***)** This function returns the *right*most *n%* number of characters from the string *str$*. The format is

```
newstr$=RIGHT$(str$,n%)
```

and as with LEFT$(), RIGHT$() can be used as part of another statement. If *str$* held the string "What a good idea", then after the statement

```
newstr$=RIGHT$(str$,4)
```

newstr$ would hold the string "idea".

MID$(***str$,start%,n%*)** This function returns a string of *n%* number of characters, beginning with the character at the *start%* position in the string *str$*. The format, as before, is

```
newstr$=MID$(str$,start%,n%)
```

As you will realise by now, MID$() can also be used as part of another statement such as

```
PRINT MID$(str$,start%,n%)
```

Here is a procedure to demonstrate how MID$() could be used. It asks for the user's complete name, then isolates the first Christian name (if more than one) and displays the result.

```
PROC midtest1:
 LOCAL name$(24),monica$(24),m$(1),c%
 PRINT "Enter your full name:",
 INPUT name$
 DO
```

```
    c%=c%+1
    m$=MID$(name$,c%,1)
    IF m$=" "
      CONTINUE
    ELSE
      monica$=monica$+m$
    ENDIF
    UNTIL (m$=" ") OR (LEN(monica$)=24)
    PRINT "Your Christian name is",monica$
    GET
ENDP
```

Notice how the LEN() function is used to prevent problems occurring should a name be entered without any spaces! This particular routine checks each character in the string in turn, until it comes to a 'space' character (code 32). As each character is taken, if it isn't a space, it is added to a new string which builds up to the first name entered.

When run, you will find that the 'search' for the space is very fast: the result will appear to be displayed instantaneously. Nevertheless, there are several looped operations to go through before the result is found. For this particular type of application - searching for a specific character or characters- there is an alternative method, discussed in the next paragraphs.

Where's that piece of string?

In the last example, we had a loop of instructions to find out where the first space occurred in a given string. This helped to demonstrate how the MID$() function worked. In practice, however, there is a much easier way to find out where one string occurs within another - and that's with the function LOC().

LOC(*large$,little$*) This function returns an integer value representing the position - number of characters from the start - where the *little$* string occurs within the *large$* string.

The 'search' is *case sensitive*: that means if the *large$* string holds "What a good idea" and the *little$* string holds "GOOD", it *won't* be found. If the *little$*

string isn't found in the *large$* string, then the value returned is '0' (zero). The format is

$$p\% = LOC(large\$, little\$)$$

and, it can be used with other commands, such as

$$PRINT\ LOC(large\$, little\$)$$

The string variable *little$* can be any length from 1 to the length of *large$*, though there's obviously no point in having it the same length.

Here is the 'midtest' procedure again, this time using LOC(): notice the different variables used, and that a *literal* string is used for *little$*.

```
PROC midtest2:
    LOCAL name$(24),p%
    PRINT "Enter your full name:",
    INPUT name$
    p%=LOC(name$," ")
    IF p%                          ┌──────────────────┐
                          ◄────────┤ If a space is found │
       PRINT "Your Christian name is",
       PRINT LEFT$(name$,p%-1)     ┌──────────────────┐
    ELSE ◄─────────────────────────┤ No space found    │
       PRINT "You're just called",name$
    ENDIF
    GET
ENDP
```

This procedure includes a test to catch those situations where just one name is entered: in this case, LOC() will return '0' (zero), to indicate that the space between the Christian and Surnames hasn't been found. If we didn't allow for this, there would be an error when the procedure is run, the offending line being 'PRINT LEFT$(name$,p%-1)'. p%, the variable used to hold the position of the space character, would be zero and we would be asking Series 3a to print up to the '-1' character in the string *name$*. It is these types of potential 'bug' that you have to try to allow for when writing your programs.

Repeating strings

If you wanted to produce a dotted line on the screen, you could have an instruction like

```
PRINT ".........................."
```

OPL provides an easier way to repeat characters and strings, and that's with the function REPT$().

REPT$(***str$*,***num%***)**   This returns the string *str$*, the number of times indicated by *num%*. So if *str$* held the string "Good" and *num%* held the value '4', REPT$(str$,num%) would return a string "GoodGoodGoodGood". The format is

```
newstr$=REPT$(str$,num%)
```

and, as before, REPT$() can be used as part of other statements such as PRINT.

Chapter 10
Creating a library

This Chapter introduces the concept of Library routines.
The OPL words covered are
    LOADM, UNLOADM

The library concept

It has already been stated that a program can comprise one or more *files*. Although there are still several *basic* topics to cover, this is a convenient point to discuss the use of library routines for commonly or often used procedures.

Just as there will be routines that are *called* several times within one program, there can also be routines which, once written, you will want to use in several programs. OPL allows you to do this, by creating Libraries of such routines in separate files. When a program needs to use one of those routines, then the appropriate file can be 'loaded' along with the rest of the program (using the appropriate OPL instructions), so giving access to the routines concerned. Up to three Library files can be loaded at a time: should a program require access to more, then one or more of the files will have to be 'unloaded' first.

How programs use memory

Broadly speaking, when a program is run, the *active* procedures - those in which the instructions are actually being executed - are copied from the area in memory where they are saved to a special *operating* area. When all of the instructions in a procedure have been completed (i.e., ENDP is reached), the procedure is removed from the *operating* area: it always remains, of course, in the saved area. Thus only the procedures being executed are kept in the operating area. In this way, very long programs with a high number of procedures can be run in a reasonably small space. The operating area is necessary since it must contain details, for example, about all of the variables used: in the area where the programs are saved, these details are, in effect, 'all over the place'. In some respects, it can be likened to the operation of a desk top computer, where the programs to be run are transferred first from the hard disk to the RAM operating memory: they are said to be 'loaded'. The Series 3a technique makes more use of the space available.

To illustrate what happens, consider a program of five procedures, which has the following structure of procedure 'calls'.

PROC a	PROC b	PROC c	PROC d	PROC e
calls Proc b	calls Proc e	calls Proc e	ENDP	ENDP
calls Proc c	calls Proc d	ENDP		
calls Proc d	ENDP			
ENDP				

The following table shows how the various procedures are loaded into and removed from the operating area of memory as the program progresses from beginning to end: the first 'controlling' procedure is PROC a.

INSTRUCTION BEING EXECUTED	PROCEDURES IN OPERATING MEMORY
PROC a *starts*	a
PROC a *calls* PROC b	a,b
PROC b *calls* PROC e	a,b,e
PROC e *ends*	a,b
PROC b *calls* PROC d	a,b,d
PROC d *ends*	a,b
PROC b *ends*	a
PROC a *calls* PROC c	a,c
PROC c *calls* PROC e	a,c,e
PROC e *ends*	a,c
PROC c *ends*	a
PROC a *calls* PROC d	a,d
PROC d *ends*	a
PROC a *ends*	all gone!

As you can see, although this particular program has five procedures, no more than three are loaded into the operating area at any given time. The number of procedures loaded into the operating area at any one time depends, of course, on the structure of your program, but generally speaking, programs with a large number of procedures will usually have only a few of them loaded at a time.

The situation is slightly different when a library file is 'loaded' into the program: a *listing* of the procedures in the file is loaded into the active area, and when a particular procedure is called, *then* it is loaded for execution.

> **Note:** You can ensure that a procedure remains in active memory *after* it has been executed, by *caching*. This can make programs run faster, since it saves the time required to load and unload frequently called procedures. Caching is a more advanced technique, dealt with in a later Chapter.

Loading a Library file

To load a Library file into a program, at the appropriate point (i.e., before the required procedure is to be called), use the OPL command LOADM.

LOADM *file$* This command loads a *translated* file, the name of which is specified by *file$* (which can be a literal string or a string variable of the required name): after the instruction has been executed, all of the procedures in that file can be used within the program. You can load up to three other library files at a time (making four files in all, with the program file) - if you need another to be loaded, unload one that is currently not in use first (using UNLOADM *file$*).

If the file you wish to load isn't in the same directory as the procedure that will use it, you must also specify the *path* in *file$*. Thus, if you keep Library files in a directory that you have created called '\LIB', and wish to load a file in that directory called 'Lib5', *file$* would be '\LIB\Lib5'. Most of the time, however, it is probably more convenient to save library files in the same directory as all other program files. Details about the library file's procedures are moved into the active area, with 'pointers' to the actual procedures: the file itself remains in memory at its stored location.

> **TIP** When creating Library files, it makes sense to place routines of a similar nature or purpose in the same file. Thus, you might keep all the string handling utilities you write in one file, mathematical utilities in another, and so on. In this way, you can build up several shorter library files, rather than have just one library file - which would be more space consuming when the program calling it is run.

To unload a file, the instruction is simply UNLOADM.

UNLOADM *file$*   This command removes the details about the library file specified by *file$* from the operating area.

Remember that, when creating a library file, the procedures in it (usually *functions*) will need to be *called* rather than run directly. Having written and translated the file therefore, it cannot be run as with other program files: it must, however, be *translated* for the procedures to be called - they must be available to the Series 3a in their translated version.

Once a library file has been created, you can add procedures to it at any time (provided you haven't deleted the *source* code!) and, equally, you can delete procedures or amend them at any time. After each such change, the file must be *translated again*, otherwise the original translated file will be used when the library is loaded into a program.

Example library routine
By the centre

It is often desirable to centralise text on the screen. Here is a simple procedure to centralise a single message line on any *text* screen. To create it in a library file:

1. Create a new File in the Program Editor, called Lib1. (Refer to Chapter 2).
2. Name the *procedure* 'cntr'
3. On the *same line*, and after the colon, enter (msg$, row%)
4. Enter the rest of the procedure. The complete procedure looks like this (don't type in the REM stuff):

```
PROC cntr:(msg$,row%)
 LOCAL w$(80),r%,info%(10)
 SCREENINFO info%()
 IF row%>info%(4)            REM Is specified row too high?
  r%=info%(4)                REM Yes, so set to bottom row
 ELSE r%=row%                REM No, so use specified row
 ENDIF
 w$=LEFT$(msg$,info%(3))     REM Cut to screen width max.
 AT 1+(40-LEN(w$))/2,row%
 PRINT w$
ENDP
```

111

Note how this program uses the SCREENINFO function to determine the depth and width of the current text screen (in terms of the current font size), and to arrange the message position and length accordingly.

Translate the procedure, but *don't* run it. (You can't, anyway).

Now we'll test the cntr Library routine, and at the same time, show how to *load* a file into a program. Create a *new* file (PSION and '$\boxed{N}$' keys) called 'cntrtest', and enter the following test procedure:

```
PROC cntrtest:
 LOCAL m$(80),r%
 FONT 12,8              REM Experiment with different font sizes
 PRINT "Enter Message"
 INPUT m$
 PRINT "Which row?"
 INPUT r%
 CLS
 LOADM "Lib1"
 cntr:(m$,r%)
 UNLOADM "Lib1"
 GET
ENDP
```

You can translate and run this procedure: it will load the Lib1 library file you have just written, and call the cntr:() procedure in that library.

In the cntrtest procedure, the Lib1 file is unloaded immediately after it is used. This isn't absolutely necessary unless you want to load more than three other modules: it was included to demonstrate how it is done.

Tip: When you've written a procedure that accepts inputs, test it *thoroughly* by entering a wide range of test values. Make unlikely entries - try entering a character when a number input is required, for example, and see what happens to your procedure. This way, you can cater for mistakes that can (and do) happen when the program is running, and adjust your procedure accordingly. Error handling is an important part of programming, discussed in a later Chapter.

As mod:(n,p), (given in Chapter 4) is also a useful function, you may like to enter it as *another* procedure in the Lib1 file, for use in all your programs.

CHAPTER 11
Converting variables

This Chapter deals with the conversion of variables from one type to another. OPL words covered are
VAL, EVAL, FIX$, GEN$, NUM$, SCI$, HEX$, INT, INTF, FLT, ABS, *and* IABS

When change is needed

There are numerous occasions when the information stored in one type of variable needs to be converted so that it can be used or stored in another type of variable. A typical example is when a number is stored as characters in a string: if you want to make a calculation using that number then generally speaking it must first be transferred to a numeric type of variable. Similarly, if you want to print or display part of a number - limiting it, perhaps, to just two decimal places - then the easiest way is to convert it to a string first.

OPL offers a variety of commands to convert variables from one form to another and there's even a way to perform mathematical operations on values and functions that are stored in strings.

Converting a string to a number

You have already seen that the *code* for a character - its 'ASCII' value - can be obtained by the ASC() function. This is not really of much use, however, if you want make a calculation of some kind on a *value* that's stored as a string - and you'll find there are many occasions when it is preferable to hold numeric values in strings. As just one example, you can keep sums of money in a 'fixed' type of format within a string - so you could have strings something like "£14.00" and "£145.45". By using the RIGHT$() or MID$() functions, you can strip out the amount of pounds and or pence, and convert those values to numeric variables for some possible calculation.

VAL(*str$*) This OPL function returns the *floating point* value of the number stored in the string variable *str$*. The string must contain only numbers: strings such as "123-456" or "£123A" or "12.234.56" or even "12,345" will produce an error when you try to run the program. The string can, however, use 'scientific notation', so something like "1.23E4" is acceptable. The format is

$$v=VAL(str\$)$$

If the string $str\$$ holds an integer value, it is still returned as a floating point value. However, you can force Series 3a to store the value held by $str\$$ as an integer by using the format:

$$v\%=VAL(str\$)$$

In this case, if $str\$$ holds, say, "123.456", the value stored in $v\%$ will be '123': the decimal part will be lost.

Evaluating a string

Whilst you cannot perform mathematical operations on numbers that are held in string variables, what OPL will allow you to do is to evaluate a valid *calculation* contained entirely within a string or concatenated strings.

EVAL($str\$$**)**   If the string $str\$$ holds a mathematical expression, then EVAL($str\$$) will return the result of evaluating that expression. The format is

$$v=EVAL(str\$)$$

The expression can contain any mathematical operator or function, such as '+', '/', 'LOG()' or 'SIN()', and $str\$$ can be a single string variable or a concatenation of string variables. It is possible, therefore, to build up a 'formula' evaluator using this function, where the formula is entered by the user at the keyboard. Here is a very simple example.

```
PROC evaltest:
 LOCAL func$(6),n$(12),eq$(20)
 DO
  CLS
  PRINT "Press Space to stop, or"
  PRINT "Enter a function: ",
  INPUT func$
  IF func$=" "
   CONTINUE
  ENDIF
  PRINT "Enter the value: ",
```

```
 INPUT n$
 eq$=func$+"("+n$+")"          REM brackets added round value
 PRINT eq$,"=",EVAL(eq$)
 AT 4,5
 PRINT "Press a key to continue"
 GET
UNTIL func$=" "
ENDP
```

When this procedure is run, you will be invited to input a mathematical function (such as 'SIN', 'LOG', 'COS', 'TAN' and so on), and then a value for that function to operate on. The answer is then displayed. So that you can test the operation of this procedure a few times without having to re-run it each time, it continues accepting inputs until the SPACE key is pressed in place of a function name. Be sure that when you enter the function name you enter *a valid OPL mathematical function*, without any brackets at all: the procedure is written to add the brackets for you.

Try running the program with, say, the 'MEAN' function, entering not one value when prompted, but a series of them separated by commas, pressing ENTER only at the end. You can also try your hand at changing the 'AT 8,5' and 'PRINT "Press a key..."' lines to load and call the CNTR: function in the Lib1 file (assuming you've entered it and translated it, of course!).

Converting a number to a string

Converting a character *code* to the actual character using the OPL function CHR$() has already been dealt with. We're now going to look at the various ways numbers can be converted into strings. The OPL words available allow you to determine how many decimal places will be contained in the string, to *position* the number within the string - that is to say have it at the start, or at the end with preceding spaces - and so on. In all instances it is essential, of course, that the string variable that will hold the converted value has been declared of adequate length.

FIX$(*value,dplaces%,length%*) This function converts the floating point variable *value* into a string. The number of decimal places is determined by *dplaces%*, and the maximum length of the stored value, *including* the decimal

115

point, is determined by *length%*. The *dplaces$* parameter enables you to trim the actual number of decimal places in *value*. So if value is '123.456' and *dplaces%* is '2', then the returned string will contain the value "123.46". If *value* is '123' and *dplaces%* is '3', then the returned string will contain "123.000". Notice that Series 3a will always 'round up' if there are to be less decimal places in the stored string than in the original value, and it will add zeroes if more decimal places are called for than in the original value.

If the value specified by the *length%* parameter is insufficient to hold the stored number string, then Series 3a will return a *length%* number of asterisks instead. If *length%* has a *negative* value, then the number will be justified to the *right* of the string: in other words, it will have leading spaces. This probably gives you a clue to the reason for incorporating the *length%* parameter: when 'formatting' a column of figures to be displayed, it is neater to have them with all the decimal points lined up. This can be achieved quite easily with the FIX() function. The formats are as follows:

```
f$=FIX$(value,dplaces%,length%)
PRINT FIX$(value,dplaces%,length%)
```

Here is a procedure that will let you test the effects of FIX$().

```
PROC fixtest:
 LOCAL f$(20),v,dp%,length%
 DO
  CLS
  PRINT "Enter any number:",
  INPUT v
  IF v=0
   CONTINUE
  ENDIF
  PRINT "How many decimal places?",
  INPUT dp%
  PRINT "How long for the string?",
  INPUT length%
  PRINT "FIX$(";v;",";dp%;",";length%;")="
```

```
PRINT FIX$(v,dp%,length%)
GET
UNTIL v=0
ENDP
```

When run, you can keep testing inputs until you enter a '0' for the number. The following examples demonstrate results achieved with FIX$ () for various values of v, dp% and length%:

FIX$(123.456,1,5)	=	123.5
FIX$(123.987,0,5)	=	124
FIX$(123,2,8)	=	123.00
FIX$(123,2,-8)	=	123.00
FIX$(123.4,2,4)	=	****"

Notice that in the first two examples Series 3a rounds up the result, since less decimal places are requested than actually exist in the original value.

In the third example, two decimal places are requested, and since the value to be converted has none, two trailing zeroes are added after the decimal point: this feature is particularly useful when dealing with currency values that have to be displayed.

The fourth example shows what happens when a *negative value* for length% is specified: the numeric value is lined up to the right hand side of an eight character string.

Finally, the last example shows what happens when the length% parameter is inadequate for the conversion. The value to be converted has three *integer* digits, to which must be added two decimal places and a decimal point - 6 characters in all. The length% parameter specifies only 4, which is not enough. Consequently Series 3a displays asterisks, to show that the number cannot be represented as a string as requested.

**GEN$** (*value, length%*) This is very similar to FIX$ (), the difference being that the number of decimal places is not specified. All the decimal places in the value will be represented in the stored string, and trailing zeroes will not be added to 'pad out' the string to a given length.

The *length%* parameter can be *negative*, which has the effect of 'justifying' the converted value to the right, filling the left side of the returned string with the appropriate number of spaces. As with FIX$(), if the value of the parameter length% is inadequate, Series 3a stores asterisks instead.

The formats are

```
g$=GEN$(value,length%)
PRINT GEN$(value,length%)
```
and typical results of using the function are:

```
g$=GEN$(45.6,6)          g$ holds "54.6"
g$=GEN$(45.6,-8)         g$ holds "    45.6"
g$=GEN$(45.678,5)        g$ holds "*****"
```

In the second example, there are four spaces in the string before the first digit.

**NUM$** (value, length%) This is very similar to GEN$(), only this time the value is converted to an *integer* before being stored as a string. In performing the conversion, Series 3a will 'round up' if necessary. If a *negative* value is specified for length%, then the string will be right justified. If the result has more digits than specified by the length% parameter, then the string will contain just asterisks. The formats are

```
n$=NUM$(value,length%)
PRINT NUM$(value,length%)
```
and typical results are:

```
n$=NUM$(123.456,5)       n$ holds "123"
n$=NUM$(123.456,-5)      n$ holds "  123"
n$=NUM$(123.9,4)         n$ holds "124"
n$=NUM$(12345,4)         n$ holds "****"
```

**SCI$** (value, dplaces%, length%) This function is the same as FIX$(), the only difference being that the *value* is changed to scientific notation before being converted to a string. The length% parameter must be at least *six* greater than the dplaces% parameter, to allow for the integer part, the decimal point, and the 'E+00' part of the notation. Otherwise, a string of asterisks will be returned. If a negative value for length% is used, the resulting representation is right justified within the string. Here are some examples:

```
s$=SCI$(123456,2,8)  s$ holds "1.23E+05"
s$=SCI$(12,3,12)     s$ holds "1.200E+01"
s$=SCI$(12,3,-12)    s$ holds "   1.200E+01"
s$=SCI$(1,2,3)       s$ holds "***"
```

HEX$ (`decimal&`) This one is really for the more experienced programmer. It returns a string containing the *hexadecimal* equivalent of the value `decimal&`, which although indicated here as a long integer, can also be an integer. Where the binary system has *2* digits (0 and 1), and the decimal system has *10* digits (0 to 9), the hexadecimal system has *16* digits - 0 to 9, followed by A to F. So A is 10, B is 11, C is 12 - up to F which has the value 15.

The hexadecimal system is important in computing, since it provides an easier way to understand what's happening in the computer (believe it or not), and in fact the system has a very close relationship with the binary system (as explained in an earlier Chapter).

Here's a little procedure that will help you to explore the hexadecimal values of decimal numbers.

```
PROC hextest:
 LOCAL h&
 DO
  PRINT "Enter 0 to finish"
  PRINT "Decimal value?",
  INPUT h&
  IF h&
   PRINT "In HEX that's",HEX$(h&)
   GET
   CLS
  ENDIF
 UNTIL h&=0
ENDP
```

Converting number types

There are several ways that numeric variables can be converted from one type to another. In assignments, it is possible to force a floating point result to an integer or a long integer by using the appropriate assigned variable, thus

```
i%=12.5*3.6
l&=123.456*.123
```

119

In both of these cases, only the integer part of the result will be stored. However, this method will not always be adequate, for there will be occasions when you will want to convert a value to an integer *in the middle* of an expression. It would be cumbersome (and unnecessary) to first make an assignment to an integer variable, and then use that integer in the expression. OPL provides the alternative.

INT(*fltexp***)**   This converts the expression or floating point value *fltexp* into a *long* integer. Thus, the two lines

```
a%=12.345
v=4.5*a%
```
can be replaced by the single line

```
v=4.5*INT(12.345)
```
Notice that while an integer variable `a%` was used in the two line example, in the one line example `INT(12.345)` would actually be converted to a long integer.

It can sometimes happen that you want the integer of a floating point value - but still wish to retain the number as a floating point value: the 'range' of values a floating point variable can have is considerably greater than the range provided by long integers, remember. OPL caters for this situation as well.

INTF(*fltexp***)**   This function is used the same way as `INT()`, the only difference being that the value returned is a *floating point* integer. Thus, after

```
i=INTF(1234.567)
```
the floating point variable *i* will hold the number '1234' as a floating point value (i.e. with a decimal point after the last digit). Notice there is no rounding up with this function.

This brings us to the conversion of any integer variable to a floating point value.

FLT(*integer%***)**   As you might expect, this converts the value of `integer%` to a floating point value. Long integers can also be used, so the formats are:

```
            v=FLT(integer%)   or
            v=FLT(integer&)
```

Knowing the way that Series 3a works when evaluating expressions (if one value is floating point, then floating point arithmetic is performed prior to the actual assignment), you may be wondering why FLT() is needed. If you have a procedure that *expects* a floating point value as a parameter and you wish to pass to it the value of an *integer* variable, then you would use FLT() to convert that variable first. Similarly, if the value you wish to pass is already a floating point value, but you wish to have only the integer part of it passed as the parameter, then you would use INTF().

There are two functions which allow the *absolute* value of a number to be returned. The absolute value is simply the 'positive' value, whether the number is negative or not.

ABS(v)   Here, v can be a value or an expression. Whatever the value of v (or the result), the returned value is '+v', where v is a floating point variable. This is useful when you have to deduct one number from another to find the difference, but don't know (and perhaps don't care) which of the two numbers is the larger. The format is

a=ABS(v)

Here's a little procedure to explain this: when you run it, enter two numbers as and when prompted, and irrespective of whether you enter the larger number first or last, you will be given the difference between those two values.

abstest allows you to continue putting the theory to the test until you've had enough, at which point, simply enter a zero for the *first* value.

```
PROC abstest:
 LOCAL n1,n2
 DO
  CLS
  PRINT "Enter 0 for to stop"
  PRINT "Enter first number",
  INPUT n1
  IF n1=0
   STOP
  ENDIF
  PRINT "Enter second number",
  INPUT n2
```

```
  PRINT "The difference is:",ABS(n1-n2)
  GET
 UNTIL n1=0
ENDP
```

IABS(v&) This similar to ABS(), the difference being that IABS() operates on integer values or expressions and returns an integer value. The integer can be normal or long. The formats are, therefore:

a%=IABS(v%), and a&=IABS(v&)

Using hexadecimal

Series 3a will allow you to enter hexadecimal values as constants, by *prefixing* them with a '$' if they're 16-bit (up to 'FFFF' in hexadecimal), or with a '&' if they're 32 bit (up to 'FFFFFFFF' in hexadecimal). Thus you could enter $1F (equivalent to 31 decimal), or &FFFFF (equivalent to 983040 decimal). You can also use these 'converters' to assign values to integer or long integer variables (such as d%=$FF, and d&=&FFFFF).

Using masks

A *mask* is a binary number which can be used to filter out unwanted 'bits' of another binary number. For example, lower case letters all have character codes exactly 32 greater than their upper case counterparts. To simply *deduct* 32 from a character to produce an upper case letter would mean having to check first that it is in fact a character code for a *lower case* letter, but that's a long winded way to do it. 32 (or $20 hexadecimal) looks like this in binary:

00000000 00**1**00000

If that particular bit of a character code is set, it means it's a lower case letter. To make it an *upper case* letter, we simply need to remove the '32' bit. We can remove it without actually *deducting* 32 and without any tests as to whether it exists or not. We simply prepare a *mask* which *excludes* the crucial 'bit'. In binary, our mask will look like this:

11111111 11**0**11111

All the 'bits' are set, except for the one we want to exclude. If we AND this value with *any* character code value, the result will be the character code *less* 32 if that bit is set, and without any change if it isn't. The hexadecimal value of binary 11111111 11011111 is 'FFDF' - which is the value we needed for the 'capital letter' mask. Thus to convert a lower case character to upper case - without affecting any other character - you could use

```
char%=char% AND $FFDF
```

The Carpet Program

This is a suitable point to include the 'Carpet' program discussed in a previous Chapter. Start by creating a new file in the Program Editor, called 'CARPET', then enter the following program in its entirety before translating and running it.

```
PROC carpet:
 LOCAL area,ppyard,tcost,q$(1)
 area=getarea:
 ppyard=getcost:
 DO
  tcost=area*ppyard
  cls
  AT 1,2
  PRINT "You need",area,"sq yards"
  AT 1,3
  PRINT "Which will cost £";
  PRINT FIX$(tcost,2,8)
  AT 1,4
  PRINT "at £";ppyard,"per sq. yard"
  AT 1,6
  PRINT "Another (C)ost, (A)rea, or (E)nd"
  q$=UPPER$(GET$)
  IF q$="C"
   ppyard=getcost:
  ELSEIF q$="A"
   area=getarea:
  ENDIF
 UNTIL q$="E"
ENDP

PROC getcost:
 LOCAL cpsy
 CLS
 PRINT "Cost per sq. yard:",
 INPUT cpsy
 RETURN cpsy
ENDP
```

```
PROC getarea:
LOCAL w,h,area
CLS
PRINT "Room Width (in feet:)",
INPUT w
PRINT "Room Length (in feet):",
INPUT h
area=w*h/9
IF area>intf(area)
  area=INTF(area)+1
ENDIF
RETURN area
ENDP
```

This program follows the structure discussed in Chapter 3. It starts by getting in the room dimensions and cost of the carpet per square yard, then enters a loop which enables you to 'test' out other carpet prices or room areas.

Notice how a check is made to see whether an extra square yard is needed (getarea procedure): if the *area* is not the same as the *integer* of the *area*, then it must be rounded up to the next square yard above. This is done in the line area=INTF(area)+1. Notice, too, how the FIX() function is used to limit the number of decimal places to two, for the 'pence' figure.

The options offered after the cost of a carpet has been displayed are for another cost (enter 'C'), another area (enter 'A'), or to end altogether (enter 'E'). If any other key is pressed, the loop is repeated, re-displaying the original information.

CHAPTER 12
Mathematical functions

This Chapter examines the mathematical functions available when programming. You'll find out about
- *Using the logarithmic functions.*
- *Evaluating roots.*
- *Using trigonometric functions.*
- *Getting random sequences of numbers.*
- *Working on lists of numbers*

The OPL words covered are

LOG, LN, SQR, EXP, COS, SIN, TAN, ACOS, ASIN, ATAN, DEG, RAD, RND, RANDOMIZE, MAX, MIN, MEAN, SUM, STD, VAR

Calculator functions, at the ready

Many of today's calculators are blessed with a range of engineering and scientific functions, to help simplify problem solving. Series 3a has such functions too, for inclusion in your programs. Whilst these functions are also available in the Series 3a's calculator mode, for lengthy, repeated calculations it is quicker to prepare a short program: the user can be prompted for the inputs required, and the rest of the calculation can then be performed under program control, displaying the answer with no further ado.

Remember that *functions* can be used in an assignment, or as a part of other statements or expressions, where the value returned by the function is used for further calculation or display. Only the assignment formats will be given in this Chapter: previous Chapters will have given you an idea of the other ways that functions can be used.

We'll start by looking at the basic mathematical functions.

Logarithms

Series 3a covers logarithms to the base 10 and *natural* logarithms to the base *e*. The functions are:

LOG (x) This returns the logarithm of x to the base 10. The format is

$$a=LOG(x)$$

where a is a floating point variable that will hold the returned value, and x is the value for which the logarithm is required. If a is made an integer variable, then only the *exponent* of the logarithm will be returned, and the *mantissa* will be lost.

LN (x) This returns the natural logarithm - that is, the logarithm to the base e (2.71828...). The format is

```
a=LN (x)
```

where a holds the natural logarithm of x.

Roots and powers

Series 3a has a prepared function for finding the square root of any number:

SQR(x **)** This returns the square root of x, and has the format

```
s=SQR(x)
```

However, other roots are easily obtained by using the 'power' operator. For example, to find the *cube* root of a value x, you can use the format

```
c=x**(1/3.0)
```

which is the programming way to write 'x *raised to the power one third*'. Note that it is important to force Series 3a to perform a *floating point* calculation, by the inclusion of a decimal point in the value of either the '3' or the '1' (i.e. '1.0/3' will also produce the desired result). If you don't - that is, if you simply use '(1/3)' as the power, then integer arithmetic will be performed, producing an incorrect result.

EXP(x **)** This function enables you to raise the natural constant e to the power x, saving the need to remember the value of e. The format is

```
v=EXP (x)
```

Trigonometric functions

There are six trigonometric functions available - COS(*radians*), SIN(*radians*), TAN(*radians*), ACOS(*x*), ASIN(*x*) and ATAN(*x*). You'll notice that the angle for the COS, SIN and TAN must be given in *radians*. However, the OPL function RAD(*degrees*) allows you to convert from degrees to radians. The formats for these three functions, therefore, are

```
v=COS(radians)          v=COS(RAD(degrees))
v=SIN(radians)          v=SIN(RAD(degrees))
v=TAN(radians)          v=TAN(RAD(degrees))
```

ACOS(*x*), ASIN(*x*), and ATAN(*x*) are the *inverse* of the COS, SIN and TAN respectively (i.e. ACOS = (COS^{-1})), and the value returned will be an angle in *radians*. This can however be converted to degrees, using the OPL DEG() function. The formats for these three functions are therefore

```
radians=ACOS(x)         degrees=DEG(ACOS(x))
radians=ASIN(x)         degrees=DEG(ACOS(x))
radians=ATAN(x)         degrees=DEG(ACOS(x))
```

Note that, for ACOS(*x*) and ATAN(*x*), the value of *x* must lie within the range -1 to +1, otherwise you will get an error.

There is one other OPL word that should be covered here, and that is **PI**. This simply returns the value of pi (π) as a constant (3.14159265358979) and saves you from having to remember it. You use it just like any other floating point variable except, of course, you cannot change its value! Thus

$$v=4*PI/180$$

Numbers at random

For programs involving an element of 'chance' - such as games programs - one often needs a *random* number. For example, to represent the throw of a die, you'd want a random number between 1 and 6, and to represent the throw of two dice, you'd want a random number between 2 and 12.

RND   returns a value from zero to 0.9999999... to 15 significant figures, and the value returned is different each time it is used during the running of a program. This value can be used to provide a random number between *any* two specific limits. For example, multiplying the random number by 6 will produce a value within the range 0 to 5.99999999999994. If only the *integer* part of this value is taken, the range of random numbers is from zero to 5 - six possibilities in all. If you want to make these six possibilities simulate the throw of a die, then add '1' to the generated random number. Thus

```
throw%=1+INT(RND*6)
```

or, more simply - since assigning a floating point value to an integer variable will force that value into an integer:

```
throw%=1+RND*6
```

As another example, to generate a random number between 10 and 20 inclusive, a range of 11 random numbers starting with 10 is required. Hence:

```
n%=10+RND*11
```

Note that, if a program uses RND, the *sequence* of random numbers provided will be the same *each time the program is run*. You can avoid this by use of the command RANDOMIZE.

RANDOMIZE x&   This sets a 'start' point for the RND function, which will then produce a specific sequence of random numbers. On its own, RND will produce the same sequence each time a program using it is run. So if you designed a game, say, that used RND, then the random sequence during play would be the same each time the game is played. This can be useful for testing out the game, but not when you want some variety!

RANDOMIZE sets a new random number sequence, which depends on the value of the parameter x& (which can be an integer or a long integer). If you use a constant value for x&, then again, the sequence for RND will be repeated each time the program is run.

To ensure a *different* sequence is used each time, x& needs to have a different value whenever the program is run, and the easiest way to do this is to use one or two of the built-in functions (yet to be discussed), SECOND and or MINUTE. These return the number of seconds or minutes, respectively, from the system clock. By using

```
RANDOMIZE MINUTE
```

you will produce one of 60 random number sequences, depending on the minute past the hour that the program is started. To get one of 3600 different sequences - with less chance of a repeat, you can use

```
RANDOMIZE SECOND*MINUTE
```

In this case, you'd have to start the program at exactly the same minute and second past the hour to have a repeated sequence. You can also use HOUR (which returns the hour of the day): however, to use RANDOMIZE SECOND*MINUTE*HOUR could produce an error, since the result of the multiplication *could* be outside the permitted integer range. (SECOND, MINUTE and HOUR return simple integer values). You can get round this easily:

```
h&=HOUR
RANDOMIZE SECOND*MINUTE*H&
```

This will force the result of the multiplication to be a long integer, and will give a range of 80063 different sequences, with far less chance of a specific sequence being repeated.

Calculations on lists of numbers

OPL has a number of functions that enable you to perform specific operations on a series of numeric values. (These functions are also available to you in the Calculator section of your Series 3a).

MAX (*list*) This looks at a list of values, and returns the highest value in that list. The list can be included in one of two different ways. It can either be a straight list of real values, variables or expressions, each separated by a comma, thus:

```
bignum=MAX(5,9,v,4*x)
```

or it can be the elements of a floating point array. In this instance, two '*arguments*' are required: the array name (which must include the brackets), and the number of array elements to be examined. Thus:

```
bignum=MAX(arry(),n)
```

where `arry()` is the name of the array you wish to have examined, and *n* is the number of elements in the array to be examined, starting with the first. Here is a procedure to demonstrate this last example:

```
PROC maxtest:
    LOCAL a(5),c%
    DO
        c%=c%+1
        PRINT "Enter number",c%,":",
        INPUT a(c%)
    UNTIL c%=5
    CLS
    PRINT "The highest number entered =",
    PRINT MAX(a(),5)
    GET
ENDP
```

This procedure will also give you an idea of how arrays are used to store values. The *elements* of the array are a(1), a(2)...a(5), and each of these is a different variable. As you can see, by having an array, you can enter the values in a DO...UNTIL loop, rather than have a lengthy repetition of input requests for each individual variable.

MIN (*list*) This is similar to MAX(), the difference being that MIN() returns the smallest value in the list. You can edit the maxtest procedure to show the smallest number entered, by changing the PRINT MAX(a(),5) line to PRINT

MIN(a(),5). You must also change 'highest' to read 'lowest' in the message line for the displayed answer of course! (And don't forget to *translate* the procedure again before running it).

MEAN (*list***)**   This returns the *mean* value of the list. The formats for MEAN() are the same as for MAX() and MIN(): the arguments can be a list of values, variables or expressions, each separated by a comma, or an array. In the case of the array, the number of elements to be examined must be the second argument. You can edit the maxtest procedure by simply changing the PRINT MAX(a(),5) line to read PRINT MEAN(a(),5), to show the mean of a series of five entered numbers. (Don't forget the message line!)

SUM (*list***)**   This returns the *sum* of the list. The formats are the same as for MAX(), and you can put the function to the test by editing the maxtest procedure, changing the PRINT MAX(a(),5) line to PRINT SUM(a(),5), (and the message line to read 'sum' instead of 'highest') to show the sum of a series of five entered numbers.

STD (*list***)**   This returns the *sample standard deviation* of the list. The formats are the same as for MAX(), and you can put the function to the test by editing the maxtest procedure, changing the PRINT MAX(a(),5) line to PRINT STD(a(),5), (and the message line to read 'standard deviation') to show the standard deviation of a series of five entered numbers.

VAR (*list***)**   This returns the *sample variance* of the list. The formats are the same as for MAX(), and you can put the function to the test by editing the maxtest procedure, changing the PRINT MAX(a(),5) line to PRINT VAR(a(),5), (and the message line to read 'variance') to show the variance of a series of five entered numbers.

CHAPTER 13
Dates and times

This Chapter briefly examines the date and time functions available for use in your programs. The OPL words covered are
DATIM$, YEAR, MONTH, MONTH$, DAY, DAYS, DAYNAME$, HOUR, MINUTE, SECOND, DOW, WEEK, DATETOSECS, SECSTODATE.

Using the system clock
You will be well aware that Series 3a keeps track of the time and date. This information - and information based on it - is available for use in your programs. You will also have noticed that, generally speaking, OPL words indicate the particular function they perform - HOUR, for example, returns the current hour in the system clock. Tempting though it may be, you *must not* use the names of the OPL words as the names of *variables* in your programs. Thus, you cannot write a program with a variable called 'hour'. This is true of all OPL words, of course, but for those associated with time, naming one of the OPL words as a variable is a very common error. You *can* however use one of the OPL reserved words if you give it a different identifier. 'Hour', for example, would produce errors as a floating point variable, but 'hour%' would be perfectly acceptable. Now let us examine the OPL words related to the time and date.

Accessing the System clock
A series of OPL words can be used to return 'simple' data from the system clock. These are:

**DATIM$** This returns the current day of the week, date and time - including the seconds - as a string. If the entire string returned by DATIM$ is assigned to a string variable, that variable must have been declared to hold at least 24 characters. Using the string handling functions, (Chapter 9), you can 'pick off' various elements of the string, if you wish. The format for the function is

```
dt$=DATIM$
```

and you can naturally use it in statements such as PRINT DATIM$. The string returned by DATIM$ has the form

```
Mon 16 Sep 1995 11:00:15
```

Remember that DATIM$ returns the current time and date - and is being updated every second.

YEAR   This returns as an integer value the current year from the system clock. Years from 1900 to the year 2155 are covered. The format is

```
y%=YEAR
```

MONTH   This returns as an integer value the current month from the system clock. Naturally, the range of values returned is 1 to 12. The format is

```
m%=MONTH
```

DAY   This returns as an integer value the current day of the month from the system clock. The range of values is 1 to 31. The format is

```
d%=DAY
```

HOUR   This returns as an integer value the current hour of the day, using a 24-hour clock, from the system clock. The format is

```
h%=HOUR
```

MINUTE This returns as an integer value the current minute from the system clock. The format is

```
m%=MINUTE
```

SECOND This returns the current second, according to the system clock, as an integer value. The format is

```
s%=SECOND
```

Converting time and date data

Very often you will be working on 'month' and 'day' information in the form of numeric values, rather than the names of the months or days of the week. Nevertheless, you may well wish to display the *name* of the day or month rather than its number. OPL has two functions which make the conversion for you.

MONTH\$ (*mn*%)　　This function converts the month number, represented by *mn*%, into the corresponding three-letter name. Obviously *mn*% must have a value from 1 to 12. The format is

$$m\$=MONTH\$\ (mn\%)$$
$$or\ \ PRINT\ MONTH\$\ (mn\%)$$

DAYNAME\$ (*dn*%)　　This function converts a day number, represented by *dn*%, into the corresponding three-letter day of the week, The format is

$$dn\$=DAYNAME\$\ (dn\%)$$
$$or\ \ PRINT\ DAYNAME\$\ (dn\%)$$

Date calculations

Most programming languages leave it to the programmer to write routines that will enable him to evaluate, for example, the number of days between two dates. OPL has functions to help achieve this and similar tasks for you.

DAYS (*dy*%,*mn*%,*yr*%)　　This function returns as a long integer the number of days between January 1st 1900 and the date specified by *dy*%, *mn*%, *yr*%, which represent the required day, month number and year respectively. The format is

$$d\&=DAYS\ (dy\%,mn\%,yr\%)$$

To find the number of days between two dates, all that is needed is to enter the two dates in a suitable form, use the 'DAYS ()' function for each of the dates, then subtract one from the other. Here's a short program to evaluate the number of days between any specified date (your Birthday, perhaps) and the current date as determined by the system clock. You could enter a date some time in the future: the ABS() function ensures that a positive result is always given.

```
PROC numdays:
 LOCAL dy%,mn%,yr%
 PRINT "Enter year:",
 INPUT yr%
 IF yr%<100
  yr%=yr%+1900
 ENDIF
 PRINT "Enter Month number:",
 INPUT mn%
 PRINT "Enter day of month:",
 INPUT dy%
 CLS
 PRINT "There are",
 PRINT ABS(DAYS(dy%,mn%,yr%)-DAYS
same line continued          (DAY,MONTH,YEAR)),
 PRINT "days between",dy%,month(mn%),yr%,
 PRINT "and today"
 GET
ENDP
```

You'll see that this procedure allows you to enter a two-figure number for the year: if you do, then the '1900' is added to prevent an error occurring.

WEEK($dy\%,mn\%,yr\%$)   This function returns, as an integer, the week of the year in which a particular date falls, the date being specified by $dy\%$, $mn\%$, and $yr\%$. The value of $dy\%$ must be sensible for the specified month, $mn\%$ must be a valid month number, and $yr\%$ must have a value between 1900 and 2155, otherwise an '**Invalid arguments**' error will occur when the program is run.

The starting day for each week is taken from the 'Start of the Week' setting in your Series 3a (under the 'Time' utility). There must be four or more days in the 'first week' for it to count as 'Week 1': if there are less, it is returned as Week 52. The format is

$$wn\%=WEEK(dy\%,mn\%,yr\%)$$

DOW(`dy%,mn%,yr%`**)**   This function returns an integer representing the number of the day in the week, with '1' representing Monday through to '7' representing Sunday. As before, the arguments `dy%`, `mn%` and `yr%` must be valid, otherwise an error will occur. The format is

```
daynum%=DOW(dy%,mn%,yr%)
```

If you want the actual name of the day, rather than its number, you can use the DAYNAME$() function, thus:

```
PRINT DAYNAME$(DOW(dy%,mn%,yr%))
```

This is a good example, in fact, of how functions can be used as part of other functions: here DOW() gets the day of the week as an *argument* for DAYNAME$(), to return the name of the day, which in turn is an expression for PRINT to operate on in order to display the answer. Notice how each function requires its arguments to be contained within its own set of brackets.

DATETOSECS(`yr%,mon%,dy%,hr%,min%,sec%`**)** This function returns as a long integer the number of *seconds* between the turn of the year 1970 (00:00 on Jan 1st, 1970) and the date and time specified by the arguments `yr%`, `mon%`, `dy%`, `hr%`, `min%`, `sec%`. The value returned is positive up to +2,147,583,647, and then becomes *negative*, starting from -2,147,583,647, and going on until -1.

SECSTODATE(`s&,yr%,mon%,dy%,hr%,min%,sec%,dayinyr%`**)** This does the 'opposite' to DATETOSECS(): it converts the long integer `s&` into its component parts - year (`yr%`), month (`mon%`), day (`dy%`), hours (`hr%`), minutes (`min%`) and seconds (`sec%`), plus the number of the day within the year, `dayinyr%`. The variables must have been declared: this function assigns the appropriate values to them, so that you can subsequently use them, for printing out, perhaps. As with DAYTOSECS(), `s&` can have a positive value up to +2,147,483,647. For a value higher than that, you must subtract 4,294,967,296 from the value.

CHAPTER 14
The sound of music

Time for a little 'light relief': this Chapter discusses the Series 3a's capability to produce sounds. The OPL word covered is
     BEEP.

Your own Beep show

By now, you will undoubtedly have heard some of the sounds that your Series 3a can create - the chimes and 'ringing' for the alarms, and the tones used for DTMF dialling. OPL has a command - BEEP - which enables you to create sounds other than a simple 'bleep' for use in your own programs.

The format for the command is

     BEEP *length%,pitch%*

The *length%* value determines how many thirty-seconds of a second the sound will last. So for a one second sound, *length%* will have a value of 32.

The *frequency* of the sound is determined by the value of *pitch%*, as follows:

$$frequency = 512000/(pitch\% + 1)$$

which can be re-written as

$$pitch\% = (512000/frequency) - 1$$

This enables you to determine what value you should give to *pitch%* in order to produce a note of a specified frequency. Thus to play a note that has a frequency of 800 Hz for a quarter of a second, you would write

     BEEP 8,512000/800-1

Note that brackets aren't needed round the '512000/800' part, since Series 3a performs the division first anyway.

If you make `length%` negative (eg BEEP -8,500) then Series 3a first checks whether the sound system is already in use. If it is, then BEEP simply returns without making any sound at all. Otherwise, BEEP waits until the sound system is free, then plays the note.

Keyboard music-maker

As a programming exercise, BEEP is used to turn your Series 3a into a musical(?) instrument. Of sorts. This program uses many of the aspects of OPL we have discussed so far but not yet implemented, so although it is fairly crude in what it achieves, you may find it useful to enter it, if only temporarily.

The Internationally accepted frequency for the note 'A' is 440Hz. To find the frequency of a note one octave higher, the frequency is doubled. So 'A' in the next scale is 880Hz. Armed with this scant information, a formula can be devised to determine the frequency of any note in the scale.

If we say that 'A' is the first note in a scale, then 'A sharp' is the second note, 'B' is the third, and so on. Calling this the note *number*, the formula is

$$\text{note frequency} = 440 \times 2^{(\text{note number}/12)}$$

which in computer-write is

$$\text{note frequency} = 440*2**(\text{note number}/12)$$

Thus, for 'C', the 'fourth note' from 'A', the frequency is 440*2**(4/12), or 554.365.

We now have the information needed to convert your Series 3a keyboard into a musical keyboard.

There are two ways to approach the actual playing of a note. The first is to calculate the required frequency each time a key is pressed, and then calculate the value required for the BEEP command. The second is to calculate the necessary values first and store them in an array. As this is an exercise, it will be useful to demonstrate the use of arrays, and so that's the method adopted.

Ideally, each note will sound only while a key is being depressed. However, it is the nature of computer keyboards that there is a short delay before a depressed key 'auto-repeats'. This means there would be a break in the note before it repeats for the duration of the keypress. The alternative is to arrange for the note to play continuously until another key is pressed - and to use the SPACE key to turn the sound off. The ESC key is used to terminate the program when it is running.

Whilst the Series 3a keyboard doesn't resemble a piano keyboard, some measure of similarity(?) can be achieved by using one row for the 'white keys', and appropriate keys from the row above it for the 'black keys'. The 'qwerty' row will give us our 'white keys'.

It will be useful to know the name of the note being played at any particular time - and which Series 3a key produced it, so this is displayed on the screen whilst a note is being played.

The BEEP part of the program is placed in a separate procedure, so that it can be called from various places: this saves us from having to repeat the command in the program.

The variables used are as follows:

n%(18)   This array holds the calculated *pitch%* for 18 notes. It is a GLOBAL variable, since it will need to be used in the second procedure.

k$(18)   This string of 18 characters holds the keyboard letters for the notes, in ascending sequence of played note.

c$(1)   This will hold the character of the pressed key when the program is running.

nn$(36)   This string holds the musical names of each of the eighteen notes, in ascending order. To allow for the fact that some notes require two characters (A#, for example), a space will be added to those only having a single character, so that all notes are defined by two characters.

c%   This integer variable is used first as a 'counter' during the initial set up, then it is used to determine the position of a pressed key from the 18 valid key names in the k$() string.

f   This floating point variable is used in the calculation of the frequency for each note.

p%   This holds the value of the last key that was pressed, so that we can avoid the gap in the note due to the keyboard's delay in auto-repeating.

You must enter both of the procedures in the same file, before translating and running the program. Take care when entering it to ensure the variables have the correct identifiers throughout, that you have the right number of spaces in the appropriate places, and so on.

```
PROC music:
 GLOBAL n%(18)
 LOCAL k$(18),c$(1),nn$(36)
 LOCAL c%,f,p%
 k$="q2we4r5ty7u8i9op+-"
 c%=1
 DO
  f=440*2**(c%/12.0)
  n%(c%)=512000/f-1
  c%=c%+1
 UNTIL c%>18
 nn$="A A#B C C#D D#E F F#F G#"
 nn$=nn$+LEFT$(nn$,12)
 PRINT "Play now...(Space stops note)"
 PRINT "ESC quits"
 DO
  c$=LOWER$(KEY$)
  IF (c$="") AND p%
   playit:(p%)
  ELSEIF c$=""
   CONTINUE
  ELSEIF c$=" "
   p%=0
   AT 18,4
   PRINT "Play            "
  ELSE
   c%=LOC(k$,c$)
  IF c%
   AT 18,4
   PRINT c$,"=",
   PRINT MID$(nn$,c%*2-1,2)
   playit:(c%)
   p%=c%
  ENDIF
 ENDIF
 UNTIL c$=chr$(27)
ENDP
```

```
PROC playit:(a%)
  BEEP 1,n%(a%)
ENDP
```

For the second procedure, `playit`, you will have to enter the PROC and ENDP words yourself.

Here's a brief explanation of how this program works. First, as always, the variables are declared. Note how you can use more than one line to declare variables: here one line is used for the LOCAL string variables, and one for the LOCAL numeric variables.

The program starts by initialising the necessary variables and arrays. k$ is loaded with the key letter characters, in the correct sequence for the ascending notes. Then, in a loop, the frequency and pitch for each note is calculated and loaded into the array n%(). This is followed by loading the note names in the string variable nn$. Note how this is done: all of the note names are entered once, then the necessary extra notes are added using the string function 'LEFT$()'.

Then comes the part of the program that plays the notes. This is contained within a DO...UNTIL loop, which will terminate when ESC is pressed (CHR$(27)).

First a check is made to see whether a key has been pressed - storing the character in c$ if it has. Then, if a key hasn't been pressed since the last keyboard 'poll', but there *is* a previous valid keypress (so p% will have a value), the `playit` procedure is called, using the previous keypress to determine the *pitch*.

If there is neither a previous valid keypress, nor a current keypress, then a jump to the UNTIL statement is made, using the CONTINUE command, to repeat the loop until something relevant *does* happen.

Then a check is made to see whether the SPACE key has been pressed: if it has, we want to stop the note from playing, and clear the screen display. We stop the note from playing by assigning zero to p%.

Failing all that, another key must have been pressed, and so we must check whether it is a valid note-playing key. This is done by checking for its location in the string of valid notes. At the same time, we will find out which key or note of the eighteen has been pressed: this will be returned in c%. If the key isn't valid, c% will hold zero.

If it is valid, the IF c% statement is *true*, and the appropriate keyboard key and the corresponding note are displayed on the screen before calling the `playit` routine to actually create the sound. Notice how the *two* appropriate characters are selected from the 36 character string nn$.

And that's it. You may not have created a wonderful keyboard instrument. But you will have learned a bit more about the basic operation of your Series 3a!

Finally, here is a short routine to provide an alarm tone until a key is pressed.

```
PROC alarm:
 DO
  BEEP 1,400
  BEEP 1,200
 UNTIL KEY
ENDP
```

CHAPTER 15
Errors and bugs

This Chapter deals with the things that can go wrong when writing a program, and what to do about them. OPL words covered are

TRAP, ERR, ERR$, ONERR and RAISE.

When things go wrong

The programmer who has never made a mistake doesn't exist. So if one of your programs doesn't run properly - or even fails to 'translate', don't despair - you've joined the club!

There are three areas where things can go wrong.

a)   Typing errors when entering the program.

b)   Incorrect use of the programming language.

c)   The program 'logic'.

You have to become a 'detective' to resolve any of these, examining every possible clue, and studying Series 3a's analysis of the problem, when it is given.

Errors when entering

The easiest problems to detect are those caused through typing errors when entering your program. Most of these will be revealed as soon as you try to translate it, for if Series 3a finds it doesn't understand the actual instructions, it will stop the translation process, report the nature of the problem and, in most instances, place the cursor at the point where the problem occurred. You can put this to the test for yourself by entering the following procedure *exactly* as it is written:

```
PROC bugs:
  PRINT (4*5
ENDP
```

There are actually two problems with this procedure. The first one you will discover when you try to translate it: Series 3a will stop, briefly report a '**Mismatched (or)**', and will leave the cursor at the end of the PRINT line. It is telling you that it found one bracket, but can't find the other. Hence the mismatched '(' or ')'. The second problem will be revealed when you correct, translate and run the program: nothing will seem to happen. That's because, having displayed the result of the PRINT operation, the program ended - before you had a chance to see the display! Edit the program by inserting GET, on its own line, between the PRINT statement and ENDP.

If you want to review an error message again, you can do so by selecting 'SHOW ERROR' from the 'PROG' option on the MENU, or by pressing the PSION and 'E' keys at the same time.

Syntax errors

Spelling errors in OPL words and errors in the way the words are used are in most instances reported as a '**Syntax error**'. Typical errors of this nature are entering, for example, 'PRINY' instead of 'PRINT', missing out a space or a comma where a space or a comma is expected, or missing out the colon after a procedure name. What Series 3a cannot do when *translating* your program is detect errors in the spelling of your variables. You may have called a variable 'cost' in one place, and 'cast' in another. Similarly, you may have given a variable a different identifier in one place - cost% instead of cost$, for example. This type of error will show up, however, when you try to run the program - usually as an '**Undefined external**'.

During the *translation* process Series 3a will also report structural errors - finishing a 'WHILE...' loop with 'UNTIL', for example. In fact, it will report quite an extensive range of error types, to help you identify the mistake that you have made.

Generally speaking, the error message provided will give you an excellent clue to what has gone wrong, and the positioning of the cursor will often help you to locate where it has gone wrong. There are times, however, when Series 3a is unable to position the cursor near to the point of the error, so be prepared for a little searching through your program.

If you have more than one procedure in your file, Series 3a will position the cursor in the procedure that caused the trouble when it reports the error. Again, in all but a few instances, this is where the problem actually lies.

The list of error messages that can occur during the translation process is given in the Appendices. Hopefully, you won't see too many of them.

Run-time errors

The second type of problem that can occur - usually involving incorrect use of the language in some way or other - doesn't reveal itself until you attempt to *run* the program. Series 3a will find it is faced with a situation which prevents it from obeying your instructions. In such circumstances the program stops running, and a message is displayed. Here's an example:

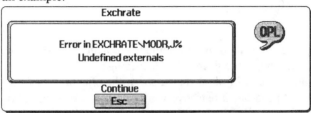

The message tells you the name of the program (in the above example, Exchrate), the procedure where the error was *detected* (in the example, modr), with further information such as a variable name (j% in the example), if relevant, and the nature of the problem. *Make a note of all the details*: after you have pressed the ESC key to return to the program editor, pressing the PSION and '🄴' keys will only repeat the *nature* of the problem.

The example shown above is a typical - and very common - error 'Undefined externals'. It means Psion Series 3a has come to a part of the program with a variable or procedure name (an 'external') which it cannot resolve.

If it is a variable name, the problem is either that you have not declared it, or it hasn't been passed into the procedure correctly as an argument, or that you have incorrectly spelt it. The trouble is, the error *may* be in another procedure altogether - if the variable concerned is a GLOBAL, for instance. If the 'external' is a procedure name, then either you have forgotten to enter the procedure in the same file, forgotten to load it in with a library file, or not spelled it correctly. Sadly, the ball is in your court to examine your program, using the clues as guidance, to find exactly what you have done wrong.

'Undefined external' is just one of a whole range of messages that Series 3a will report when it has a problem whilst running a program. The messages relate to specific situations, and will usually give you an excellent clue as to what you must do to correct the situation.

To give two more examples, a 'String too long' message means that you have tried to assign too many characters to a string variable - more than it was declared to be able to hold. Thus:

```
PROC bugs:
   LOCAL a$(4)
   a$="abcdefg"
PRINT a$
ENDP
```

This procedure will translate without problem, but when run, it will stop, give the 'String too long' message and, on re-entering the Program Editor, will place the cursor at the offending *assignment* line. You won't need much detective work to put that one right: however, if the assignment is of the form 'a$=b$', then you'll have to examine the declarations for both variables.

A 'Subscript or dimension error' message means that you are trying to use an array element that hasn't been allowed for in the array definition. Here's the 'bugs' procedure edited to demonstrate this:

```
PROC bugs:
      LOCAL a%(4),c%
      PRINT a%(c%)
ENDP
```

On the face of it, everything looks fine: however, although all of the variables have been declared, c% hasn't been assigned a value and so it is equal to zero. You are therefore asking Series 3a to print the value of the array element a%(0) - which doesn't exist. Array *subscripts* (a subscript is the bit in brackets - the element number of the array) start from '1' when the declaration is made, remember, so a declaration of a%(4) means set up variables a%() to have a range or 'dimension' of a%(1), a%(2), a%(3) and a%(4). Four variables in all. When you attempt to run the procedure, the error message will be displayed and on re-entering the Program Editor, the cursor will be positioned at the offending 'c%'.

This particular kind of situation needs a little more detective work on your part. You must ascertain *why* the value of the variable c% has caused the subscript error. In the 'bugs' example, it isn't too difficult to spot, once you realise that declared variables are zero until they are assigned a value. In different circumstances the error could equally well be that c% has been assigned a value greater than '4' or less than '1' somewhere in the program. You need to find out where, and why, and correct for the situation from occurring again.

Errors of logic

We now come to the programmer's nightmare: errors in the logic of a program. This type of error varies considerably in its degree of complexity and the ease with which it can be resolved. Sometimes, the error is fairly easy to detect. On other occasions it can take hours of work - and possibly a great deal of re-writing to detect the error and put it right.

The problem is, unless the error causes the program to stop running, it can be difficult to detect. Furthermore, the error may become apparent only under very specific running conditions.

The very first 'bugs' program in this Chapter had a very simple error of logic: the GET instruction (or some other way of 'holding' the display whilst you examined it) had been missed out.

Another common error occurs when one variable is being divided by another. As long as the second variable has a value, the program will run perfectly. But for just one value of the second variable - when it is zero (equals '0') a '**Divide by zero**' error will occur.

This particular error will be detected by Series 3a since it cannot perform such an operation: it will stop the program. But there are many times when errors of logic aren't revealed. And that's when you need to put your Sherlock Holmes hat on and winkle out the problem, carefully and methodically.

The first thing to do, always, is to examine your code to ensure that there are no obvious mistakes - such as a missing GET. Examine your 'flow-chart' and see that *its* logic makes sense. (If your program is of any length and you *haven't* prepared a flow-chart, then you are on your knees begging for trouble).

There are several techniques you can employ when trying to locate errors of logic. The object is to create 'clues' where clues don't exist, and this can usually be achieved by adding lines of code on a temporary basis. For example, you can insert statement lines to PRINT out the name and values of suspect variables at various points in the program (followed by GET of course!), and then run the program observing what happens to the values of those variables under specific running conditions.

Where programs have a number of individual *function* procedures, you can copy each of them in turn to another file, and write a *test* procedure (as the first procedure in the file) to call the function and test it out thoroughly, allowing for various types of input.

If you can get a print-out of your program, try to follow it through, step by step, for different conditions: run the program 'in your mind' as though you are the Series 3a! Check that each OPL instruction does what you think it does: if in doubt, write a short procedure to test the instruction (as indeed we have been doing in this book).

Finally, if you can identify the particular area of the program that is causing the trouble, try writing it in a different way, perhaps using different OPL instructions altogether. This may give you a clue to the problem, and then you can either go back and correct the original coding, or simply use the new instructions.

Trapping detectable errors individually

It has already been stated that with a number of 'run-time' errors, Series 3a will stop and inform you it has a problem, and will spell out the nature of the problem. Errors that Series 3a can detect *you* can also detect - and prevent from stopping the program from running. OPL has instructions specifically designed for this purpose.

The range of commands which, if used incorrectly, will cause a 'stoppable' error is quite large: most of them however are concerned with *Graphics* and *File Handling* operations, neither of which we have dealt with yet: to do so now would only confuse. However, there is one instruction that we have dealt with, INPUT, which although doesn't actually stop the program from running, will allow the 'trapping' method to be examined.

You may have noticed that, where there is an INPUT statement, an incorrect entry for the variable type concerned will cause a question mark to appear on the next line of the display. Series 3a has in effect said "Pardon?" or, more explicitly "What you have entered at the keyboard is of the wrong *type* for the variable I've been told to use. Try again". Enter the following procedure, then when you run it, enter anything you like *except* a number. Then, when the question mark appears, enter a small integer number.

```
PROC traptest:
  LOCAL a%
  PRINT "Enter a number"
  AT 18,1
  INPUT a%
  PRINT "You entered",a%
  GET
ENDP
```

Although the program doesn't stop running, the question mark that appears on incorrect entries can be a pain if you have carefully arranged for a neat display. You can avoid it with the OPL instruction TRAP.

TRAP   This instruction can precede a number of the OPL commands, to 'trap' any error that occurs when that command is executed. Such errors would normally stop the program running, with a relevant message displayed on the screen. When TRAP is used, however, any error that occurs *is handled under your control*. It is very important to remember this: the Series 3a's mechanism for dealing with the error - which is short and curt - is effectively switched off. It is up to *you* to deal with the error in your program. The benefit, of course, is that you can anticipate what *might* go wrong and prevent it from stopping the program running. How you handle the error is up to you, but usually you will want to correct the error in some way and perhaps display a message, so that the program can continue to perform the way you intended.

When TRAP is used, any error resulting from the execution of the associated command will not stop the program running. However, Series 3a will register the fact that an error has occurred, by storing an identifying 'number' for that error in an OPL variable called **ERR**. Execution will then continue with the *next* statement in your program. *This is where your 'action on an error' routine should be.* You can detect the nature of the error by examining the value held by ERR, and then act accordingly.

ERR   simply holds a number representing the last error that occurred whilst a program is running. There is also an OPL

149

function that will return the relevant *message* for a particular error number, and that's ERR$ (en%), where en% is the error number. The format normally used would be

```
PRINT ERR$(ERR).
```

Note that although it doesn't have an identifier, ERR stores a *negative* integer value for *Series 3a's* error codes.

The commands that TRAP can be used with are:

Data Entry: INPUT, EDIT

Data File Handling: APPEND, BACK, CLOSE, CREATE, DELETE, FIRST, LAST, NEXT, OPEN, OPENR, POSITION, UPDATE, USE.

Directory File Handling: COMPRESS, COPY, ERASE, LCLOSE, LOADM, LOPEN, MKDIR, RENAME, RMDIR, UNLOADM.

Graphics: gCLOSE, gCOPY, gFONT, gPATT, gSAVEBIT, gUNLOADFONT, gUSE.

Most of these OPL words are dealt with later. Now let us take a look at how TRAP can be used with INPUT. We are going to precede the INPUT command in the traptest program with a TRAP command, and then follow this statement line with our own error handling routine. Edit traptest so that it reads as follows:

```
PROC traptest:
 LOCAL a%
 PRINT "Enter a number"
 DO
  AT 18,1
  TRAP INPUT a%
  IF ERR
   AT 3,3
   PRINT "Bad input"
   GET
   AT 3,3
   PRINT "           "
  ENDIF
 UNTIL ERR=0
 PRINT "You entered",a%
 GET
ENDP
```

You'll see that the input routine is contained within a DO loop which will run until an error free input has been obtained (UNTIL ERR=0). Following the TRAP INPUT line, we are simply testing for *any* error - although in practice there are probably only two that can occur with this routine- '**General failure**' (error number -1) and '**Escape key pressed**' (-114). If no error occurs with the input, ERR is zero, and IF ERR is *not true*, so execution jumps to the UNTIL ERR=0 (which is *true*). The program will then continue the way you planned, with an acceptable input, and with the screen display entirely under your control.

Since the ESC key produces an error number when pressed during an INPUT operation, you can use it to escape from the routine altogether. To show this, delete the IF ERR line in traptest, and insert the following in its place:

```
IF ERR=-114
  STOP
ELSEIF ERR
```

Now when the procedure is run, pressing the ESC key will simply break out of the program. This gives you an easy way to terminate a program without going through the rigmarole of having statements such as "Press 0 to exit", and then testing for a zero input.

Trapping any program-stopping error

TRAP gives you control over errors that occur with a wide range of OPL commands. But there is also a universal way to trap almost any *program stopping* error, irrespective of the command that caused it. (This universal method won't trap errors occurring with INPUT, for example, since they don't actually stop the program from running).

Trapping *any* program-stopping error takes a little more care and thought, for whereas you can be fairly sure of the type of error that is likely to be produced by a specific OPL command, when spreading a broad net over a procedure, file or an entire program, you cannot be too certain of what error is going to occur. Consequently, *you* will have to test for the nature of the error. The OPL command for 'overall trapping' is ONERR.

ONERR *label::* This command (which stands for 'ON ERROR'), is followed by a label name, indicating where Series 3a is to continue to execute the program should an error occur. The label can be positioned anywhere in the current procedure

151

(even *before* the ONERR command, so that processing will 'jump back'). The format for using ONERR is

```
ONERR label or
ONERR label::
```

ONERR switches off the Series 3a's handling of errors on all the instructions that follow it, including instructions in *called* procedures. You could, therefore, protect an entire program by having ONERR as one of the first statements. This, however, is not recommended since it can result in endless loops, and it makes the handling of specific errors difficult - and prone to mistakes (errors in error handling routines? ... the mind boggles).

You can have more than one ONERR in a procedure, but only the *last* one to be executed is obeyed. You can also 'switch off' all ONERRs in one procedure, with the line

```
ONERR OFF
```

Note that this affects only the action of the ONERR commands in the *current* procedure: those in procedures that call the current procedure are unaffected.

It is important to note that, since ONERR covers all possible 'reportable' errors, it should be *switched off* as the first instruction in the actual error handling routine. If it isn't, and an error occurs *within the error handling routine*, your program will wind up with the error handling routine calling the error handling routine calling the error handling routine calling the ... you get the idea.

If you use ONERR and TRAP, the TRAP command takes precedence: the error handling routine you write following TRAP will be executed, rather than the ONERR error handling routine. When protecting an entire procedure with ONERR, it is usual but not necessary for the error handling routine to be placed either at the start or the end of the procedure. When at the start, you would probably want to have an 'IF ERR' as one of the early statements, to prevent the that part of the program from executing during the normal sequence of events. Similarly, when the error handling routine is placed at the end of a procedure, to prevent it from being executed you would most likely place a statement such as 'RETURN' *before* the error routine's label.

Both of these methods are demonstrated with the following programs, which divide 10 by an integer number. Whilst *any* error will be trapped, it is unlikely that anything other than a '**Divide by zero**' will occur. Nevertheless, these programs serve our purpose in showing how the ONERR command can be used.

First, here's the procedure with the error handling routine 'up front'. The error handling routine (fixit::) starts with an ONERR OFF, even though so far we haven't apparently switched it on yet. Point is, should an error occur later on in the program, ONERR *will* be 'on', and it is important to make sure it is switched off within the error handling routine itself. The TRAP command is used with INPUT, to show how both error handling techniques can be included within the one procedure. Remember that TRAP takes *precedence* over ONERR for all *program stopping* errors. When you run this program, first enter a letter instead of a number, then, next time you're asked for a value, enter zero, and then finally, enter a small(ish) integer number.

```
PROC traptest:
 LOCAL a%
 fixit::
  ONERR OFF
  IF ERR
   AT 1,4
   PRINT "Divide by 0 trapped by ONERR"
   PRINT ERR$(ERR)
   GET
   AT 1,4
   PRINT "                         "
   PRINT "                         "
  ENDIF
 ONERR fixit::
  CLS
  PRINT "Divide 10 by?:"
  DO
   AT 18,1
   TRAP INPUT a%
   IF ERR
    AT 1,4
    PRINT "Trapped input error"
    GET
```

153

```
      AT 1,4
       PRINT "                          "
      ENDIF
    UNTIL ERR=0
   PRINT 10.0/a%
   GET
ENDP
```

Notice how the ONERR error handling routine is prevented from being executed when the program is initially started, by checking OPL's ERR variable.

Now here's the program with the error handling routine at the end. This time, RETURN is used to prevent the error handling routine 'fixit::' from being executed during the normal running of the program (in this case, you could also use STOP). Also, you'll see that in order to give the user a chance to enter another value, the dreaded GOTO is used to jump back to the start of the program in the event of an error. Without this, the program would end after the error had been announced.

```
PROC traptest:
  LOCAL a%
redo::
  ONERR fixit::
  CLS
  PRINT "Divide 10 by?:"
  DO
    AT 18,1
    TRAP INPUT a%
    IF ERR
      AT 1,4
      PRINT "Trapped input error"
      GET
      AT 1,4
      PRINT "                          "
    ENDIF
  UNTIL ERR=0
  PRINT 10.0/a%
  GET
  RETURN                    REM or STOP will do here
fixit::
  ONERR OFF
```

```
AT 1,4
PRINT "Divide by 0 trapped by ONERR"
PRINT ERR$(ERR)
GET
AT 1,4
PRINT "                              "
PRINT "                              "
GOTO redo::
ENDP
```

The ONERR command is fairly powerful, in that it will also trap the program stoppers you may not have bargained for. Remember that you can detect the nature of the error through the ERR variable, and print it out with PRINT ERR$(ERR).

As a general strategy, in an ONERR handling routine you can use 'IF ERR=*en1%*' and 'ELSEIF ERR=*en2%*' statements to deal with the errors you're catering for (where *en1%* and *en2%* represent error code values), and an ELSE statement to deal with anything unexpected.

Raising errors

To help when testing or de-bugging a program, OPL allows you to generate an error. The effect is exactly the same as if an error had actually occurred: the requested error code is stored in the OPL variable ERR, and acted on accordingly. If you don't have an ONERR command preceding the RAISE statement, Series 3a will stop the program and report the 'raised' error just as if it had really occurred.

RAISE   The format is

RAISE errcode%

where *errcode%* is a negative code value for the error type you wish to generate (see Appendix 3).

You must be a little careful when using RAISE where loops in the program structure are involved. For example, if in the previous traptest program you include a line 'RAISE -8' (for 'Divide by zero') after the ONERR fixit:: statement, the program would go into a perpetual loop. The error would be generated, dealt with by the error handling routine fixit::, then program execution returned to the point a little before the error is generated again. Wheels will spin.

You can break out of such a loop, so that you can happily continue using your Series 3a, by pressing the PSION and ESC keys.

RAISE can also be useful in generating an error message for you. Say, for example, that at some point in your program the user is required to enter an input from 1 to 10 inclusive. Anything else is not acceptable. You can use RAISE to generate an "Out of range" message, which is quite appropriate for the circumstances. Thus

```
PROC raistest:
  LOCAL a%
fixit::
  ONERR off
  IF ERR
    PRINT "Naughty you"
    PRINT ERR$(ERR)
    GET
  ENDIF
  CLS
  PRINT "Enter a number (1-10)",
  INPUT a%
  ONERR fixit::
  IF (a%<1) OR (a%>10)
    RAISE -7
  ENDIF
  PRINT "Thank you!"
  GET
ENDP
```

Notice how the RAISE instruction is obeyed *only* if the user makes an invalid entry. Any valid entry, and the error message is not generated, so perpetual loops are avoided. Test it for yourself.

Finally you can use RAISE to generate your *own* error messages, different from those used by OPL. Psion strongly recommends that, when raising your own numbers, you avoid any negative values like the plague: they may wish to add to the list themselves!

In the raistest procedure, first edit 'RAISE -7' to read 'RAISE 1', and run the program. With an entry of over 10, the error message reported will be '**Unknown error [1]**'. Then edit the 'IF ERR' line to read 'IF ERR=1', and the 'PRINT ERR$(ERR)' line to read 'PRINT "My error message". That shows how you can 'catch' errors of your own choosing and display a message accordingly.

PART 2

The Graphics

This Part of the Book deals with the very powerful Graphics capabilities of OPL, enabling the creation of windows, menus, dialogs, icons and drawings.

CHAPTER 16
Putting you in the picture

This Chapter introduces the powerful Graphics capabilities of Series 3a, and in particular, discusses the concept of windows. The OPL words covered are
DEFAULTWIN, GPRINT *and* BUSY

Now comes the power...

All the topics discussed so far have been *basic* programming techniques, which will enable you to write *text* programs: that is, programs which use no graphics at all. But you will have realised, from the way Series 3a presents its own built-in facilities (such as the World Map or Agenda) that it is capable of far more than simple textual displays. Clocks, pull-down menus, 'dialog' boxes, little button displays that 'press down' when the appropriate key is pressed, brief on-screen messages tucked away in a corner - all these and more are available for you to use. They'll add life to your programs, give them a professional feel and help to make them easier to use, or as they say, 'user friendly'.

Why didn't we start off with all of the Graphics commands and functions, so that the programs written so far could have been made more attractive? Quite simply, instructions involving the graphics capabilities can *appear* fairly complex at first, entail a reasonable working knowledge of the language, and an understanding of the various techniques involved. To have combined learning the essential basic commands and functions of OPL, the various techniques, *and* the graphics commands would have made it very difficult to build up a clear background of knowledge.

But now you should be ready to assimilate the principles of the very extensive range of graphics commands and functions available. If you found the very first program you entered an exciting achievement (and most people do), then, to paraphrase that well known saying, "You ain't seen nuthin' yet!".

The graphics capabilities of the Psion Series 3a are vast: consequently it must be stated at the outset that this Book can do no more than explain how to use them and give demonstration examples where practical. It will then be up to you, armed with an understanding

159

of how they 'work', to incorporate them into your own programs. But bear in mind that almost anything is possible, even a Chess game with properly designed pieces...

An overview of the text window

When dealing with *text only* displays - as we have done so far - the screen area or *window* your programs can occupy is in effect a grid of characters. The number of characters per line and the number of lines displayed are governed by the font chosen and the screen size - which is determined by the SCREEN command.

You may have wondered why the SCREEN command could be needed. In this part of the book, you will see that you can have a number of windows - defined areas of the screen - where specific displays are portrayed: the text screen, either the 'whole' display area or that defined by the SCREEN command - is, in effect, just *one* of those windows, and is always available.

With the text screen (there is and can be only one), the *character* blocks within the 'grid' are 'referenced', as in the AT command, by their column and row positions. Thus, AT 1,1 defines the position of the first character block to the left of the first row of the text window.

Initially, the text window occupies the whole screen - or that part of the screen not used by the *status display* - which shows the system clock, for example. You use the SCREEN command to change the size of that window, and the SCREENINFO command to get details about it. **The text window is, actually, a part of the default graphics window and as such cannot be 'closed'. It can, however, be hidden from view.**

The graphics windows

For graphics windows, the screen should be considered *not* as a grid of 'blocks' which can each take one character (as with the text screen), but rather of 480 *pixels* (wide) by 160 *pixels* (deep). A pixel is the smallest point that can be displayed. The default graphics screen is always available - and it incorporates the text screen: both graphics and text screen characters can be displayed on it.

Just as the character blocks of the text window are referenced by their row and column positions, so the pixels of graphics screens are also referenced by two numbers, representing the column across the window, and the row down the window. For these, however, the pixel in the very top left position is not '1,1', but '0,0'. So a pixel that has its position identified as '2,3' is actually the *third* pixel across, and the *fourth* pixel down. The pixel in the bottom right hand corner of the whole screen is identified as '479,159'.

Series 3a keeps track of the current *pixel* location for *graphics* commands. For the text window displays, only one command, AT, allows you to 'accurately' position the 'cursor' or set the screen location. There are a quite a few graphics commands that will re-position the next *pixel* location to be used in a graphics window, depending on what you are doing.

You can have up to eight *graphics* windows. All of the windows can be positioned and sized anywhere on the overall screen - and can cover up other windows: you can determine which windows are to appear 'on top' when there is more than one occupying the same area. You can also determine whether a window will be 'visible' or not.

As you will see, *all* of the screens can display text. However, whereas the text window has only the PRINT command available to display text, there are several different commands to display text on the graphics screens.

When you create several windows, the window commands used relate to the *current* window: only one window can be accessed at a time, and you specify which window that is to be. Furthermore, details about *all* of the windows - for example, the pixel location for the next graphics action - are retained by the Psion Series 3a. This means you can switch back to a previously used window and carry on where you left off in that display.

The 'windowing' capability of the Psion Series 3a opens an incredible variety of possibilities for programs. We shall be dealing with some of them in this book.

Black and grey window planes

Graphics windows have two *planes*: black, and grey. That means anything displayed in a graphic window - whether it be text or graphics - can be in black or grey, or indeed, 'reversed' out of black or grey. If you want to use the grey plane as well as the black plane, then this fact must be specified when the window is created: you can specify black only, or black and grey, but you cannot request to have only the grey plane. Creating and manipulating windows is dealt with in a later Chapter.

The *default* graphics window (which is always available) uses, by default, only the black plane. In order to use the grey plane of this window, you need to use the DEFAULTWIN command.

DEFAULTWIN x%   This command determines whether or not the grey plane will be used in the default graphics window (always window number '1') according to the value of *x%*. If x%=1, then the grey plane is enabled. If x%=0, then the grey plane is disabled. Using this command also clears the graphics (and text) window. Generally speaking, you will only need to use DEFAULTWIN once in any program - to invoke use of the grey scale (the default is black only, remember), and since use of *both* planes involves more memory, it is best to use it at or near to the beginning of the program - and bear in mind that when it *is* used, the screen will be cleared.

The method for specifying the use of black only or black and grey planes in other windows is discussed in a later Chapter.

Sprites

One of the powerful capabilities introduced into the Series 3a's programming language is the use of sprites. A sprite is a drawn 'object' which can be 'superimposed' on the display, animated, moved, and cleared, without affecting the underlying display. To see a sprite in action, have a look at the WORLD application of your Series 3a: the flashing cross indicating the location of the selected city is a sprite.

The graphics commands

Generally speaking, the graphics commands can be divided into three groups:

1. Those dealing with the creation and manipulation of windows and *bitmaps* (bitmaps are windows that are in memory, not on the screen display), and displaying specially formatted text, drawing shapes and creating clock displays within those windows and bitmaps. These, collectively, are identified by an initial letter 'g'.
2. Those dealing with the creation of *dialog boxes* which look like those offered by Series 3a applications. These are identified by an initial letter 'd'.

3. Those dealing with the creation of *menus* which look just like menus in the Series 3a applications. These commands are identified by an initial letter 'm'.

To identify and help differentiate all these commands from others dealt with so far, the initial letters will be shown as lower case. You can type them in as capitals or lower case.

There are also commands for displaying the 'Status window' (the one with the clock that can be set to appear to the right of Series 3a's display), for manipulating sprites, and for displaying those 'information' and 'Busy' messages that can appear on the screen to inform the user that 'something' is happening.

CHAPTER 17
Brief screen messages

This Chapter introduces two easy ways to display a brief superimposed message on the screen for the user's information. The OPL words covered are
    BUSY *and* GPRINT

Hang on ... I'm busy

In some programs, Series 3a will spin its wheels for a while whilst it is making complex calculations. For example, in a game program, you may have written routines for Series 3a to assess the best of the possible moves available. During this period, nothing will appear to be happening at the screen, and so to assure the user that Series 3a hasn't in fact 'seized up' or gone into hibernation, you can use the BUSY command.

BUSY   This command produces a reversed out, 'flashing' message in one corner of the screen, similar to the '**Translating**' message you see when Series 3a is translating your program before it can be run. The syntax for this command is as follows:

        BUSY *msg$*, corner%, delay%
or   BUSY *msg$*, corner%
or   BUSY *msg$*
and
        BUSY OFF
where

msg$ is the message to be displayed, and can be either a variable or a string literal of no more than 19 characters. A string literal is the message you want, actually written out, between double quotes.

corner%   is a value from 0 to 3, representing the corner of the screen that you want the message to be displayed, as follows:

0   the top left corner
1   the bottom left corner (*default* location)
2   the top right corner
3   the bottom right corner.

delay%   is a delay, in half-seconds, before the message is displayed. Thus, to prevent the message appearing for two seconds, *delay* would have a value of 4.

The *delay%* argument can be used to prevent the message appearing too quickly - if the 'wheel-spinning' periods are short, then the messages will appear very briefly. If you don't specify a delay period, then the message *msg$* will be displayed immediately the command is met.

If you don't specify which corner of the screen you want the message to appear, then by default it will appear in the bottom left hand corner.

The flashing display message is 'turned off' with the BUSY OFF command at a suitable point in your program: generally speaking, immediately after the time consuming part of the program has been completed.

Note that you can have only one 'Busy' message on the screen at a time. If you issue another BUSY command whilst one is being displayed, the new one replaces the original.

A quick message

If you want your message to appear for only a limited period, without having to bother to 'switch it off', then use the GPRINT command.

GIPRINT This is very similar to BUSY, except that the message doesn't 'flash', and it automatically switches off after about two seconds, or sooner if a key is pressed. The formats are

```
        GIPRINT msg$,corner%
or      GIPRINT msg$
where
```

msg$ is the message to be displayed, and can be a string variable or literal up to 63 characters long: if it is too long for the screen display, it will be 'clipped'.

corner% is a value from 0 to 3, representing the corner of the screen that you want the message to be displayed. Use:

0   for the top left corner
1   for the bottom left corner
2   for the top right corner
3   for the bottom right corner (*default* location).

Note that the default location, if you don't have a value for *corner%*, is the bottom right corner.

This command is useful for printing brief messages on the screen - such as those like '**Syntax error**' that Series 3a displays when you have an error during the 'translation' of a program. (Surely, you *must* have seen it?!).

Like BUSY, only one GIPRINT message can be on the screen at a time, although you can have both a BUSY message and a GIPRINT message on display at the same time, if you want to.

Here is a program that makes use of both of these words:

```
PROC msgtest:
 LOCAL c%
 BUSY "I'm working!",0
 DO
  c%=c%+1
  PRINT c%;
  PAUSE 3
  IF c%=120
   BUSY "Nearly done!",2
  ENDIF
 UNTIL c$=240
 BUSY OFF
 GIPRINT "All done! (Press a key)",1
 GET
ENDP
```

In this program, the message "I'm working!" is flashed in the top left corner whilst the screen is filled slowly (the PAUSE command slows it up) with a range of numbers. Towards the end of this task, the BUSY message is switched to the top right corner, to inform you that it is "Nearly done!".

The BUSY message is then switched off, and the "All done..." message displayed for about two seconds, *unless* you have pressed a key whilst the program is running. GIPRINT, like the KEY command, doesn't wait for a keypress, but rather examines a *buffer* in Series 3a where keypresses are stored. So if a key has been pressed whilst the program is running, GIPRINT sees that keypress - but does nothing with it: program execution jumps to the next statement, GET, which also sees the keypress, removes the keypress information from the *buffer*, and so the end of the program is reached.

It's worth running this program a few times - testing it with and without a keypress, and removing the BUSY OFF statement, to see how it all works.

It is also worth trying another little test whilst the program is running: press the PROGRAM button. You will be returned to the Program Editor, with the Series 3a 'Busy' message displayed at the bottom left corner. This is telling you that whilst you are looking at your program entry, Series 3a is still carrying out your program instructions. If you then press the SYSTEM button, and select the program under the RUNOPL icon, you will be returned to the running program - which by then may well have finished, and be waiting for your final keypress.

You have seen 'multitasking' at work: Series 3a has the powerful capability of handling more than one job at a time. So if you have a program performing lengthy computations, you don't have to wait until they're finished before you use one of the other facilities available. You could, for example, dial out a telephone number whilst your program is running, and whilst *that* is happening, you could examine your Agenda. There are very few desk-top machines that offer that as a built-in capability!

As with the other explanatory programs in this book, once you are satisfied that you understand the principles involved, you can delete both the *source* code file and the *translated* code file.

CHAPTER 18
Graphic text

This Chapter explains how you can display text in different styles in a graphics window. The OPL words covered are

gAT, gFONT, gMOVE, gPRINT, gPRINTB, gTWIDTH,
gPRINTCLIP, gTMODE, gSTYLE, gXPRINT *and* CURSOR.

A different way to print

In the first part of this book, you saw how to display text in the text window, using the PRINT command. The print position can be located at any character block location within the text window by using the AT command, and you can use a comma or semi-colon seperator between the items in a PRINT statement. The font and styles available, you will recall, were rather limited.

By using *graphics* commands, you can produce a *mixed* display of text that can be bold, italicized or underlined, and in a wider choice of fonts. The start of this text can be at virtually any *pixel* window location. This is graphics text. You can use the CURSOR command to display a cursor on the current screen window (this is discussed at the end of this Chapter), and there are functions that will tell you the column and row of the pixel where the next graphics operation will take place: these are discussed in a later Chapter.

Setting a location in a graphics window

There are two basic ways to reset the current pixel location in a graphics window, ready for the next graphics operation.

gAT x%,y%   This is very similar to the text-screen command, AT. It operates on the *current* graphics window. x% can have values from 0 and 479, and y% can have values from 0 to 179 for a full-screen sized window. Pixel locations beyond the range of a window's dimensions won't cause an error, but they simply will not be 'visible'.

You'll notice that the minimum value for x% and y% is '0' (not '1', as with AT). Thus gAT 0,0 determines the top left-most pixel in the current window. The position set by gAT is *absolute*: whatever the current location in the *current* graphics window, the new location in that window will be defined by the x% and y% values of gAT.

gMOVE *dx%,dy%* Like gAT, this sets the location for the next graphics operation, but rather than setting an *absolute* position, it *moves* the current position dx% pixels to the right, and dy% pixels down. To move to the left a *negative* value for dx% is used, and to move up, a *negative* value for dy% is used.

The value of this command will be appreciated more when the drawing capabilities of Series 3a are discussed. If the move makes the current pixel fall outside the range of the current window, then any graphics produced from that pixel will not be seen.

Displaying graphics text

Generally speaking, when you use a *graphics* print command, the pixels are 'set' to display the characters. *They do not automatically 'clear' any pixel that has been previously set.* This is quite different from the text PRINT command, which automatically clears any character at the print position. However, for the graphic printing commands you can govern the way that the pixels are set - whether they are turned 'on' (made 'black' or 'grey', depending on the window plane being printed on), they can be turned 'off' (made 'clear'), or their current pixel state can be reversed. Let us first examine the gPRINT command.

gPRINT *itemlist* This is similar in some respects to PRINT, in that the item list can be variables or literals, separated by commas or semi-colons. The effect of a comma is to leave a space between two items, whilst a semi-colon simply separates the items: no space is left between them in the display. However, unlike PRINT, the *next* print or graphics position is at the next pixel location, usually the end of the printed data: using gPRINT on its own, for example, *doesn't* start a new line.

The first character to be printed in a gPRINT statement is located so that its *left side* and *baseline* are at the current pixel location. The baseline is rather like a line on writing paper: most characters 'sit' on the line, but some, like the letter 'g' or 'y' will descend below the line. The following short procedure will show you the difference in characters between text printing and standard font graphics printing:

```
PROC gprint1:
 PRINT "This is text print"
 gAT 1,40
 gPRINT "This is graphic printing"
 GET
ENDP
```

After you have run this procedure, edit the gAT line to read gAT 30,12: you will see that the graphics print line is *overwriting* part of the text print line.

To clear an area of the window before printing graphics text, use the gPRINTB command:

gPRINTB *text$,w%,align%,top%,bot%,marg%* In the last procedure, you saw how gPRINT can overwrite anything on the screen without clearing it first. That can be a pain. One solution is the gPRINTB statement. This 'clears' a box for the printed message. However, *you* have to specify information about the box to be cleared, and how the text will appear within it. Also, gPRINTB displays only *one* text message, as defined by *text$*, although this could be a concatenation of strings (my, how musical that sounds!), and you can of course use the string conversion functions to turn numbers into strings. The permissible formats you can use are:

```
gPRINTB text$,w%,align%,top%,bot%,marg%
gPRINTB text$,w%,align%,top%,bot%
gPRINTB text$,w%,align%,top%
gPRINTB text$,w%,align%
gPRINTB text$,w%
```

w% determines the *width* of the box, in *pixels*, that you want cleared for the text. Does that mean you have to know how many pixels there are in your text message? Yes, it does. If your box isn't wide enough, part of the message will be lost. But ascertaining the minimum width that the box must be to display all of the message is no problem, because there's an OPL function to handle it for you - gTWIDTH. We'll deal with this function in a moment.

align% controls the alignment of the text within the cleared box. The permissible values are:

1	Aligned to the right of the defined box.
2	Aligned to the left of the defined box.
3	Centred within the defined box.

The default value if you don't include the parameter is 2 - left aligned. If you don 't provide a value for the `align%` parameter, then you cannot provide any information for the parameters that follow it either - look at the permissible formats for gPRINTB.

top% and **bot%** determine the clearances above and below the text in the box: again, the measure is in pixels. These values, together with the height of the *current* font (which you can also choose through another OPL command) determine the overall height of the cleared box. If you create an *above* clearance area that, with the font size, will be greater than 255 pixels, you'll get an error. The use of `top%` and `bot%` can give your graphics text a clearer space to 'sit' in: if you don't specify values, the defaults are '0'.

marg% controls the size of the left or right margin within the box, measured in pixels. If the alignment is set to the left (`align%=2`), then `marg%` controls the space between the left edge of the box and the start of the text. If the alignment is set to the right (`align%=1`), then `marg%` controls the space between the end of the text and the right edge of the box. If the alignment is set to be centred (`align%=3`), `marg%` gives an offset to the part of the box in which centering is to be effected: positive values place the offset to

171

the left, and negative values place the offset to the right of the box. If you ignore this parameter, the default value is '0'.

OPL also has a print command, gPRINTCLIP, for displaying text in a 'limited area' - for example, where the start location is near the edge of the window and you don't want the text to vanish 'off screen'.

gPRINTCLIP(text$,width%**)**   This print *function* prints the text string text$, but only as many whole characters as the number of pixels determined by width% allows. It *returns* the number of characters *actually* printed. This function is designed more for use with 'narrow' windows or window areas, which could inhibit the printing of a complete text line. Knowing the width of the window area, you can limit the number of text message characters printed to fit the space available, ascertain how many characters were *actually* printed, then start on a new line (using gAT) to print more of the text message. In this way, a graphical text display can be formed within a window area. The format for the function is

$$pc\% = gPRINTCLIP(text\$, width\%)$$

You can use pc% as a parameter of RIGHT$() (or MID$()) to select the part of text$ that hasn't been printed. Thus, the next line could read something like

$$gPRINTCLIP(RIGHT\$(text\$), pc\%), width\%)$$

The width of text

You will often need to ascertain the width of a string of text on the graphic screen - when formatting, and typically when using the gPRINTB command. The OPL word for this is gTWIDTH.

gTWIDTH(text$**)** This function returns the width of the text$ string. The value returned is in pixels, and takes into account the current font and style settings for the current window. The format is

$$w\% = gTWIDTH(text\$)$$

172

Setting the style and font for graphics printing

Text displayed using the graphics gPRINT, gPRINTB and gPRINTCLIP words can be in any a huge range of different 'styles' - all combinations, in fact, of monospaced, bold, underlined, inverse, double height, or italic. This is irrespective of the *font* that's used: 13 fonts are built into the Series 3a, and there is a facility to 'load' your own fonts.

You set the *style* of the printing with the gSTYLE command:

gSTYLE style% This sets the style for all subsequent gPRINT, gPRINTB and gPRINTCLIP commands. The style is determined by the style% variable, which can be a combination of the following values:

style% value	value in binary	Displays text as
0	0	Normal
1	1	Bold
2	10	Underlined
4	100	Inverse
8	1000	Double height letters
16	10000	Monospacing
32	100000	Italicised lettering

You select the combination you want, then simply add the relevant style% values together. For example, if you want bold, italicised letters, you'd add 1 and 32 to have a value for style% of 33. The monospacing style ensures each character is placed within a block of the same width (much the same as the way PRINT prints characters) - even if the font selected is a proportional font.

Note that gSTYLE has no effect on the *text* PRINT command - for text window styles, use the STYLE command.

The binary equivalents of the decimal values show how each style has its own 'bit flag'.

To select the required font for the subsequent *graphics* print commands, the OPL word is gFONT.

gFONT *fontId%* This command sets the font that will be used by ensuing graphics print commands, in the *current* window. Thirteen fonts are built into the Series 3a, so they are *always* selectable. Apart from these, there is a facility to load your own fonts, using the command **gLOADFONT**: when used, this function returns an 'ID' value which can be used with gFONT to select your loaded font. Such fonts can be removed by the command **gUNLOADFONT**. The creation of fonts is fairly complex, and well beyond the scope of this book, and so these two commands will not be discussed any further. For built in fonts, *fontId%* can have values as follows:

FontId% Value	Font type	Pixel size
1	Series 3 normal.	8
2	Series 3 bold	8
3	Series 3 digits	6x6
4	Monospaced	8x8
5	Serif *	8 x Character width
6	Serif	11 x Character width
7	Serif	13 x Character width
8	Serif	16 x Character width
9	San serif	8 x Character width
10	San serif	11 x Character width
11	San serif	13 x Character width
12	San serif	16 x Character width
13	Monospaced	6x6

*This font, although 'Serif' is too small to display the serifs.

The first three fonts are really Series 3 fonts - which the Series 3a uses when running in compatibility mode. Note that the third font will display only numbers, and a space. There is also a special font number - $9a. This is set aside to provide the default graphics font for the machine - and will vary among the different model types. For example, on the Series 3, font $9a is the same as Font 1, whilst on the Series 3a, it is the same as Font 11.

Here is a program to let you study the large number of graphic styles available, and how they look when used with the different fonts. This program uses a *dialog box* to get in the required information: although dialog boxes haven't been discussed yet, there is no reason why you shouldn't, now, get a taste of the graphics power that is available.

The selected font is displayed first as a *text window* font, then as the graphics font in the selected style. To see the effect of monospacing a font, try font 7 with style 16. Note too, say with font 12, how the text window characters each sit in the same width - monospaced, whilst the graphics characters occupy only the amount of space required - proportionally spaced

```
PROC gprint2:
 LOCAL f&,s&,d%
 DO
  dINIT "Graphic Text"
  dLONG f&,"Which Font (1-3):",1,13
  dLONG s&,"Style Combination (0-63):",0,63
  dBUTTONS "Do it",13,"Quit",27
  d%=DIALOG
  IF d%
   FONT f&,0
   AT 1,1
   PRINT "Text screen Font",f&
   gFONT f&
   gSTYLE s&
   gAT 10,50
   gPRINT "This is Font:",f&,"Style:",s&
   GET
   gCLS
  ENDIF
 UNTIL d%=0
ENDP
```

As this program uses OPL words not yet discussed, please be extra careful when entering it.

You'll notice that, for the gFONT and gSTYLE commands, *long integers* are used (with the '&' identifier) instead of ordinary integers (identified by '%'). This is necessary for the dialog box instructions - and is quite in order provided the values aren't allowed to exceed the *integer* values that can be accepted by gFONT and gSTYLE.

Setting the way characters print

So far, you have seen that the gPRINT command prints on the screen by setting the appropriate pixels: any pixels that are previously set will remain set. It's rather like writing or drawing on a page that already has writing or drawings on it. However, you can change the way that gPRINT, gPRINTB and gPRINTCLIP perform their printing operations. You can arrange, for example, for the pixels to be 'cleared' if they were already set.

gTMODE *mode%* This command determines how the pixels will be changed when the graphics print commands are executed, and hence how the characters will be displayed on the screen. Four possibilities are available, governed by the value of *mode%* as follows:

mode% value	Pixels are
0	Set
1	Cleared
2	Inverted
3	Replaced

mode%=0 is the default: this is the way that the graphics print commands normally work.

When **mode%=1**, any clear pixels remain clear, whilst any 'set' pixels are cleared. Thus, this mode can be used to provide 'white' print on a previously darkened display. (The word 'darkened' is used here, since the printing action may be directed to either the black or the grey plane - which will be dealt with later).

When **mode%=2**, the pixels are 'reversed': those that were clear are darkened, whilst those that were darkened are cleared. This is a useful mode when running print from across clear area into a darkened area, and vice versa.

When **mode%=3**, the space for a character is cleared first, then the character pixels are set. The 'replacing' effect is fairly similar to that when using the text PRINT command - the difference being that you can set the style for the graphics print display.

Note that gTMODE determines the way the graphics print commands operate in the *current* window: at the moment, we are considering just one 'window' - the default window.

Here is a procedure that will let you examine these four modes. It includes another command that hasn't been discussed yet - gFILL - to darken an area of the screen so that you can see the effects of text printed across it and into clear space.

```
PROC gprint3:
 LOCAL x&,d%
 DO
   dINIT "Graphic Text Modes"
   dLONG x&,"Select Mode:",0,3
   dBUTTONS "Do it",13,"Quit",27
   d%=DIALOG
   IF d%
     gAT 0,0
     gFILL 60,20,0
     gAT 5,12
     gTMODE x&
     gPRINT "This goes over a black box"
     GET
     gCLS
   ENDIF
 UNTIL d%=0
ENDP
```

Special inverse and underline printing

In addition to all the options provided by the gSTYLE command, there is yet another way to display a text string either underlined or inverted, and that's with the gXPRINT command.

The current font and style - as set by gFONT and gSTYLE - are still effective with gXPRINT, even if the style itself happens to be inverse or underlined. The text mode used is as if gTMODE had been set to '3' - that is, the relevant screen area is cleared before the characters are printed.

gXPRINT *text$,display%* This displays the string *text$* according to the variable *display%*, as follows:

177

display% value	Displays text as
0	Normally, as with gPRINT
1	Inverse, with 'square corners'
2	Inverse, with 'rounded' corners
3	'Thin' inverse, square corners
4	'Thin' inverse, rounded corners
5	Underlined
6	Thin underlined

The 'thin' options are for those occasions when lines of text are separated by a single pixel.

gXPRINT can be used only with a single text string: you can of course build up a string by concatenation for display.

You should also note that the print display starts from the current graphics location.

Here's a procedure to demonstrate the seven different styles available in turn:

```
PROC gprint4:
    LOCAL c%,m$(40)
    DO
        m$="This is display "+num$(c%,1)
        gAT 15,50
        gXPRINT m$,c%
        GET
        CLS
        c%=c%+1
    UNTIL c%=7
ENDP
```

Sizing the Cursor

The cursor display on the text screen is a fixed size. On the graphics screens, however, you can determine the size of the cursor, and its position relative to the *baseline* of any text displays. One window can have a cursor: you must specify which it is to be, and specifically switch the cursor on. The cursor is switched off by the CURSOR OFF command.

CURSOR `id%,ascent%,wid%,ht%,type%`   This form of the `CURSOR` command enables you to switch on a graphics cursor, and set its shape and positioning on the screen.

id% is the identification number of the window you wish to set the cursor in.

type% is an optional parameter which can have a value that is any combination of

1   oblong shape
2   not flashing
4   grey

Thus, if `type%` has a value of 3 (1+2), it will be non-flashing oblong.

ascent% - together with `wid%` and `ht%` - is also optional, and determines the number of pixels that the *top* of the cursor should be above the baseline of the current font, and has a range of -128 to 127.

wid% and *ht%* are the width and height respectively you want the cursor to be - both of which must be in the range 0 to 255, although you probably would not want to use high values!

If you don't specify `ascent%`, `wid%` and `ht%`: then the default values used are the font ascent for `ascent%`, the font height for `ht%`, and 2 for `wid%`.

You can, if you wish, simply turn a graphics cursor on by just specifying `id%`, in which case the default values are used. The cursor is turned off by the `CURSOR   OFF` command.

Here's a procedure to let you examine the way this command works. It again uses the dialog box technique to obtain the required input information, and uses another command that also has not yet been discussed, to draw a line across the screen display.

Enter the program carefully, then experiment with different (permissible) values. Remember that the *ascent* is the height of the top of the cursor above the baseline, and that *height* is the actual height (in

pixels, of course) of the cursor. Make sure you give your cursor a
reasonable width!

```
PROC cursor:
 LOCAL a&,w&,h&,t&,d%
 DO
   dINIT "Cursor size"
   dLONG a&,"Ascent (-128 to 128):",-128,128
   dLONG w&,"Width (1 to 255):",1,255
   dLONG h&,"Height(1 to 255):",1,255
   dBUTTONS "Do it",13,"Quit",27
   d%=DIALOG
   IF d%
     gAT 0,12
     gPRINT "Cursor ascent:",a&
     gAT 0,24
     gPRINT "Cursor width :",w&
     gAT 0,36
     gPRINT "Cursor height:",h&
     gAT 0,48
     gPRINT "Cursor type  :",t&
     gAT 0,70
     gPRINT "Text baseline"
     gAT 0,70
     gLINEBY 300,0              REM New command draws line
     gAT 200,70
     CURSOR 1,a&,w&,h&,t&
     GET
     CLS
   ENDIF
 UNTIL d%=0
ENDP
```

Note: Technically speaking the CLS command, four lines up from the
bottom, should be a gCLS command. However, this hasn't been
discussed yet, and since the default text/graphics window is being
used, CLS will clear the screen adequately. In fact, it will miss out
four lines of pixels all round the edge of the window.

CHAPTER 19
Time for a dialog

This Chapter deals with 'Alert' and Dialog boxes.
The OPL words covered are:
ALERT,   dINIT,   dPOSITION,   dTEXT,   dEDIT,
dXINPUT, dFLOAT, dLONG, dFILE, dDATE, dTIME,
dCHOICE, dBUTTONS *and* DIALOG

The 'friendly' way to get an input

In the last Chapter some of the program samples used a graphic method for obtaining information from the user - the *Dialog box*. Dialog boxes offer an easy way for options to be selected or edits to be made, and they cater for a wide variety of different types of input.

For example, with a dialog box, the user can be given the facility to input and 'edit' specific types information, with the display formatted to suit that information. You can also provide a display of 'buttons', suitably labelled, to help the user make a choice by pressing particular keys - you can choose what the active keys are to be.

As well as the dialog box, there is also a simpler type of display which gives the user from one to three options to choose from - the choice being made by a single keypress. This is called an *'Alert box'*, since it is most often used to alert the user to something with a simple message. We'll examine this type first.

Creating Alert boxes

Although far simpler than dialog boxes, Alert boxes have a variety of useful applications. For example, you can use them just to inform that an error has occurred. Or you can give the user a choice of two or three options, with specific keys to press to make those options. The specific keys used are ESC, ENTER and SPACE, and are displayed as 'buttons', suitably labelled with words of your choice.

Unlike dialog boxes, an Alert box completely fills the screen. It appears 'over' anything else you have on the screen, the previous display being restored when the Alert box is cleared.

The OPL word to use is **ALERT**, and the formats are as follows

```
a%=ALERT(line1$)
a%=ALERT(line1$,line2$)
a%=ALERT(line1$,line2$,escbt$)
a%=ALERT(line1$,line2$,escbt$,entbt$)
a%=ALERT(line1$,line2$,escbt$,entbt$,spbt$)
```

where

line1$	is the message you want displayed on the top line.
line2$	is the message you want displayed on the second line.
escbt$	is the annotation you want to appear over the ESC button display.
entbt$	is the annotation you want to appear over the ENTER button display.
spbt$	is the annotation you want to appear over the SPACE button display.

Note the permissible formats: if you want to use one or more button displays at the bottom with your own annotations, the strings *line1$* and *line2$* (either as literals or as variables) must be present, although they can be 'null' strings - in other words equal to " " (Two quote marks with nothing between them).

If you choose to use one or two lines of message without annotating any buttons yourself (the first two formats listed), then Series 3a automatically creates a single, centred button marked as the ESC key, and annotated '**Continue**'. The messages are centred, and the lines can be as long as you like: howver, if the message is too long for the screen width, then only the *central* part of the message is displayed - so there's no point in having over-length messages.

When the buttons are used, the value returned by this function when one of the displayed keys is pressed is as follows:

ESC key	returns '1'
ENTER key	returns '2'
SPACE key	returns '3'

To make life easy for the user, you should make your annotations appropriate for the keys displayed. For example, if you wish to provide two options 'Cancel' and 'Continue', then it makes more sense to annotate the ESC button with 'Cancel' and the ENTER button with 'Continue', rather than the other way round.

Here is a short procedure to demonstrate the use of the ALERT function with three options. It also demonstrates the use of a string array, and how an element of the array can be selected by use of a variable. (Note the long line, which must be entered as one line in your Series 3a).

```
PROC alert1:
 LOCAL a%,but$(3,10)
 but$(1)="Cancel"
 but$(2)="Go forward"
 but$(3)="Go back"
 a%=ALERT("Top line","2nd line",
same line continued        but$(1)$,but$(2),but$(3))
 PRINT "OK. I'll",but$(a%)
 GET
ENDP
```

You may like to experiment by editing this program - first deleting but$(3), then but$(2) and finally but$(1) from the ALERT line statement - translating and running it each time.

Using dialog boxes

Unlike Alert boxes, Dialog boxes are automatically sized to take the messages and lines they contain. In other words, they don't necessarily fill the screen. Furthermore, you can within reason determine the location on the screen that the dialog box is displayed, so that you can avoid overprinting an important part of the background display

As well as the 'dialogs' that can be displayed, you can, like ALERT, have up to three 'exit' buttons - or none at all. However, *you* can define which keys are used: they are not pre-defined, but under your control.

Generally speaking, the use of a dialog box therefore makes for a more versatile and neater display on the screen, and you will probably find that you prefer its use.

Creating dialog boxes

Fortunately, much of the formatting and display 'work' is done for you automatically by the Series 3a. Nevertheless, the number of possibilities available can make the process look a little forbidding at first. The entire dialog must be created in one 'chunk' and it must all be in one procedure.

The steps involved are as follows:

a) Get the Series 3a ready to receive a dialog operation, using the dINIT command.

b) If you don't want the dialog to appear in the absolute centre of the screen, use the dPOSITION command to re-position it. Actually, this command can be used *anywhere* between the dINIT and DIALOG statements, but for convenience, we'll take it to be our second step.

c) Set up each line of the dialog with the functions you want. The options available are

dTEXT	To display formatted text messages - which can also be options for selection.
dEDIT	To edit string data.
dXINPUT	To input a 'secret' string of data, such as a password.
dFILE	To select or enter a filename.
dLONG	To enter an *integer* number (it can be an ordinary or long integer).
dFLOAT	To enter a floating point number.
dDATE	To enter a date.
dTIME	To enter a time.
dCHOICE	To select from a prepared list of options.

Which just about covers every possibility! However, there is a limitation: the *entire* dialog must *not* exceed nine lines. This number includes the three lines necessary for displaying 'exit' buttons, if you choose to use them, the 'title' line, and *two* lines for the filename editor. You should also note that, unlike ALERT which prints the central part of any over-length line, if a line is too long for the screen you will get a '**Too wide**' error when the program is running.

d) If you want 'exit' buttons - and you can have up to three - they must be defined as the penultimate step, using the dBUTTONS function.

e) Finally, switch on the dialog display using the DIALOG function.

The use of the commands and functions that are available for each of these steps is now discussed in detail.

Initialising the Dialog

Series 3a has to be prepared for the fact that it is about to display a dialog, and this is achieved quite simply by the single statement dINIT.

dINIT *title$*   Only one Dialog box can appear on the screen at a time. The formats for initialising a Dialog are

```
dINIT
dINIT title$
```

Use the *title$* format if you choose to give your dialog box a title. The string literal or variable will be displayed at the top of the box, centred, and with a line beneath it across the entire box. If you choose to include a title, remember that it counts as one of the nine lines which are the maximum permissible for a dialog box.

Positioning a dialog

The 'default' location for a dialog is the dead centre of the screen. However, you may not want the dialog in this position: you may wish to position it so that it doesn't cover other vital information on display. You can do this with the dPOSITION command. Note that, irrespective of how your screen display is made up (i.e. whether you're using 'windows' and specified display areas), the dialog will *always* appear 'on top'. When the dialog is cleared, the original screen display is restored for you.

dPOSITION *hp%, vp%*   where *hp%* and *vp%* represent the horizontal and vertical positions respectively. These can each have one of three values, as follows:

	-1	0	1
hp%	Left	Centre	Right
vp%	Top	Centre	Bottom

Thus, the statement dPOSITION −1,1 would position the dialog box at the bottom left corner of the screen. Remember that the default position is the centre of the screen (equivalent to the statement dPOSITION 0,0), so if that's where you want the dialog box to appear, you don't need to use the dPOSITION statement at all.

The dialog 'action' lines

As previously noted, there is a variety of different 'action' lines you can have in your dialog box. For *some* of them, you *must* use a variable declared previously as LOCAL or GLOBAL to receive data: using a string literal or an actual value is *not permissible* for these, although you can assign values to the variables so that they are displayed when the dialog box appears. Neither can you use a variable that has been *passed* to the procedure as a parameter, or a *field* variable (these are special variables used when creating data files). The reason is that, when the dialog is actuated, certain information will be entered by the user, and this information must be stored in a variable: if you have a string literal or a value instead of a variable, there will be nowhere for Series 3a to store the entered information, and a 'Function argument' error will occur when you try to translate the program.

Where *only* variables are permissible rather than values or strings, the variables will be identified by the use of a preceding emboldened 'v', (thus: *vfloat*) in the descriptive name.

The 'action lines' commands and functions are as follows.

Displaying text. Apart from any title you may give the dialog box when using the dINIT command, you can have lines of text as messages, or as 'selectable items'.

dTEXT *prompt$,body$,type%* This command is extremely versatile and very flexible: it can be used to simply display a text message in various ways, and it can also be used to provide one of a series of options for selection, as on a drop-down menu. You need one dTEXT statement for every line of text you wish to include in the dialog box, (except for the 'title' - which can be provided by the dINIT statement). The formats are:

```
dTEXT prompt$,body$
dTEXT prompt$,body$,type%
```

where

prompt$ provides the message that will appear on the left side of the text line as a 'prompt'. This can be a null string ("") if you don't want a prompt.

body$* This is the main part of the message that will be displayed on the line. If *prompt$ is a null string, then *body$* will assume the whole width of the line for itself - its position within the line being determined by *type%*, if present. Otherwise, if *prompt$* is not a null string, the text of *body$* is positioned on the *right* side of the dialog box, either left-aligned, or as specified by the *type%* variable. Note that you *cannot* have a null string for *body$*.

type% This determines the *position* of the *body$* text within the line, and also what *type* of display the line is to use. There are three options for the *position* of *body$*:

Type% value	Effect
0	Aligns *body$* to the left.
1	Aligns *body$* to the right.
2	Centralises *body$*.

Any unit values for *type%* outside of this range will result in an '**Invalid arguments**' error when translating the program. You can also use *type%* to select a combination from three *styles* for the way that *body$* will appear. These are best considered as their *hexadecimal* values, and are as follows:

Type%	Effect
$100	Displays *body$* in bold text.
$200	Draws a line below this item, across the dialog box.
$400	Places a 'bullet point' in front of *prompt$*, provided that it is *not* a null string.

You can use all, any or none of these three, by simply adding the effects you want to the value of *type%*. For example, if you want a bullet point and bold lettering for *body%*, then *type%* would be '$500'. If you also wanted *body%* to be

187

aligned to the right, then *type%* would have the value '\$501'.

Note that, apart from the title line, there can be only *one* other horizontal line across the dialog box: the last one to be specified is the one that takes effect.

When you give a line a bullet point, it can be selected by using the arrow keys. Lines that aren't given a bullet point cannot be selected in this way. The following demonstration procedure simply shows the type of dialog produced by dTEXT statements using some of the *type%* values discussed.

```
PROC dialog1:
  dINIT "Text Choices"
  dTEXT "Line 1","Can't choose",$200
  dTEXT "Line 2","Can Choose this",$400
  dTEXT "Line 3","Ditto",$402
  dTEXT "Line 4","Bold unselectable",$100
  dTEXT "","That's all",2
  DIALOG
ENDP
```

When you translate and run this demonstration, you'll see that lines 2 and 3 have a bullet point to the left, and that you can use the up or down arrow keys to switch between them: the other lines are not selectable. When you use this kind of selection process in your dialogs, on exit *provided you haven't used 'buttons' as a means of exiting* (or pressed ESC), the *line number* for the highlighted line is returned by the DIALOG function. If ESC is pressed, then '0' is returned.

Entering or editing text. Three commands facilitate the entry of text within the dialog: dEDIT covers plain text, dXINPUT covers 'secret' information, and dFILE covers the entry of a file name.

dEDIT *vedit\$,prompt\$,len%* This function will display the string variable or literal *prompt\$* to the left of the line, and the initial contents of *vedit\$* (which *must* be a previously declared variable) to the right of the line. The contents of *vedit$* can then be edited or entered, as the case may be, using the usual editing keys. The number of characters that can be entered is determined when the variable is declared.

The formats for the function are

```
dEDIT vedit$,prompt$
dEDIT vedit$,prompt$,len%
```

As you can see, the variable *len%* can be ignored, if you wish, in which case the editing area is made wide enough to cope with the number of characters declared for *vedit$*, allowing for the widest character in the font (proportionally spaced characters are used).

If you specify a value for *len%*, then that's the number of characters wide the editing area will have, *based on the pixel width of the widest character in the font*. If the value of *len%* is less than the declared length for *vedit$*, then the *vedit$* string will scroll sideways within the editing area as you edit. If *len%* is made greater than the number of characters declared for *vedit$*, then all that will happen is you get extra width to the editing box - it *doesn't* mean you can add extra letters.

If your *prompt$* and edit width are such that the line would have more characters than the maximum possible width of a dialog box, you will get a '**Too wide**' error.

When you exit the dialog box, *vedit$* will contain the newly entered or edited string, *unless* the ESC key is used to make the exit. In this case, *vedit$* is left unchanged.

Here's a short demonstration procedure to show how dEDIT works. When you've entered and translated it, run it a few times to see the effects of editing, and test what happens when you press ESC to exit instead of ENTER.

```
PROC dialog2:
 LOCAL str$(18)
 str$="Series 3a"
 dINIT "Editing Box"
 dEDIT str$,"Change it:",8
```

```
DIALOG
PRINT "You changed it to",str$
GET
ENDP
```

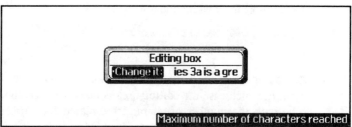

Trying to enter too many characters into the edit box

dXINPUT *vedit$,prompt$*   This function enables you to enter *eight* characters of 'secret' information, such as a password. The *prompt$* string is displayed to the left of the line.

vedit$ *must* be a variable declared to hold *at least eight characters*. Declaring less than eight characters won't produce any error messages, but could cause problems in your program. Anything previously assigned to **vedit$** is *not* displayed when dXINPUT is used. The edit area *always* has eight blank 'spaces' for *character* entry *irrespective of the number of characters defined for* **vedit$** *when it was declared*. You can thus enter up to eight characters only, even though **vedit$** may have been declared to hold more.

As the entry is being made, special 'lock' characters appear instead of the actual characters, to preserve the secrecy. When you exit the dialog box, the newly entered information will be stored in **vedit$**, *unless* the ESC key is used to exit. In this case, the original contents of **vedit$** remain unchanged. Here is a simple demonstration procedure that will enable you to put this function to the test.

```
PROC dialog3:
      LOCAL str$(8)
      dINIT "Secret Edit"
      dXINPUT str$,"Password:"
```

```
        DIALOG
        PRINT "You entered",str$
        GET
ENDP
```

When you run this, try it a few times, using both ESC and ENTER to exit the dialog. Note that, whilst the entry is kept 'secret', your program can access the information. This is obviously necessary, to enable you to compare the entered string with another!

dFILE   *vedit$,prompt$,ftype%* This powerful function is generally for use in *file handling* situations, and offers an extremely wide variety of options for entering or selecting a file name, or examining *directories*. The actual display and the way it 'operates' depends on the options - and combinations of options - that you select. All the features which by now may be familiar to you when using the Series 3a's file handling features, are available for you to use: the good news is, they are provided automatically. The bad news is - there's a lot of options to assimilate!

Note that although the actions of dFILE are programmed in just one statement, the screen display occupies *two* lines (as you will see with the demonstration program given later). Both of these lines count towards the maximum number of nine permitted for a dialog box.

vedit$ must have been declared as a LOCAL or GLOBAL variable, and dimensioned to hold *at least* 128 characters: you will get an '**Invalid arguments**' error when the program is run with any less. If ***vedit$*** is assigned a string before the dFILE statement, that string is displayed: if the number of characters is too great for the display, it will sideways scroll as required.

The contents of ***vedit$*** in fact define the *path* to the file you're interested in, or to a file you may wish to create or open. This *path* can include the 'drive' and directories. If ***vedit$*** is a null string (or simply hasn't been assigned a string), then the path set by another OPL command

191

SETPATH is used: failing that, the '\OPD' directory on the default drive (usually the 'internal drive', 'M:') is used.

***prompt$*** holds a 'prompt' message that will be displayed to the left of the line: but note, the word 'Name' is automatically added to your message (so you don't need to include it). For example, if you want the prompt to be 'File Name', all that *prompt$* needs to be assigned is 'File '.

ftype% determines how the line is going to operate - that is, the type of display, and the inputs allowed. The range of options can be used in any combination by simply adding together the appropriate values. You can therefore tailor the actions to suit the needs of the program. The options are:

ftype% =	Function
0	Simply allows the *selection* of (matching) files in the file path defined by *vedit$*. The TAB key can be used to list all the selectable files. The name of the selected file, with its path, is stored in *vedit$* on leaving the dialog (unless ESC is pressed).
1	Enables the contents of *vedit$* to be *edited*, as well as permitting file name selection as in '0' above. The name of the selected file, with its path, is stored in *vedit$* on leaving the dialog (unless ESC is pressed).
2	Allows directory names to be used.
4	Allows *only* directory names to be edited into *vedit$*. This is useful if you're getting in the directory for a file- copying operation.
8	Stops an *existing* file from being named when editing the contents of *vedit$*. A warning is given if an existing file is named, and re-entry of the name requested.
16	*Queries* when the file specified or edited in *vedit$* is the same as an existing file: you are asked if you want to 'overwrite' the existing file, on the assumption the file name being entered will be used to create a new file.
32	Allows a null string to be entered for *vedit$* (ie, when the edit area is being used).

One of the first two options (0 or 1) will, of course, *always* be applicable. The other options you 'add' as required: note that the last three options, 8, 16 and 32, only have relevance when option 1 is also selected.

As an example, if the dialog is asking the user to supply a name for a *new* file that is to be created, you might choose options 1, 2 and 8, or 1, 2 and 16 - assigning '11' or '19' to *ftype%*: this would either prevent the use of an existing file name (11), or warn the user and allow him to overwrite an existing file name (19).

Pressing the TAB key whilst a file edit line is highlighted will switch the display to a directory listing, which you can move around with the cursor keys.

The following program will allow you to experiment a little with this dialog function, and will display the results so that you can see what is happening. It will also allow you to check the size of each of your OPL source ('*.OPL' files), compared with the corresponding translated files ('*.OPO' files). Note the use of the *backslash* - don't use the ordinary 'oblique (/)' character.

```
PROC dialog4:
      LOCAL fnopl$(128),fnopo$(128)
      fnopl$="\opl\*.opl"
      fnopo$="\opo\*.opo"
      dINIT "File Name Edits"
      dFILE fnopl$,"Source file",0
      dFILE fnopo$,"Coded file",0
      DIALOG
      PRINT fnopl$
      PRINT fnopo$
      GET
ENDP
```

When you translate and run this program for the first time, perform the following operations: they will help you to understand the facilities and actions involved, and will help you to find your way around the directories. (It is assumed that you have a number of program files and a number of translated files saved).

1) Notice that an *extra* line - 'Disk' - appears in the dialog for each dFILE line, and that the lines have a 'bullet' point to the left,

indicating that they can be 'selected'. The up and down arrow keys will allow you to run up and down through each line - except for the 'Title' line, of course.

2) With the flashing cursor on the top line, press the left or right arrow keys to run through the saved program source files in your Series 3a.

3) With the flashing cursor still on the top line, press the TAB key: you will see a list of all the files as a table, with the size of each file and the date it was last changed. (This is much the same as the operations you can perform from the 'File' option on the System display menu). Press TAB *again*, and a 'Specify Filelist' dialog will appear, requesting a 'Filename pattern' or a different directory path: you can at this point obtain a *selective* display of filenames. For example, if you want to see all the files you have that begin with the letter 'm', enter 'm*.*' as the Filename pattern, and press ENTER. Now all the files that begin with the letter 'm' (and 'M') will be shown. (In case you're wondering, the '*' stands for *all letters and numbers here*, and is called a 'wild-card' in computer jargon). ESC clears the Specify Filelist dialog.

4) Whilst still in the listing display, use the arrow keys to move the highlight bar up to the top line - which will have a '\' symbol on the left side - and press ENTER. You will now see a list of all the *directory* names in your Series 3a: typically '\OPL\, '\OPO\', '\WDR\' and so on. Use the up and down arrow keys to select one of them - say '\DAT\' and press ENTER. If no files are shown, press TAB, and set the 'Filename pattern' to ' *.* ' and press ENTER: you will now see the name, size and the 'last changed' date of your Database files. Notice that heading the list is the name of the current directory, and above that, the directory selector symbol '\'. Select this symbol again, choose the '\OPL\' directory and press ENTER. Notice that at the top of the dialog there is a line which will be saying 'Disk Internal, ???k free', with arrows at each side. Press the right or left arrow keys, and you'll cycle through the drives available: 'Internal' is in the RAM area, 'A' and 'B' are the two slots, and 'C' is for the expansion socket. Unless you have Solid State Disk(s) fitted, these drives will be marked as 'Absent!'.

5) Return to the files listed under '\OPL\', select one and press ENTER. You will now be returned to *your* dialog box, with the selected file name (excluding the 'extension - the bit that comes after the 'dot') between the two selector arrows.

6) Now 'arrow' down to the 'Coded file name' line, and press TAB again. This time you will see a list of the *translated* file names you have in Series 3a. Note that this listing was selected by the assignment of the appropriate path to the *fnopo$* variable in the program. Browse through the list as before: note how, for most files, the *translated* length of a program is less than its source code - the program file you actually entered.

7) Select a file name from the list, and press ENTER: you'll now be back at *your* dialog box again. Press ENTER once more, and the screen will display the names of the two files that you have selected, together with their complete 'paths' and the full extension names. The 'LOC::' at the beginning stands for 'LOCal' - meaning within the Series 3a: you could equally well be accessing files on a computer connected to your Series 3a, in which case instead of 'LOC::' you will see 'REM::', which is short for 'REMote'. In other words, your Series 3a can create or access files on *other* computers too, provided they follow the MS-DOS file format.

8) Press any key to return to the Program Editor and your program listing.

Having completed that exercise - a good demonstration of the power behind the dFILE function - edit the dFILE lines of the program by changing the '0' at the end of the dFILE lines to a '1'. Now when you translate and run the program, in addition to all of the features mentioned in the explorations (1) to (8) just given, you will also be able to actually type in a file name - or a 'pattern', using the '*' as before. The TAB key works as before, so you can continue browsing and experimenting.

Now return to the Program Editor and edit the end of the dFILE lines to read '9' instead of '1'. This says you not only want to be able to input a file name as well as select it ('1'), you also want to prevent an *existing* file name from being selected or entered ('+8'). Translate and run the program as before, and using the TAB key, select an existing file name and press ENTER to return to your dialog. When you press enter again, to say 'that's the information I want stored in the *fnopl%* and *fnopo$* variables', a warning will be given that the '**File already exists**', and instead of leaving the dialog box, it will remain on display for you to make another choice - that is, enter the name of a file that *doesn't* exist. This is the effect of having '8' as part of the *ftype%* value: selection of an existing file name has been prevented.

Press the ESC key to abandon the dialog box.

It is left to you to experiment with the other *ftype%* options available - in particular, try '17'. Note that values of 8, 16 and 32 are only effective when '1' has also been selected. Note too that if you use the 'prevent existing files' option (8), the 'query overwriting an existing file' option (16), is ignored so there's not much point in using these two in combination.

Entering numbers. Two commands are available for entering numeric values: one covers *ordinary* and *long integers*, and the other covers *floating points*. With both functions the minimum and maximum acceptable values are defined, so the input can be restricted to any range you wish.

dLONG *vlng&,prompt$,minimum&,maximum&* This allows a long integer or an ordinary integer, between two defined limits, to be entered.

> **vlng&** - is the long integer variable that stores the result, and must have been declared as a LOCAL or GLOBAL long integer variable. If it is assigned a value before this command is executed, that value will be displayed - it can of course be edited and changed.

> **prompt$** is the prompt that will appear to the left of the displayed line.

> **minimum&** and **maximum&** define the smallest and largest values that the user is permitted to entry: the minimum value must be less than the maximum value. If these limits are exceeded then the appropriate limit value will be used

dFLOAT *vfp,prompt$,minimum,maximum* This permits the entry of floating point numbers - which can have a decimal point in them somewhere.

> **vfp** must have been defined as a LOCAL or GLOBAL *floating point* variable, and will store the input value when you exit the dialog, *unless* the ESC key is used for the exit.

prompt$ displays a prompt message, to the left of the edit area in the dialog box.

minimum and *maximum* define the minimum and maximum values for the entered value, and can have a decimal point in them. Both must be specified, and the *minimum* value must be less than the *maximum* value, otherwise you'll get an error. If a value outside the specified range is entered, a warning message is displayed: this is different from dLONG entries outside the permitted range - where the minimum or maximum value, as appropriate, is used.

Here is a short program to demonstrate the use of these two commands.

```
PROC dialog5:
   LOCAL fl,lng&
   dINIT "Entering numbers"
   dFLOAT fl,"Enter decimal",1,100
   dLONG lng&,"Enter integer",2,10
   DIALOG
   PRINT fl,lng&
   GET
ENDP
```

Entering the time or date. The two functions that enable you to enter a date or a time both work on the 'time since' principle used within Series 3a. The entry can be made in the same way that you set the date and time on your Series 3a. However, the values actually stored on leaving the dialog box are 'days since 1st January 1900' for the date, and 'seconds since 00:00 on the same day' for the time. In other words, once you have the stored values, you'll have to convert them (using the appropriate OPL words) for 'conventional' displays of the date and time.

dDATE *vdt&,prompt$,minimum&,maximum&* The three numeric arguments required for this function are all *long integers*, and relate to the number of days since 1/1/1900.

vdt& must have been declared as a LOCAL or GLOBAL variable. Whilst the display shows the date in a normal form, *vdt&* holds a value representing the chosen date - the value is the number of days from 1st Jan 1900 to the date. To have a date shown when the dialog box is displayed, you must assign the appropriate value to *vdt&* (don't panic - this is not a problem, as you will see later).

prompt$ provides a prompt message that will be displayed on the left side of the line.

minimum& and *maximum&* give the limits of the date entry - entries of dates before the *minimum&* date or after the *maximum&* date will be rejected by Series 3a, and the user invited to re-enter. Note that the statement line requires these to be long integer *values*: this is no problem, since the DAYS() function will convert an actual date into the long integer value required. No function is provided for converting a value back to the equivalent date, but as we shall see, this is quite achievable using existing functions.

When the dialog box is displayed, if *vdt&* hasn't been assigned a value, then the *minimum&* date appears in the edit area, in whatever format you chose when you set up your Series 3a.

Here's a routine that will allow you to calculate what the date will be (or was) a given number of days from a specified date. The display starts with the current date, but you can edit the date (from 1st Jan 1970 onwards). You then enter the number of days - either as a positive value or, for days previous, a negative value. On pressing ENTER, the appropriate date is displayed. This program uses some new OPL words (which will be discussed in a later Chapter), and the built-in capability of Series 3a to display a date from a given value, using the dDATE function. Note that the value for the maximum date is set as 73413: this is 31st December 2100, which should be far enough ahead for most people! Note that the display of the actual date is within an 'edit' area: the program as written won't allow you to change the date. Exit by pressing the ESC key.

```
PROC datefind:
 LOCAL dl&,nd&,fd&
 fd&=DAYS(1,1,1970)
```

```
d1&=DAYS(DAY,MONTH,YEAR)
dINIT "Date Finder"
dDATE d1&,"Start Date:",fd&,73413
dLONG nd&,"Days ahead/back:",-30000,30000
dTEXT "","(Negative for days previous)",2
IF DIALOG
  d1&=d1&+nd&
  dINIT "Date Finder"
  IF d1&>fd&
    dDATE d1&,"The Date is:",d1&,d1&
    dTEXT "","Press ESC to exit",2
  ELSE
    dTEXT "","Date out of range",2
  ENDIF
  DIALOG
ENDIF
ENDP
```

In particular, notice how a different dialog display is set up if the number of days takes the date outside the permitted range. As you can see, this is possible provided that the dialog instructions are properly completed, and they all occur within the same procedure.

dTIME *vtm&,prompt$,type%,minimum&,maximum&*

This function allows the user to enter a particular time of day, between the limits set by *minimum&* and *maximum&*. Note that the values of *maximum&* and *minimum&* represent the number of *seconds* from midnight to the specified time. (This should not be confused with the value returned by DATETOSECS - which gives the number of seconds since 00:00 on Jan 1st, 1970).

vtm& *must* be a LOCAL or GLOBAL declared variable. Any value assigned to this variable - as a number of *seconds* since 00:00 - will be displayed as an actual time, for editing. The time that is entered will be stored in this variable on exiting the dialog.

minimum& and **maximum&** are the minimum and maximum values that you are going to allow: again, these must be expressed as a number of seconds from 00:00.

type% determines the nature of the displayed time, as follows

Type% value	Time Display
0	Absolute time, without seconds.
1	Absolute time, with seconds
2	Duration period, without seconds
3	Duration period, with seconds.

Absolute time here means a specific time-of-day display, such as 10:35. Duration period means just so many hours, minutes and (if requested), seconds. In terms of the display, *absolute* time will appear according to the format you set for your Series 3a: for example, if you've set Series 3a for a 12 hour clock, 'am' or 'pm' will appear after the time period, but not after a duration period.

Offering a choice. Series 3a enables you to offer a variety of options in one line of a dialog box - selection of the required option being made by using the left and right arrow keys, or the TAB key and up and down arrow keys. The same way, in fact, that Series 3a offers such options when selecting a file name, for example.

dCHOICE *vchoice%,prompt$,list$*   In this function:

prompt$ is a prompt message that will be displayed to the left of the line.

list$ is your list of options. Each item in the list must be separated from the next by a comma - but with no comma after the last item. The entire list must be enclosed by a single pair of quotation marks.

vchoice% *must* be a LOCAL or GLOBAL declared variable. On leaving the dialog, the option that has been selected will be stored in **vchoice%** as a number - '1' for the first item in the list, '2' for the second, and so on. If you assign a value to **vchoice%** before the dCHOICE command, the relevant option item will be the one that is displayed within the selector arrows. If you don't assign a value, the first option is displayed (this may vary with different models of Series 3a). Here is an example of the use of dCHOICE: in this program, the dialog part is in a separate procedure of the same file, to show how it can be called from other procedures which set up the necessary lists.

```
PROC choice:
    LOCAL d%,item$(4,12),list$(52)
    item$(1)="Drive A,"
    item$(2)="Drive B,"
    item$(3)="External,"
    item$(4)="Internal RAM"
    DO
        d%=d%+1
        list$=list$+item$(d%)
    UNTIL d%=4
    d%=listqry:(list$)
    IF d%
        PRINT "You selected",item$(d%)
    ELSE
        PRINT "You ESCaped!"
    ENDIF
    GET
ENDP

PROC listqry:(list$)
    LOCAL ch%
    dINIT
    dCHOICE ch%,"Choose:",list$
    IF DIALOG
        RETURN ch%
    ELSE
        RETURN 0
    ENDIF
ENDP
```

Notice how the list is constructed in this program: the commas, essential for the dCHOICE function, are made a part of each *item$ ()* string assignment, except the last. This was necessary for this program since it displays the actual choice made. But in practice, your programs would probably operate on the numeric value returned to perform an operation of some kind, and so you could simply assign the string to a variable such as *list$*. Thus

```
list$="Drive A,Drive B,External,Internal RAM"
```

Then, IF choice%=2, say, you'd know that 'Drive B' had been selected and your program could act accordingly.

Providing exit buttons. So far, all of the dialog functions that we have discussed have used either the ENTER or ESC key as the means of leaving the dialog box. When the ENTER key is pressed, the entries that have been made are assigned to the appropriate variables, and the line number for the highlighted line is returned by the DIALOG function. ESC cancels the operation, leaves the various variables unchanged, and the DIALOG function returns '0' or zero.

You can however define up to three of your own exit keys, thus offering another range of options. In fact, you could use simply the 'exit buttons' as the main purpose of your dialog box. DIALOG doesn't return the highlighted line number when exit buttons are used, but rather a code related to the button.

When you use buttons as the means of leaving the dialog, you define which key on the keyboard must be pressed to activate the button, and the annotation or message that goes above it. The keyboard character (or key name) appears on the button itself.

Only the keys that you have defined will permit an exit, plus, if you *haven't* defined it, the ESC key. You can if you wish include both the ESC or ENTER keys as buttons. The ENTER key works *only* if you define it. If you don't define the ESC key as one of your exit buttons, you can have four different ways to terminate the dialog - your three buttons *and* the ESC key.

dBUTTONS *text1$,key1%,text2$,key2%,text3$,key3%*

This command *must* be the last item to appear in your dialog set up before the DIALOG function itself, and there can be only *one* dBUTTONS command per dialog box. Also, you should remember that it takes up three of the permitted nine lines maximum for a dialog (which includes the Title line).

You can use one, two or all three of the button pairs *textx$,keyx%*.

textx$ This variable in each pair defines the *annotation* that is to appear over the associated button.

keyx% This specifies the *character code* for the key that must be pressed to 'activate' the button. It also specifies the character (or key name) that will appear on the key itself, and, apart from ESC, *determines the value returned by* DIALOG *on exit.* This means that you cannot use dTEXT to have a highlighted line number returned. As well as the letter (or number) keys, the following can be used:

Character code	Appearing on Button
9	Tab
13	Enter
27	Esc
32	Space

Note that ESC will *always* return zero, whether you define it as a key or not. Note too that it is the character *code* that must be used: the easiest way to do this is to use the form '%A' - which gives the character code for the letter 'A' without you having to look it up. When using letters, the actual value returned is *always* for the *lower case letter.* It is important that you realise this: for example, if you use '%A' to put a letter 'A' on the key, (the character code for which is 65), the *actual* code returned when the key is pressed is 97 - the code for the *lower case* 'a'. The character code for numerals is returned as expected: '%1' for example will return '49' if that key is pressed.

You should also note that, if you use the character code for a *lower case* letter, such as '%a', the *capital* letter ('A') will actually appear on the button.

If you want to use a key *other* than ESC to cancel the dialog - and disregard any input entries that may have been made, then use a *negative* value for the character code. Thus, to have a key with the letter 'C' on it to cancel any inputs, use '-%c' for the *keyx%* variable. When this key is pressed, it acts as though the ESC key had been pressed.

The buttons can be used to provide a simple 'what now' type of dialog: here for example is how they could be used to provide the options 'Price', 'Area' or 'Quit'.:

```
PROC whatnow:
     LOCAL wn%
     dINIT "What next?"
     dTEXT "","Another...",2
     dBUTTONS "Price",%p,"Area",%a,"Quit",-%q
     wn%=DIALOG
     PRINT "You selected",wn%,"=",CHR$(wn%)
     GET
     ENDP
```

This procedure simply shows what button was pressed (it shows zero, and a bent arrow for ESC): you would of course use the returned value to determine the next step to take in the program.

Completing the dialog

As you will have realised by now, the dialog you have prepared is displayed when you use the DIALOG function.

DIALOG   This completes the dialog box set-up, displays it, and waits for an *exit* key (ENTER or ESC) or, if used, a button key to be pressed. The formats are

     d%=DIALOG

     DIALOG

The information returned on leaving a dialog is as follows.

Pressing the ESC key - or any 'button' that is given a *negative* character code value, such as '-%a', simply exits the dialog box, leaving everything as it was. DIALOG returns zero ('0').

Pressing ENTER when **not** *using 'buttons'*   If you have used 'action' lines involving a declared variable (such as dEDIT), any information entered in those lines will be stored in the appropriate variable. Since such variables must be either LOCAL or GLOBAL, their contents can therefore be used by the rest of your program.

     DIALOG 'returns' the *row number* of a highlighted line (if any) when ENTER is pressed. If there is no highlighted line, then DIALOG returns '1'. If you have used dTEXT lines with the '$400' option for the *type*, the line can be highlighted, and its row position returned. Note that rows are counted from the top, and that if you have included a 'Title' (with the dINIT command), the title line is row 1. All visible lines have a row number: only those selectable by the up and down arrow keys can be highlighted and returned by DIALOG.

Pressing ENTER when using buttons. If you have used 'action' lines involving a declared variable (such as dEDIT), any information entered in those lines will be stored in the appropriate variable. In this instance, however, DIALOG itself returns the *lower case* of the *character code* associated with the pressed key.

Since DIALOG is a function, the value it returns can be used in a variety of ways. The following program demonstrates how it could be used to provide a Library function that simply asks a question for a 'Yes' or 'No' response:

```
PROC qrytest:
    LOCAL q%
    DO
        PRINT "Clever stuff!"
        PAUSE -20
        q%=yornqry:("Again?")
    UNTIL NOT q%
END

PROC yornqry:(msg$)
    dINIT msg$
    dBUTTONS "No",%n,"Yes",%y
    RETURN DIALOG=%y
ENDP
```

Notice how DIALOG is used in 'yornqry' to return a *true* condition only if the 'Y' key is pressed: pressing the 'N' *or* ESC keys will produce a *not true* condition. Notice too how the 'title' for the displayed dialog can be passed to the yornqry procedure. The function yornqry could be a useful routine for your Library file.

Here's the Carpet program discussed in Part 1 of this book, using dialogs. Note that the program prevents 'zero' values from being entered.

```
PROC carpet2:
 LOCAL a,ppy,q%
 a=getarea:
 ppy=getcost:
 DO
  dINIT "Carpet Prices"
  dTEXT "Sq Yards needed: ",num$(a,3)
  dTEXT "Cost:£",fix$(a*ppy,2,7)
  dBUTTONS "New Cost",%c, "New Area,%a,"Quit",27
  q%=DIALOG
  IF q%=%c
   ppy=getcost:
  ELSEIF q%=%a
   a=getarea:
  ENDIF
 UNTIL q%=0
ENDP

PROC getcost:
 LOCAL cpsy
 DO
  dINIT "Cost of Carpeting"
  dFLOAT cpsy,"Per sq.yd:£",1,100
  DIALOG
 UNTIL cpsy
 RETURN cpsy
ENDP

PROC getarea:
 LOCAL w,h,a
 DO
  dINIT "Enter Room Dimensions"
  dFLOAT w,"Width (feet):",1,100
  dFLOAT h,"Length (feet):",1,100
  DIALOG
  a=w*h/9
  IF a>INTF(a)
   a=INTF(a)+1
  ENDIF
 UNTIL a
 RETURN a
ENDP
```

As you can see, creating dialogs is a reasonably straightforward and very graphic, 'user friendly' way not only to obtain necessary data from the keyboard, but also to display the results of calculations along with appropriate messages.

It is well worth your while practising with dialogs, for you will undoubtedly want to use them in your programs, rather than the text screen methods of obtaining data from the keyboard.

CHAPTER 20
Windows and bitmaps

In this Chapter you'll discover how to create, manipulate,
use, save and restore Windows and bitmaps, and you'll
be introduced to the use of the grey window plane. OPL
words covered are:

gBORDER, gCLOSE, gCLS, gCREATE, gCREATEBIT, gGREY,
gHEIGHT, gIDENTITY, gINFO, gORDER, gORIGINX/Y,
gPEEKLINE, gRANK, gSETWIN, gUSE, gVISIBLE, gWIDTH, gX,
gY.

Windows galore

So far, the whole screen has been used for program displays. As
mentioned at the beginning of this Part, you can select specific areas of
the screen to use for your displays. Each area is known as a 'Window'.

Graphic window areas can be defined such that they overlap, cover
each other up, or are all occupying their own discrete part of the screen.
When a graphic window is defined or 'created', it is given an identity
number - a number by which that window can be referenced when you
wish to display something in it. As you will see in a moment, you can
also create *bitmaps* - which are like *hidden* windows in memory. The
whole screen is always available as one graphics window, and up to
seven more windows and bitmaps can be created for *graphics* displays:
remember that you can have the whole screen for *text* displays, or define
one area using the SCREEN command.

It may be easier to consider the *graphics* windows as rectangles of
'paper' placed over the screen, each of which can be used to display
graphics: anything on areas of paper hidden behind other 'paper
rectangles' will not be seen. You can, however, specify which 'pieces of
paper' will appear on top. The *text* window (always identified as
number 1) must appear as one of the 'top' areas if its textual displays
are to be seen.

Only one window (or *bitmap*) can be *active* at a time: that means
you can only *write* information to one window at a time - and that is
whichever window happens to be *current*. You can, of course, select the
window or bitmap you want to be *active* or *current*.

The current window is not necessarily a *visible* window. That means you can write to window that is not visible, then make it visible for a faster, crisper display. A window may be *invisible* because it is hidden behind other windows, or because you *choose* to make it invisible.

When writing information to a window or bitmap, it has its own pixel referencing system: pixel '0,0' is always the top left corner of the *window*, whatever the position of the window on the screen. The whole screen is 480 by 160 pixels in size, but the windows you define may be smaller or larger - and anything written 'outside' of the defined window area or outside of the screen area will not be seen.

Each window can be created with a black only plane - where everything that is 'written' to the window is in black, or it can be created with both black and grey planes. In this instance, your program determines which window plane - black or grey - the next action will be directed to, using appropriate OPL language words.

Using windows enables you to create and manage sophisticated displays more easily, and can also make animation appear smoother and faster: successive movements can be written to different windows of the same size and occupying the same screen area, then the windows selected for viewing in turn. This is quicker than writing the animation data each time.

About bitmaps

A *bitmap* is the same as a window - except that it is always hidden from view: it is a window in the *memory* area of Series 3a.

Bitmaps are a useful way to build up images 'off screen' for subsequent transfer to a screen window - or for saving in a file for use in other programs. Generally speaking, images can be created faster in a bitmap area than in a window, and of course, the 'build-up' process is hidden from view. Bitmaps are created in much the same way as windows, and are referenced much the same way too: the 'top left corner' of a bitmap is referenced as '0,0', just like the top left corner of a window.

Like windows, bitmaps are identified by a reference number when they are created: remember, you can define up to seven windows *and* bitmaps altogether.

Psion refer to bitmaps and windows as 'drawables', meaning areas on which graphics can be drawn. We shall refer to them the same way, to avoid confusion.

Creating and closing windows and bitmaps

When you create a new window, you must specify where it is to appear on (or even off) the screen, and how large it is to be. Creating the window returns a 'reference' number, so that you can identify that window again for subsequent usage. For bitmaps, you don't have to specify the screen location (because there isn't one!). However, you still need to know its reference number for subsequent use. The functions for creating windows and bitmaps are gCREATE and gCREATEBIT.

gCREATE (*xloc%,yloc%,width%,height%,vis%,grey%*)

This creates a window with its top left corner at the pixel location defined by **xloc%** (distance in pixels from the left of the screen) and **yloc%** (distance in pixels from the top of the screen). Remember that the topmost row and leftmost columns are '0', so the top left position is '0,0'. If you make one or both of the values of *xloc%* and *yloc%* negative, then they will be 'off' the main screen area - and so part of the window will not be visible. (But there are ways to 'scroll' the hidden part of the window into view).

width% and **height%**, which relate to dimensions in pixels, determine the size of the window. You can define the window area such that it is not completely 'on the screen' - which you may wish to do for large displays: these can be 'scrolled' or moved into the screen area for viewing. As typical example, you might create such a window for use in a spreadsheet type of program or for a map, where the area you wish to work on is larger than the screen display area.

vis% determines whether or not the window will be visible or invisible immediately after it has been created: if *vis%* has a value of '1', it will be visible, if it has a value of '0', it will be invisible (you can always change this status later with other OPL commands). Even though the window may be invisible, you can still write to it.

grey% is an *optional* parameter that determines whether or not the window will have a grey plane. If *grey%* is not given, or is zero, then the window will not have a grey plane.

If *grey%* has a value of '1', then the window will have a usable grey plane.

The format for the function is

id%=gCREATE(*xloc%,yloc%,width%,height%,vis%,grey%*)

The reference number for the window is returned in *id%*, which will have a value between 2 and 8. The whole screen or default window is *always* identified as number 1.

When you create a window, it is immediately made *current* or active, ready for you to write information to, and the pixel location for graphics commands is set to the '0,0' position within the window. Note that, if you have several windows, each will have its own 'cursor' or pixel location for the next graphic command.

gCREATEBIT(*width%,height%*)   This function is very similar to that for creating a window: however, with gCREATEBIT, you don't need to specify a screen location, or whether it will be visible or not. And bitmaps don't have a grey plane: if you want a bitmap that will be used to transfer data to and from a grey plane, then it must be created separately, and you must remember that it is a bitmap for use with a grey plane. The format is

id%=gCREATE(*width%,height%*)

The reference number of the bitmap is returned in *id%*.

There is another way to 'create' a bitmap in memory, and that is to load a bitmap *file* that has been previously saved. We will deal with this method later.

As with a window, when you create a bitmap it is immediately made *current*, and the 'cursor' or pixel location within the bitmap is set to pixel '0,0' - the top 'left hand corner' of the bitmap area.

With these functions you can create up to seven windows and bitmaps ('*drawables*') altogether. If your program needs to know whether or not

211

a specific drawable is a window or a bitmap, there is an OPL function available (gINFO - dealt with later). However, if you specifically want a bitmap to write to a grey plane of a window - or store grey plane data - then you must know which bitmap it is.

There may be times when you want more than the permitted eight windows and bitmaps: if this is the case, then you will have to *close* one or more of them, in order to create new ones. The command is:

gCLOSE *id%*   This closes the window or bitmap identified by *id%*. If you close the *current* window or bitmap, then the default window (*id%*=1) is made the current window. Obviously you cannot close the default window (you'd be trying to shut down the screen!) - and if you do try, a program-stopping error will occur.

Clearing windows and bitmaps

To completely wipe out anything displayed in a window or stored in a bitmap, use the gCLS command.

gCLS   This is very much like the CLS command used to clear the text window. gCLS clears the *current* window or bitmap of any displayed graphics and text.

Getting information about windows and bitmaps

When working with windows and bitmaps, it will often be necessary to know exactly where the 'cursor' is for the next graphics command, where the window is on the screen, which window is current, which window is 'on top', and so on. There is a range of functions in OPL that enable you to determine such information, so that you don't have to keep track of it: indeed, if the user is given the facility to change things around (such as shifting a window from one place on the screen to another), it will be difficult and fairly complicated for your program to keep track without the *information* facilities.

Where's the graphics cursor?

The pixel location where the next graphics command will take effect from within the *current* window or bitmap can be determined by the functions gX and gY.

gX   The format is

$$x\%=gX$$

x% will hold the current horizontal pixel location, from the left edge of the current window or bitmap. Remember that the leftmost edge is '0'.

gY   The format is

$$y\%=gY$$

y% will hold the current vertical pixel location from the top edge of the current window or bitmap. Remember that the topmost edge is '0'.

Where's the window?

The location of the *current window* on the screen can be determined by the two commands gORIGINX and gORIGINY, which can only be used with windows, not bitmaps. (It makes sense, if you think about it: bitmaps don't have a screen location. If a bitmap is the current 'drawable' when either of these functions is invoked, you'll get an error which, unless trapped, will stop the program from continuing).

gORIGINX   The format is

$$x\%=gORIGINX$$

x% will hold the pixel location on the *overall* screen of the leftmost edge of the *current* window. Remember that the leftmost edge of the screen is '0'.

gORIGINY   The format is

$$y\%=gORIGINY$$

y% will hold the pixel location on the overall screen of the topmost edge of the *current* window. Remember that the topmost edge of the screen is '0'.

Which window or bitmap is current?

Your program can identify which window or bitmap is currently being used.

gIDENTIFY   has the format

$$id\%=gIDENTIFY$$

After executing this function, `id%` will hold the identification number of the current window or bitmap. The default window is number 1..

How big is the current window or bitmap?

Two functions enable you to ascertain the size of the current window or bitmap.

gWIDTH   The format is

$$width\% = gWIDTH$$

`width%` will hold the width, in pixels, of the current window or bitmap.

gHEIGHT   The format is

$$height\% = gHEIGHT$$

`height%` will hold the height, in pixels, of the current window or bitmap.

What 'level' is the window?

You will recall that *windows* can be placed 'on top of each other' on the screen - and that those windows concealed by others will not be seen. You can determine how far 'down' or 'back' a window is by the function gRANK:

gRANK   The format is

$$rank\% = gRANK$$

`rank%` will hold the depth position of the *current* window, with '1' being the topmost or the one that's in the foreground, and '8' being the window that's 'right down at the back'. A program-stopping error will occur if you try to use this function when a bitmap is current.

Full information about the current window or bitmap

As well as the *position* information provided by the previously discussed functions, you can obtain more sophisticated data about the current window or bitmap: full details about the *font*, the *current text* or *graphics* mode, whether it is a *window* or a *bitmap*, and so on. Much of this information is for fairly advanced use - particularly the font data, and you will be unlikely to need it for most of your programs.

gINFO `vid%()` This function requires `vid%()` to have been declared as a LOCAL or GLOBAL *array*, with at least 32 elements - the last two elements (32 and 32) will not contain any relevant data: they are reserved for later use. After executing this command, the `vid%()` array holds data as follows:

vid%() element	Data held
1	The lowest character code in the current font.
2	The highest character code in the current font.
3	The height of the current font.
4	The descent of the current font.
5	The ascent of the current font.
6	The width of the zero character '0'.
7	The width of the widest character.
8	Font details (additive hexadecimal values): $1=font uses standard ASCII characters 32-126 $2=font uses Code Page characters 128-255 $4=Font has been enboldened $8=Font has been italicised $10=Font has serifs $20=Font is monospaced $8000=Font is stored expanded for fast drawing
9-17	Font name as a string **(Note 1)**
18	The graphics mode, as set by gGMODE.
19	The text mode, as set by gTMODE.
20	The text style, as set by gSTYLE.
21	Cursor state (0=off, 1=on) **(Note 2)**
22	ID of window containing the cursor display **(Note 3)**
23	The cursor width.
24	The cursor height.
25	The cursor ascent.
26	The cursor's x position in the window.
27	The cursor's y position in the window.
28	Window (0) or Bitmap (1).
29	Cursor effects (additive values) 1=oblong cursor 2=non-flashing cursor 4=grey cursor
30	Window pane, as set by gGREY
31	Reserved
32	Reserved

Note 1 The value in vid%(9) is an *address*. You can get the name of the font by a lines such as

```
PRINT PEEK$(ADDR(vid%(9)))
font$=PEEK$(ADDR(vid%(9)))
```

PEEK and ADDR are two of the OPL words that 'access' the ROM or RAM areas of Series 3a. These are discussed in more detail in Part 4 of this book, which covers more advanced details about the programming language.

Note 2 If the cursor is switched off, then vid%(22) to vid%(27) should be ignored.

Note 3 The *text* screen cursor is identified by the value '-1'.

Reading a line of pixels

There is a function for the more advanced programmer that enables a horizontal line of pixels to be read from a window or bitmap. The information is stored 16 pixels at a time in an integer array, which must have been declared as a LOCAL or GLOBAL variable.

gPEEKLINE id%$,x$%$,y$%$,varray$%$(),ln$%   With this function:

id% is the identification number for the required window or bitmap. If id% is set to zero, then the pixels are read from the whole screen, not any particular window. If $8000 is added to the value of id% (that's 8000 hexadecimal), then the *grey* plane rather than the black plane pixels will be read. Remember that bitmaps don't have grey planes.

x% and **y%** define the pixel location from which the information is to be read.

ln% is the number of pixels to be read.

varray%() is the array that will hold the data. The line is read from the left, information regarding the first 16 pixels being stored in the first element ($varray$%(1)), the next 16 pixels are stored in the second array element ($varray$%(2)) and so on. The first or leftmost pixel in each instance is stored in the *least significant* (lowest valued) bit of the array element: a set bit ('1') indicating that the pixel is switched on, and a zero value ('0') indicating that the pixel is switched off. The dimension or number of elements that the array must have when it is declared can be calculated from the formula:

$$((\text{ln\%}+15)/16)$$

using integer arithmetic.

Selecting and positioning windows

We have seen how to get information about the current window or bitmap: now let us look at the various ways there are to *select, resize* and *reposition* windows.

Making a window or bitmap current

To select a window or bitmap and make it current for the next action, the command is gUSE:

gUSE *id%* This command makes the window or bitmap identified by *id%* current, ready to receive graphics or text commands, or to be resized and repositioned. It *doesn't* however make a selected window visible: the window may still be hidden behind other windows, or be designated to be 'invisible'.

Setting a window's position and size.

The gCREATE command allows you to define a window's size, and to position it within the overall screen. It doesn't end there, however: you can, through your program, shift it somewhere else if you wish - perhaps under 'user control' - and also change its size.

gSETWIN *x%,y%,width%,height%*   With this command, you can move the *current window* to a new location, as defined by the values of x% and y% - which represent the horizontal and vertical pixel locations respectively of the top left corner of the window within the *overall* screen. The width% and height% arguments are optional: however, if you specify one, you must specify both. As expected, they will change

217

the size of the window. The command cannot be used with bitmaps: it will cause an error.

Note that if this command is used on the default window (1), and you are also using ordinary text print displays (which are also on the default window), you will also have to invoke the SCREEN command, to ensure that the area used for PRINT statements is kept within the newly sized window.

The position for the next action within the newly positioned and possibly resized window remains unchanged.

Setting the window level

When you have a number of windows opened, invariably some of them will be hidden behind others. You can change the depth or level of a window - bringing it nearer to the top (so that it is visible), or sending it further back.

gORDER *id%,level%*   This command sets the level of the window (it causes an error if used with bitmaps) identified by *id%*, to the level specified by *level%*. The topmost level, guaranteed to be clear of all other windows, is at level '1'. If the value of *level%* is greater than the number of windows in use, then the window with the highest identification number is used. Thus, if *id%* has a value of '6', but only windows up to an id of '4' have been created, then window '4' will be placed at the specified level. The current level of a window can be obtained by gRANK, remember.

Setting a window's visibility

When you create a window, you determine whether or not it will be immediately visible. Naturally, the situation can be changed at any time within your program.

gVISIBLE ON/OFF   To make the *current* window visible, use gVISIBLE ON, and to make it invisible, use gVISIBLE OFF. If a bitmap is the current drawable, you'll get an error.

Window frames

When a window is created, it is 'frameless' -it has no visible edges - which can make it difficult to see. There is, of course, a solution: the gBORDER command.

gBORDER *type%, width%,height%*   This command enables a window to be framed in a variety of different ways, depending on the value of `type%`.

type% value	Border effect
0	No shadow, no gap, slightly rounded corners
1	A single pixel shadow is drawn
2	A *gap* for a single pixel shadow is drawn
3	A double pixel 'drop' shadow is drawn
4	A *gap* for a double pixel shadow is drawn

You can have any *one* of the above values with or without any combination of the following two hexadecimal values:

type% value	Border effect
$100	Leaves a single pixel gap all round the border
$200	Makes the corners more rounded

Thus for a single pixel gap all round, more rounded corners and a double pixel drop shadow, `type%` will have a value of $303. The options available enable you to frame a window in a variety of ways- and to differentiate it from other windows, to show it is the 'selected' window, perhaps. For example, you can use a drop shadow to indicate an active window, then use the *gap* option when another window is made active. However, when and if you do this, be sure to use related commands. If you have 'rounded corners' when the window is active ($200), but not when it is de-activated, then you will get unwanted lines on the display.

The `width%` and `height%` are optional arguments. If used, instead of the border being drawn 'round the window', it is drawn to the specified width and height (in pixels) with the top left corner at the *current* drawing location within the window. This makes it similar to the `gBOX` command (discussed in a later Chapter), the difference being that `gBORDER` allows you to have drop shadows and so forth.

Here is a procedure which will enable you to examine the different ways you can frame a window using `gBORDER`. So that you can see the effects of the shadows and gaps, the screen is first filled with a pattern.

```
PROC borders:
 LOCAL id%,r%,f&,g%,c%
 DO
  r%=r%+8
  gAT 0,r%
  gPRINT REPT$(CHR$(176),60)
 UNTIL r%>=153
 id%=gCREATE(20,20,120,80,1)
 DO
  f&=f& AND $F                         REM See Note 1
  dINIT "Border types"
  dPOSITION 1,0
  dLONG f&,"Type (0-4):",0,4
  dCHOICE g%,"Gap all round?","Yes,No"
  dCHOICE c%,"Round corners?","Yes,No"
  dBUTTONS "Do it",13,"Quit",27
  r%=DIALOG
  IF r%
   f&=f&-$100*(g%=1)-$200*(c%=1)       REM See Note 2
   gBORDER f&
   gAT 5,30
   gPRINT "Border type",HEX$(f&)
   GET
   gCLS
  ENDIF
 UNTIL r%=0
ENDP
```

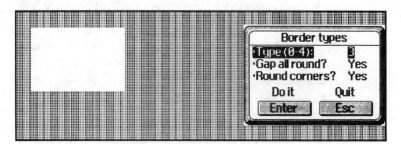

Selecting a border type to examine

Note 1   This line selects the 0 to 4 part only of any previously value
             assigned to f&. Without it, f& will reset to '4' (the highest
             unitary permitted value) if one of the high hexadecimal
             values has been selected.

Note 2   This type of construction - which saves a series of 'IF' statements, is discussed in the *'Making Decisions'* Chapter, under the heading of *'The Logic of it all'*.

Here's another program that will allow you to see the action of the gSETWIN, gORDER, gORIGINX, gORIGINY and gBORDER commands. It creates a series of seven windows (numbered 2 to 8), then invites you to select a window number for moving. Notice how the gBORDER command is used to show which window is selected (and brought to the 'top'), and the gORIGINX/Y functions are used as the reference point for the desired movement. This program also demonstrates the use of KMOD function to detect whether the SHIFT key has been pressed (the program is written so that pressing SHIFT enables you to move a window 'faster', but with less precision).

The program comprises two procedures, both of which must be entered - in the same file - before it is translated and run. You have to type in the PROC and ENDP for the second procedure. Don't enter the **REMarks** - shown in a different type face. They're there to help you understand how the program works.

When you run the program, press the ENTER key to clear the instruction Dialog box so that you can select and move windows.

```
PROC windmove:
 LOCAL c%,f%
 c%=2
 DO                          REM Create 7 windows within a loop
  gCREATE(c%*3,c%*5,120,50,1)
  gBORDER 2                  REM No drop shadow yet
  gAT 20,17
  gPRINT "Window",c%         REM Name that window
  c%=c%+1
 UNTIL c%=9
 dINIT "Instructions"
 dTEXT "","Press a number key (2-8) to",2
 dTEXT "","select a Window and bring it",2
 dTEXT "","to the top. Use the",2
 dTEXT "","arrow keys to move it",2
 dTEXT ""," (arrow+shift key=faster)",2
 dTEXT "","Press ESC to quit",2
 DIALOG
 DO
  c%=GET
```

```
f%=1+5*(KMOD AND 2)      REM f%=1, or 11 if SHIFT is pressed
IF (c%>49) AND (c%<57)   REM Is it a number key?
 gBORDER 2               REM Yes - clear the Border
 gUSE c%-48              REM Make selected window current
 gORDER c%-48,1          REM ...put it on top
 gBORDER 1               REM ...and give it a shadow
ELSEIF c%=256            REM Code for the UP key
 posit:(0,-1,f%)
ELSEIF c%=257            REM Code for the DOWN key
 posit:(0,1,f%)
ELSEIF c%=258            REM Code for the RIGHT key
 posit:(1,0,f%)
ELSEIF c%=259            REM Code for the LEFT key
 posit:(-1,0,f%)
ENDIF
UNTIL c%=27              REM Code for the ESC key
ENDP

PROC posit:(x%,y%,f%)
 gSETWIN gORIGINX+x%*f%,gORIGINY+y%*f%
ENDP
```

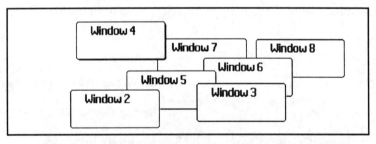

Windmove in action - showing Window 4 as the current window

Window planes

You will recall that *windows* (but not bitmaps) can have two planes, black and grey, and that you must specify a grey plane is to be used when you create the window (using gCREATE). For the default window to have a grey plane, you need to use the DEFAULTWIN command.

If your window has both a black and a grey plane, then you must specify in your program which plane or planes graphics (including graphic text) will be displayed on. The command to use is gGREY.

gGREY *mode%*   This command controls whether all subsequent graphic and graphic text commands are directed to the black only, grey only, or both black and grey planes when dealing with the *current* window, according to the value of *mode%*.

mode% value	Plane
0	Black only (default)
1	Grey only
2	Black and grey

The black plane is, in effect, 'on top' of the grey plane. This means if both pixels are set, the appearance will be black. If the black plane pixel is then cleared, then the grey pixel will be seen.

CHAPTER 21
Copying windows and bitmaps

In this Chapter you will learn how to copy data to and from 'drawables', scroll their contents, and how to save a drawable to a file and reload it. The OPL words covered are:

gCOPY, gLOADBIT, gPATT, gSAVEBIT, gSCROLL, gUPDATE

Transferring drawable data

There will be many occasions when you will want your program to transfer the contents (or part of the contents) from one drawable to another - and to save the contents to a file. It is much easier to construct an image in a window - where it can be seen - then transfer it to a bitmap or file for subsequent use.

Two commands are available for copying drawables: the first, gCOPY, enables you to transfer an entire area or a selected part of it, and the second, gPATT, enables you to have a particular area copied as a pattern - that is, repeated as often as possible in the new area.

gCOPY id%,x%,y%,width%,height%,mode%   With this command, you can copy a rectangle from the window or bitmap identified by id%, to the *current* pixel location in the *current* window or bitmap, and you can set the way the copying process is to be executed. Remember it is the drawable you are copying *to* that must be current.

id% is the reference number of the window or bitmap *from* which the data is to be copied.

x% and **y%** define the top left corner of the area to be copied within the drawable identified by id%.

width% and **height%** define the size of the rectangle to be copied, in pixels.

mode% determines *how* the copying process is to be executed. Both set (darkened) and clear pixels can be copied, but the *way* they are copied depends on the value of `mode%` as follows:

mode% value	Copying method
0	Copies set pixels as set pixels.
1	Copies set pixels as *clear* pixels: these will be seen only over darkened areas in the new location.
2	Set pixels invert the current pixel settings, so in darkened areas they will be cleared, in clear areas they will be set.
3	The whole of the specified area is copied 'as is' so that the copy is duplicated exactly at the destination area.

As you can see , for `mode%` values of 0 to 2, only the *set* pixels are copied, either as they are, as clear pixels, or inverting anything that's at the destination. After the command has been executed the 'cursors' at both locations are restored to their original positions.

It is important to remember that windows can have *two* planes. If you have specified that a grey plane is to be used for the current window, then the copying action will be to the *plane* or *planes* as selected by `gGREY`:

`gGREY 0`   Copies a black plane to a black plane.

`gGREY 1`   Copies a grey plane to a grey plane. If the source has only a black plane (or is a bitmap), then that plane is copied to the grey plane.

`gGREY2`   Copies the black plane to the black plane, and the grey plane to the grey plane. If the source has only a black plane (or is a bitmap), then that plane is copied to both the black and the grey planes

gPATT `id%,width%,height%,mode%`   This command is used to create repetitive patterns. The entire bitmap or window identified by `id%` is copied into the current window or bitmap, into a box area specified by `width%` and `height%`.

The top left corner of the box is determined by the current cursor location. The copied pattern is repeated as many times as will fit within the box area.

The way that the pattern is copied into the box is determined by *mode%*, which has exactly the same effects as detailed for gCOPY on the previous page. The plane or planes that the pattern is copied to is determined by the setting for gGREY - as described on the previous page.

If you give *id%* a value of '-1', then a built-in grey pattern is used.

Here is a procedure to give you a feel for the potential of the gPATT command, and to demonstrate one or two of the other commands dealt with so far. When you have run this program, experiment by editing, for example, the *mode%* value of gPATT and the size of the area in which the pattern is to be reproduced. You can use also the program to practice creating your own patterns in the bitmap, altering the size of the bitmap at the gCREATEBIT command as necessary. Don't enter the REMark parts set in a different type face.

```
PROC pattern:
 LOCAL id%(2),c%
 id%(1)=gCREATEBIT (20,20)       REM Create a Bitmap
 gCLS                            REM Ensure it's clear
 DO                              REM Create a pattern
   gAT c%,c%
   gBOX 2+c%,2+c%
   c%=c%+2
 UNTIL c%>=10
 id%(2)=gCREATE(2,2,400,140,1)
 gBORDER $203                    REM Window and border
 gAT 100,10
 gFILL 50,50,0                   REM Black box in the window
 BUSY "Press a key"             REM Wait for the moment!
 GET
 BUSY OFF
 gAT 2,2
 gPATT id%(1),400,140,2         REM Pattern the window
 GET
 ENDP
```

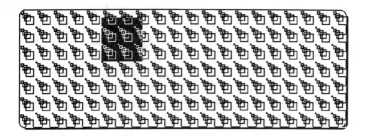

The Pattern program as written

Scrolling every which way

You will probably have seen how, in the text window, Series 3a scrolls text upwards when new lines are added at the bottom of the screen. This doesn't happen automatically on graphics screens: anything you 'send' to the screen overprints what was already there, according to the *mode* selected. Scrolling is made possible, however, in any direction you choose, by the gSCROLL command.

gSCROLL *dx%,dy%,x%,y%,width%,height%*   The formats for this command are

```
gSCROLL dx%,dy%
gSCROLL dx%,dy%,x%,y%,width%,height%
```

If you just specify *dx%* and *dy%*, then the display in the *entire* current window (or bitmap) is scrolled by *dx%* pixels horizontally, and by *dy%* pixels vertically. As with other commands, negative values for *dx%* move to the left, positive values move to the right. Similarly negative values for *dy%* move up, and positive values move down.

Note that if your window has a border (gBORDER command), then as this is *within* the window area, it too will scroll.

You can limit the scrolling area to a rectangle within the window or bitmap, by specifying *x%* and *y%* (to determine the top left corner of the rectangle), and *width%* and *height%* (to determine the size of the rectangle).

The area 'left behind' by a scrolling action is always cleared, and anything scrolled 'beyond the edge' of the *defined* window area is lost: scrolling back again *doesn't* bring it back into view. You can have a *defined* window that is larger than the actual screen: the screen then becomes a 'viewport' on your defined window. In this case, anything previously 'hidden' - because it is beyond the limits of the *screen* - can be scrolled into view. Nevertheless, areas 'left behind' are still cleared. It is up to your program to prevent wanted information from being scrolled beyond the limits of the window, or to replace cleared areas with new information, if that's what you want.

The gPEEKLINE function can be used to 'read' a horizontal line from, say, a bitmap, for inserting into a cleared horizontal line in a window: this calls for a slightly more advanced programming technique, as you must be able to 'convert' an integer value into pixel display information. We shall examine the process involved a little later.

Note that the position of the window is unaffected by the scrolling action. Also, the current cursor location within the window is not affected by the scrolling action, even if a rectangular scroll area is specified.

Here is a program that will demonstrate the scrolling process. A larger-than-screen window is created and filled to the brim with letters. You use the arrow keys to scroll in any direction - and reveal the stuff 'hidden' beyond the screen. At first, everything is scrolled: pressing 'R' will limit scrolling to a rectangle, pressing 'A' will scroll the entire window. By scrolling to the limits of the *window* and back, you should be able to see how 'off screen' displays can be brought into view, and also how scrolled data is lost when it is taken beyond the limits of the window. When you've had enough, press the ESC key to Quit.

Enter the program carefully - both procedures must be entered in the same file, and you will have to type in the PROC and ENDP for the second procedure. you don't have to enter the REMarks, shown in a different type face.

```
PROC scroller:
 LOCAL c%,a%
 gCREATE(-40,-40,520,200,1)        REM Window limits 'off screen'
 c%=-20
 gFONT 9
 DO                                REM Fill window
  c%=c%+9
  gAT 1,c%
  gPRINT REPT$("AbCdEfGhIjKlMn",8)
 UNTIL c%>=300
 DO                                REM Now for the scrolls
  c%=GET
  IF c%=256                        REM Up
   doscroll:(0,-1,a%)
  ELSEIF c%=257                    REM Down
   doscroll:(0,1,a%)
  ELSEIF c%=258                    REM Right
   doscroll:(1,0,a%)
  ELSEIF c%=259                    REM Left
   doscroll:(-1,0,a%)
  ELSEIF c%=%A OR c%=%a            REM 'A' pressed?
   a%=0                            REM '0' for 'all screen'
  ELSEIF c%=%R OR c%=%r            REM 'R' pressed?
   a%=1                            REM '1' for rectangular area
  ENDIF
 UNTIL c%=27                       REM 'ESC' pressed
ENDP

PROC doscroll:(horiz%,vert%,area%)
 IF area%
  gSCROLL horiz%,vert%,100,50,60,30
 ELSE
  gSCROLL horiz%,vert%
 ENDIF
ENDP
```

Replacing 'lost' scrolled displays

Here's a scrolling procedure, this time using a smaller window, to show how the data that's 'lost' as a result of a *vertical* scrolling action can be replaced using the gPEEKLINE function.. Scrolling is limited to vertical directions only. Don't enter the REMarks, shown in a different type face.

```
PROC scroll2:
 LOCAL k%,row%,id%
 id%=gCREATE(40,20,160,40,1)
 k%=8
 DO                              REM Fill window
  gAT 1,k%
  gPRINT "AbCdEfGhIjKlMnOpQrStUvWxYz12"
  k%=k%+8
 UNTIL k%>=48
 DO                              REM The 'action' loop
  k%=GET
  IF k%=256                      REM Up
   row%=0                        REM so TOP line goes
   scrollit:(id%,row%)           REM Go do it
  ELSEIF k%=257                  REM Down
   row%=39                       REM so BOTTOM line goes
   scrollit:(id%,row%)           REM Go do it
  ENDIF
 UNTIL k%=27                     REM esc key pressed
ENDP

PROC scrollit:(id%,row%)
 LOCAL ne%,bp&,a%(10)            REM Note 1
 gPEEKLINE id%,0,row%,a%(),160   REM Read line
 IF row%                         REM Means row%=39 = down
  gSCROLL 0,1                     REM so scroll down
 ELSE                            REM Otherwise...
  gSCROLL 0,-1                    REM Scroll up
 ENDIF
 ne%=1                           REM Set counter to '1'
 DO                              REM For each array element
  bp&=0                          REM set bit position to '0'
  DO                             REM For each bit position
    IF a%(ne%) AND 2**bp&               REM See Note 2
     gAT ((ne%-1)*16)+bp&,39-row%       REM See Note 3
     gLINEBY 0,0                         REM Plot it
    ENDIF
   bp&=bp&+1                     REM Next Bit
  UNTIL bp&=16                   REM Bits are 0-15
  ne%=ne%+1                      REM Next array element
 UNTIL ne%=11                    REM End of the array
ENDP
```

Note 1: *ne%* is used to select the elements of the array *a%()* (which will hold the 'peeked' information). *bp&* is a 'bit position' variable which must be a long integer to handle the large multiplications. The window is 160 pixels wide, so array (*a%()*) must be dimensioned to hold lines of 160 pixels: using the formula, '(ln%+15)/16', you'll see ten array elements are needed.

Note 2: Each *bit* in the stored value must be tested, to see if it represents a *set* bit (value of '1') or a *clear* bit (value of '0'). Each *bit* position from the lowest to the highest represents an increasing *power* of two. The first bit (bit zero) represents 'two to the power *zero*' - and *any* number to the power of zero is equal to 1. It's a fact of life. The next bit - (bit *one*) - represents 'two to the power *one*' and the next bit represents 'two to the power *two*' and so on. Thus, each bit represents 'two to the power of its position in the *binary number* stored in the array element'. If we AND the *total* value stored in the element with the different powers of two, each bit can be tested in turn to see if it is set. If it *is* set, then the result of

```
IF a%(ne%) AND 2**bp&
```

will be *true*, and so the corresponding pixel can be plotted in the window. Easy, huh?

Note 3: Having ascertained that a particular *bit* in the array element is *set*, the corresponding pixel must be plotted on the display. So we need to calculate where, along the row, that bit is. Knowing the row itself is easy - we passed that information down from the main procedure. To find out which pixel along the row needs to be 'switched on' or darkened, we need to make a calculation. You will recall that gPEEKLINE stores the leftmost 16 pixels in the first array element, the next 16 in the second array element, and so on. You will also recall that the *first* pixel information in a group of 16 goes into the lowest or least significant *bit* of the number in its binary form. Thus, the very first pixel will be in the '*bit zero*' position of the first element of the array. Similarly, the very first pixel in the *second* element of the array will be *sixteen pixels along*. So, if '1' is deducted from an array element number and it is then multiplied by 16, the *band* of 16 pixels being represented by the value stored in that array element can be determined. All that has to be done then is to add in the actual bit position, and the position the pixel that must be turned on is determined. Finally, for the gAT command, the row number must be set. If *row%* is zero, it means the pixel row from the top line was read- but now needs to be replaced at the bottom line, which will be '39'. Similarly, if *row%* was 39, the pixel row on the top line - '0' - must be replaced. By deducting *row%* from 39, the required result is obtained. And that's it!

Armed with the remarks given in the program and the notes above, you should be able to follow the process involved in creating a 'rolling scroll'. This program reads the information from the same window, but you could read it from a *bitmap* which would be the same width as your window, but which is 'longer' or deeper, to hold all the information. In this case, you would need to keep track of which 'row' in the bitmap needs to be read - slightly more tricky, but not too difficult if you remember that the top and bottom rows that may need to be read will be the same 'distance' apart as your window's depth.

It must be said at this point that the example above is just *one* solution, and the result, although it works, is a fairly slow scrolling action: Series 3a has to make a large number (160 in this case) of calculations and plots to replace a line of pixels.

Finally you should note that, if you place a border round your window, that too will scroll unless you limit the scroll area to a rectangle *within* the border area: you would also need to adjust the row numbers being read and replaced, of course.

Saving and loading windows and bitmaps

Your programs can be quite lengthy if they use graphic displays of some kind, and these displays have to be created each time the program is run. Far better is to create the displays once, either in a bitmap or window, and then save them as a 'picture' file. When your program needs the saved display, it can be loaded quickly, easily and directly into a bitmap for copying entirely or in part to a window. Once a display has been saved, the 'display generating' part of your program can deleted, of course, saving space as well as speeding things up.

gSAVEBIT *name$,width%,height%*   This saves the current window or the bitmap to a file. If a window is current and it has both black and grey planes, *both* are saved to the file separately - the black plane first. The formats are

```
gSAVEBIT name$
gSAVEBIT name$,width%,height%
```

If you use **width%** and **height%**, then the area saved is a rectangle of the specified size, with its top left corner at the current pixel location. If you don't specify `width%` and `height%`, then the whole of the window or bitmap is saved.

name$ is the name that the file will have when it is saved, and this name must follow certain rules (the same rules, in fact, as for file names used on desk top computers). In essence the file name can consist of three parts:

a) A *path* to the directory in which the file is to be saved.

b) The *file name*, which must be no more than eight letters or numbers, always starting with a letter.

c) The *extension*, which is a dot followed by three letters, usually to denote the type of file.

Of these, `name$` need only specify (b) - the name you wish to give to the file. If you don't specify the *path*, then the default 'bitmap' directory '\OPD\' will be used. If you don't specify an *extension*, the default extension '.PIC' will be used.

Note that if any file with the same name already exists at the saved location, it will be replaced by the new file.

gLOADBIT(`name$,write%,i%`)   Once you have bitmap files saved, you can load them again with this function. The formats are

```
id%=gLOADBIT(name$)
id%=gLOADBIT(name$,write%)
id%=gLOADBIT(name$,write%,bmnum%)
```

The file is loaded into a *bitmap* (not a window) in memory, and the function returns the reference number for the bitmap in `id%`. As with gSAVEBIT, if `name$` doesn't specify the path or the extension, then the default directory (\OPD\) and extension (.PIC) will be used.

If you want to prevent the bitmap restored into memory from being changed in any way, then use the *write%* argument and make it equal to '0': this makes the bitmap *'read-only'*, so any attempts to write new information to it will be ignored. The default value for *write%* is '1' - which means it can be changed and re-saved.

If the file you saved had both black and grey planes, then you will need to use the *bmnum%* argument. Files can have more than one bitmap 'embedded' in them, and the bmnum% argument selects the particular bitmap to load. For black and grey plane windows saved using the gSAVEBIT command, to restore the black plane, *bmnum%* should have a value of '0', and to restore the grey plane, *bmnum%* should have a value of '1'. This means that *two* gLOADBIT statements are required to load both the black and grey planes of the file back into memory: each will be a separate bitmap with its own *id%* number. To restore the bitmaps to a *window*, you would then use the gCOPY command *twice*: once to restore the black plane, and once to restore the grey plane - remembering of course to use the gGREY command to set the planes written to black and grey respectively during the copying action.

Now let us examine a way these two commands can be used. If you have a program which requires drawings or window displays, you probably won't want the program to generate those drawings each time it runs. If you don't have a special 'drawing' program which enables you to create displays and save them, a typical technique could be:

1)   Write your program, with all the drawing instructions.

2)   Test that it works - and the drawings appear as required.

3)   Add commands to *save* the windows and bitmaps, either placed soon after the required drawings have been created, or as a 'called' procedure.

4)   Translate and run the program again.

5)   Check that the required files have been saved: you can do this by

a) switching to the system screen

b) pressing the TAB key whilst over any file name

c) use the arrow keys to select the '\' symbol at the top of the file listing

d) press the ENTER key, then use the arrow keys to select the '\OPD\' directory (or whichever directory you used to save the files).

e) press the ENTER key again: you should see a listing of all the files in that directory - and your newly saved file.

6)   Make the 'drawing' and 'saving' lines of your program 'REMarks', by adding the word REM at the beginning of each line. Before the drawing sections of your program, add commands to *load* the relevant bitmaps and, if necessary, create windows and copy the bitmaps to them.

7)   Test the program again. If it works, you can delete all of the drawing and save commands completely.

Let us put this to the test. First, enter the following procedure

```
PROC mapsave:
 LOCAL c%,id%,g%
 id%=gCREATE(10,10,235,93,1,1)
 gBORDER 0
 DO
  gGREY g%
  DO
   gAT c%*3+(g%*4),c%+(g%*4)
   gBOX 20,20
   c%=c%+10
  UNTIL c%>=80
  g%=g%+1
  c%=0
 UNTIL g%=2
 BUSY "Press a key"
 GET
 BUSY OFF
ENDP
```

That's the first step: you have created a window with a simple border, and filled it with a few boxes, using black and grey planes. (The command to create boxes is dealt with in detail in the next Chapter). Translate and run it, to prove it works.

Now edit the program by adding a line after the GET function and before the BUSY OFF statement, as follows

```
gSAVEBIT "boxes"
```

then translate and run the program again. This time, you should have a bitmap file called 'boxes' saved in memory. Check it out as previously detailed: it should be in the '\OPD\' directory.

Now edit the program again, so that it looks like this (notice the changes to id%()), and that g% is no longer needed:

```
PROC mapsave:
  LOCAL c%,id%(3)
  id%(1)=gLOADBIT("boxes",1,0)
  id%(2)=gLOADBIT("boxes",1,1)
  id%(3)=gCREATE(10,10,235,93,1,1)
  gUSE id%(3)
  gGREY 0
  gCOPY id%(1),0,0,235,93,0
  gGREY 1
  gCOPY id%(2),0,0,235,93,0
REM gBORDER 0
REM DO
REM   gGREY g%
REM   DO
REM     gAT c%*3+(g%*4),c%+(g%*4)
REM     gBOX 20,20
REM     c%=c%+10
REM   UNTIL c%>=80
REM   g%=g%+1
REM   c%=0
REM UNTIL g%=2
  BUSY "Press a key"
  GET
REM   gSAVEBIT "Myboxes"
ENDP
```

Translate and run this - and you should get the same box display as before (*including* the border, even though it has been REM'd out. The border is saved as part of the bitmap). Once that has been proved, you can delete all the statement lines with a REM in front: they're no longer needed. Then translate and test it again.

The revised program is a few lines shorter - and should be a tad quicker in displaying the 'picture'. The real benefit, of course, is that once saved, your pictures can be used in *any* program that you write.

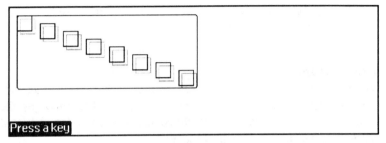

The Mapsave program, with the 'boxes' file restored.

Speeding up graphic displays

The Series 3a usually updates the screen whenever something is displayed to it. You can cause the screen to be updated less frequently by using the gUPDATE command.

gUPDATE OFF	switches off continuous updating.
gUPDATE	causes the screen to be updated.
gUPDATE ON	returns the display to normal continuous updating

The use of these commands can result in a speed improvement when a large number of graphics instructions are used. However, with gUPDATE OFF, the location of errors can be reported incorrectly: it is advisable, therefore, to use the command only when your program is in the final stages of development.

CHAPTER 22
Drawing things

This Chapter deals with the graphics commands available for drawing. The OPL words covered are
gBOX, gDRAWOBJECT, gFILL, gGMODE, gINVERT, gLINEBY, gLINETO, gPOLY.

Setting the mode

You have seen (Chapter 18) that the way the graphics print commands work - whether they set or clear pixels - can be determined by the command gTMODE. There is a similar command to control the way that the Series 3a *drawing* commands operate.

gGMODE mode%   This command determines the way that the subsequent drawing commands work in the *current* window: if you change the window, then for the new window you will have to use gGMODE again to set the way the drawing commands work in *that* window. The action depends on the value of mode%, as follows

mode% Value	Pixels are
0	Set (darkened)
1	Cleared
2	Inverted

The default condition, if you don't use the command, is '0' - that is, the pixels are darkened. Normally speaking, you would use a value of 1 for mode% if you want to clear existing lines, or create white lines in an already darkened area. A mode% value of 2 would be used if you want a line to appear across darkened and clear areas.

Drawing the line

There are two ways to set the position or pixel where the next graphics command will operate from. There is the *absolute* way, using gAT, which takes the co-ordinates you give as being absolute positions in the current window, with '0,0' being in the top left corner. Then there is the *relative* way, using gMOVE, which takes the co-ordinates you give and adds them to the current position in the window.

For most drawing situations, the gMOVE option is probably to be preferred, since it makes the construction of drawings easier. You don't have to worry so much about where in the window a line, for example, is to end, only how long the line is to be. Also, it is easier to define particular shapes by the relative positions of each line within the shape - and to position (or re-position) that shape as an entity by simply resetting the start position.

Note that any part of a drawing or text that is positioned outside the area of the current window simply isn't seen.

Three commands are available to enable you to draw straight lines in any direction, in the window plane(s) determined by gGREY.

gLINETO x%, y%   This is the way to draw lines from one *absolute* position within a window, to another *absolute* position. The start position is the current pixel location, as may have been determined by gAT or gMOVE, for example. The end position is determined by x% and y%, which give the horizontal and vertical co-ordinates respectively. The pixel at the *current* location can be switched on (or off, depending on gGMODE) by giving x% and y% the values for the current location. For example,

```
gAT 40,50
gLINETO 40,50
```

would set the pixel at the point 40 across and 50 down in the current window.

When the line is drawn, the location for the next graphic command is the point at the *end* of the line: in other words, the location specified by x% and y%.

gLINEBY dx%, dy%   This command draws a line from the current pixel location to a *relative* location determined by dx% and dy%. The value of dx% determines how many pixels away the line will end in the horizontal direction: with negative values the end point is to the left of the start point, while with positive values the end point is to the right. Similarly, dy% determines how many pixels away the vertical end point will be from the start position. Negative values position the end point towards the top, while positive values move it down.

The pixel at the current location can be set (or reset, depending on gGMODE) by using zero values for dx% and dy% - thus

```
gLINEBY 0,0
```

This is obviously a far simpler method than using gLINETO, since you don't have to worry about the current location. When the line is drawn, the end position of the line becomes the *new* current pixel location for further graphics commands.

gPOLY *a% ()*   There will undoubtedly be occasions when you will want to draw a series of connecting lines. You could do this using a series of gLINEBY line drawing commands. There is, however, an alternative, and that is to use an array to hold all of your line drawing information, and to use the gPOLY command.

The command works in much the same way as gLINEBY and gMOVE, that is to say, each point position is determined as a *relative* location to the previous point. It also allows you to move to a new position, without drawing a line. First, however, let us examine the way that you set up the array *a% ()* to draw your shape. The number of 'elements' in the array will be 3 plus *twice* the number of points in your drawing, and the array is set up as follows:

a%(1)   Holds the starting *horizontal* position.
a%(2)   Holds the starting *vertical* position.
a%(3)   Holds the number of *points* that will be defined.
a%(4)   Holds *twice* the dx% value for the first point.
a%(5)   Holds the dy% value for the first point.
a%(6)   Holds *twice* the dx% value for the second point.
a%(7)   Holds the dy% value for the second point.
              ... and so on.

You'll notice that the *start* location has to be specified for this command: in this respect, the first two elements of the array behave rather like the gAT command. When the line has been completed, the *current* location is returned to the *start* location. In other words, when the command has been executed, the values in a%*(1)* and a%*(2)* determine the new current pixel location.

It was stated earlier that this command could be used to *move* to the new location as well as *draw* the line. How does it know the difference? The answer is in the way that you define the values for all of the dx% (horizontal) positions.

To draw a line the dx% values (only) must be multiplied by two.

To simply move to the new position the dx% value must be multiplied by two, and then have '1' added to it. Series 3a knows that a line is not to be drawn because it sees an *odd* number for dx%.

Thus a dy% value of 50, and a dx% value of 20*2 will target the point 50 pixels down and *20* pixels to the right, and will draw a line to that point, which then becomes the current pixel location. If the dx% value were made 20*2+1, then the targeted point will become the new current point, but a line will *not* be drawn. Remember though that once the command has been executed, it is the *start* location that becomes the current location for further graphics commands.

Here is how this command can be used to draw two diamond shapes.

```
PROC diamonds:
      GLOBAL a%(11)
      draw:(50,10)
      draw:(75,10)
      GET
ENDP

PROC draw:(dx%,dy%)
      a%(1)=dx%
      a%(2)=dy%
      a%(3)=4                    REM The number of points being plotted
      a%(4)=-30*2
      a%(5)=30
```

241

```
        a%(6)=30*2
        a%(7)=30
        a%(9)=-30
        a%(10)=-30*2
        a%(11)=-30
        gPOLY a%()
ENDP
```

Notice how, as with the other line drawing commands, a negative value for dx% moves the horizontal point to the left, and a negative value for dy% moves the vertical point upwards. Notice too that all of the *horizontal* values (the even elements of the array, from element '4' onwards) are multiplied by two.

When you have run this program, edit a%(4) by adding one to the statement line (a%(4)=-30*2+1), then translate and run it again. This time, you'll see that the shape is the same, but the line referenced by a%(4) hasn't been drawn.

The operation of a gPOLY command is faster than a series of gLINEBY and gMOVE commands, although you do need to take a little care in setting it up. In particular, remember to define the array with sufficient elements, and to ensure you set the element '*a%(3)*' to the correct number of points or pairs of offset co-ordinates.

Boxing clever

By drawing lines or by using gPOLY, you could construct box shapes - oblongs or squares. OPL however provides five different types of box drawing command, to make life easier.

gBOX *width%,height%*   This draws a box that is *width%* pixels wide and *height%* pixels deep, in the current window, with the top left corner at the current pixel location. The lines are drawn according to the setting of gGMODE, if present for the current window, and in the window plane determined by gGREY, (provided that both planes are in use).

Once the box has been drawn, the *starting* point is again made the current point for further graphics commands.

gFILL `width%,height%,mode%` This fills a rectangle `width%` pixels wide and `height%` pixels deep in the current window and the selected plane, starting from the current position. How it is filled is determined by `mode%`, which operates in the same way as gGMODE. Thus, a value of '0' darkens the filled area, a value of '1' clears the area, and a value of '2' inverts the area - clears all the darkened pixels, and darkens all the clear pixels. Because of the presence of the `mode%` argument, the gGMODE command *has no effect on* gFILL. The current cursor position is unchanged: it remains at the top left corner of the filled area.

gINVERT `width%,height%` This operates rather like gFILL with the *mode* set to '2' - the pixels are inverted within the defined area. The difference is that the four corner pixels are left clear to give a slightly 'rounded' effect.

gDRAWOBJECT `type%,flag%,width%,height%`

This command produces a box with rounded corners, a drop shadow with a highlight on the top and left edges, and filled in grey: the window in which it appears *must* have been created with a grey plane. (For the default window, use the DEFAULTWIN 1 command). The top left corner of the box is at the current cursor location within the window.

type% defines the type of object drawn: for the Series 3a, this argument is academic, since only one type is available - '0'. Thus the value for `type%` will always be a zero - unless further types have been added in subsequent models.

flags% defines the 'roundness' of the corners, as follows:
0   normal
1   more rounded
2   a single pixel is removed from the corners.

width% and **height%** determine the size of the box, in pixels

Here is a short program that demonstrates the use of gDRAWOBJECT, and shows how to produce lettering with a drop shadow.

```
PROC drawobj:
      LOCAL flags%
      DEFAULTWIN 1
      gDRAWOBJECT 0,2,300,120
      gFONT 12
      gSTYLE 9
      gAT 100,70
      gGREY 2
      gPRINT "S H A D O W S !"
      gTMODE 1
      gAT 97,67
      gPRINT "S H A D O W S !"
      GET
ENDP
```

Producing drop shadow lettering in a shaded box

Remember too that the **gBORDER** command, discussed in Chapter 20, can be used to create boxes within windows as well as providing a border for the window. When used to create a box within a window area, gBORDER also allows you to have drop shadows.

CHAPTER 23
Clocks

This Chapter deals with the many ways you can have a clock displayed in your programs. The OPL words covered is
gCLOCK

Time on your hands

You will be well aware that your Series 3a can display a digital or analog clock - in various different sizes and forms. You can have a display of a clock or clocks in your own programs - and can even reproduce the Status window on the right hand side which shows the current time, date and an icon indicating the current function or program in use (this is covered in the next Chapter).

With this facility you can, for example, show the time in two or more places in the world simultaneously, rather than having to select them individually in the 'World' function. Or you can give your programs the same 'feel' as the Series 3a's facilities, where the system time panel can be made to appear (or disappear) 'permanently' by pressing the CONTROL and MENU keys. (It will always appear temporarily when the PSION and MENU keys are pressed).

Choice of clock style and size

OPL offers you an extremely wide choice of both *digital* and *analog* clocks - in a variety of sizes and forms. Depending on the type of clock you select, you can have the date, seconds and am/pm information also displayed.

Digital clocks will use the 24-hour or 12-hour format depending on the setting in the TIME application (Settings Menu, Time format option). The choice of a *system* digital or analog clock is made from the System screen, Control menu, Status Window option.

Whatever the clock type selected, it is displayed in the top left corner of the *current* window: you can have only one clock displayed in a window. Also, clocks that include grey in their design *can* be used in windows that have been created without a grey plane.

All the different clock styles and types available are generated by the
gCLOCKS command, which can be used in a variety of formats, as
follows.

gCLOCK ON,*mode%,offset%,format$,font%,style%*
     The formats you can use for this command are as follows.
Note that the *format$*, *font%* and *style%* arguments
are for a formatted digital clock only (mode%=10): for this
reason, the actual *value* for mode% is used in the following
format options.

```
gCLOCK ON
gCLOCK ON,mode%
gCLOCK ON,mode%,offset%
gCLOCK ON,10,offset%,format%
gCLOCK ON,10,offset%,format$,font%
gCLOCK ON,10,offset%,format$,font%,style%
gCLOCK OFF
```

If you simply use the gCLOCK ON command, you will get a
small analog clock showing the hour and minute, positioned
in the top left corner of the current window.

The *mode%* argument allows you to select a *type* of clock, as
follows

mode% value	Clock type
1*	Small digital, black only
2*	Medium size digital or analog according to system setting, black only
3*	Medium sized analog, black only
4*	Medium sized digital, black only
5*	Large analog, black only
6	Medium sized digital or analog according to system setting, black and grey.
7	Medium sized analog, black and grey
8	Medium digital, black and grey
9	Extra large analog, black and grey
10	Formatted digital clocks: this mode also requires the *offset%* and *format$* arguments.

* These modes provide compatibility with the Series 3

You can also use combinations of the hexadecimal values $10, $20, $40 and $80 to OR with the value of *mode%* to add features or produce different effects: however, the features or effects produced are not available for all modes, as the following table shows:

Hex value	Modes used with	Effect
$10	2 to 8	Shows the date
$20	1, 5, 6 (if analog), 7, 9	Shows seconds
$40	1,2, 3, 4	Shows am or pm
$80	1, 2, 3, 4, 5, 8, 10	Shows clock in grey plane only

Thus, if *mode%* has a value of $94 ($10+$80+4), you will have a medium sized digital clock displayed together with the date, all in grey, while a *mode%* value of $D4 ($10+$40+$80+4) shows a medium sized digital clock with the date and am or pm, all in grey. ('D' is hexadecimal for 13)

offset%: Normally, the clock will display the time from the current system setting, but you can change this by using the *offset%* argument. The value of *offset%* determines how many *minutes* before (negative values) or ahead (positive values) the time on your clock display will be in relation to system clock. This enables your program to set up a clock representing the time in a different part of the world. Remember that the offset is in minutes, whilst time differences are generally in hours. So for a two hour time difference, *offset%* would have to be 120.

format$*: if you wish to use this argument, then you must also use the offset% argument - assigning it '0' if you don't want a time difference on the clock. *format$ is used with a *mode%* value of 10, to give a digital clock formatted exactly how you want - with text if required. *format$* can be a string of up to 255 characters, and in addition to any text you may wish to have, can contain a variety of different *specifiers* to provide the time and date information required. The specifiers are identified by a '%' sign, or '%*' for an abbreviated form of the information. The specifier letters can be upper or lower case.

Specifier (%)	Displays	Abbreviated form (%*) Displays
%: and %/	Time and date separators	No abbreviated form
%A	'am' or 'pm' text	'a' or 'p'
%D	Day of month as two digits	Leading zeroes removed
%W	Week of the year as two digits	Leading zeroes removed
%M	Month of year as two digits	Leading zeroes removed
%E	Day of week in full	First three letters of week day
%N	Month name in full	First three letters of month
%H	Hour in 24-hour format, two digits	Leading zeroes removed
%I	Hour in 12-hour format, two digits	Leading zeroes removed
%S	Seconds as two digits	Leading zeroes removed
%T	Minutes as two digits	Leading zeroes removed
%X	suffix for day number (1*st*, 2*nd*, etc)	No abbreviated form
%Y	Year as four digits	Year as two digits (no century)

In addition, you can also use numbers - such as %1 - as detailed in the following table. These provide results depending on the setting of the system TIME application (Settings menu, Formats option). The abbreviated forms require the use of *another* specifier rather than an asterisk, and act as 'toggles' affecting the *remainder* of the format string *format$*, or until changed again.

You may wonder why these are provided, since they seem to duplicate the letter specifiers detailed in the previous table - in a more complex way. They enable you to construct your program so that the day-month-year can be in the sequence chosen by a user, so making your program 'international'.

Specifier %	Displays
%1	The *first* item in the Date Format sequence set in the TIME application, as a number.
%2	The *second* item in the Date Format sequence set in the TIME application, as a number
%3	The *third* item in the Date Format sequence set in the TIME application, as a number.
%4	The day or month number, whichever comes *first* in the Date Format sequence set in the TIME application.
%5	The day or month number, whichever comes *second* in the Date Format sequence set in the TIME application.

The variety of abbreviation specifiers available for use with these 'number' specifiers is as follows. Remember that these are 'toggles' acting on all of the ensuing items they affect in the *format$* string: to switch them on, therefore, they can be placed at the *beginning* of the string.

Abbreviation specifier	Affect
%G	Abbreviates the *day*, whether it is a number or a name, and whether it is %1,%2,%3,%4 or %5
%P	Abbreviates the *month* whether it is a number or a name, and whether it is %1,%2,%3,%4 or %5
%U	Abbreviates the year by removing the century, whether it is %1, %2 or %3
%F	Toggles *days* between numeric and name formats, whether they are %1,%2,%3,%4 or %5
%O	Toggles *months* between numeric and name formats, whether they are %1,%2,%3,%4 or %5
%L	Toggles the *suffix* on a day *number*, whether it is %1,%2,%3,%4 or %5

The time can also be defined within the *format$* string, of course, as follows.

If a 12 hour format has been set in the TIME application
%6 sets the hour and
%7 sets am or pm

If a 24-hour format has been set in the TIME application
%6 sets the hour and %7 has no effect.

Here are a couple of examples.

First, assuming that the DATE FORMAT has been set to Day-Month-Year and the TIME FORMAT has been set to am/pm, **gCLOCK ON,10,0,*format$***, with *format$* =:

```
"Today is %E the %D%X of %N, %Y"
```
the display is of the form

Today is Monday the 15th of May, 1995

and

```
"Today is %*E the %*D%X of %N, '%*Y"
```
displays

Today is Mon the 15th of May, '95

Secondly, assuming the DATE FORMAT is set to Month-Day-Year, and the TIME FORMAT is set to am/pm, with *format$* =

```
"%F%U It is %6%:%T%7 on %E, %F%L%O%1 %2, '%3"
```

you get

It is 10.45am on Monday, May 15th, '95

If the DATE FORMAT is then set to Day-Month-Year, the same *format$* will produce:

It is 10.45am on Monday, 15th May, '95

As you can see, there is an extremely extensive variety of ways you can display a date and time message. And it doesn't end there! If *format$* is specified, you can also optionally specify a value for *font%*, and if you specify a value for *font%*, you can also set a style with *style%*! The values and effects for these are the same as for gFONT and gSTYLE, discussed in Chapter 18. For example, add "12,10" to the end of your gCLOCK...format$ line, to produce a large, underlined san serif display.

To switch off a clock display, use the gCLOCK OFF command.

Here's a program that sets up a display of four large clocks, to show the time in four different places round the world. The way this program is written, you can easily modify it to have your own four places, if you wish: simply enter the place name for the appropriate element of variable place$(*x*), with the time difference in the associated element of variable td%(*x*).

```
PROC clocks
LOCAL id%(4),c%,place$(4,12),td%(4)
place$(1)="London"
td%(1)=0
place$(2)="New York"
td%(2)=-5
place$(3)="Athens"
td%(3)=2
place$(4)="Perth"
td%(4)=8
c%=1
DO
```

```
            id%(c%)=gCREATE(115*(c%-1),0,105,140,1,1)
            gCLOCK ON,$29,td%(c%)*60
            gBORDER 3
            gAT 20,120
            gPRINT place$(c%)
            c%=c%+1
        UNTIL c%=5
        GET
ENDP
```

Notice how arrays can help to shorten and simplify the program (they save having to set each clock, and name the places individually). The use of arrays also makes it easier for places and time differences to be entered from a dialog, if you wished.

You'll see, too, that the array counter (c%) is also used to position the windows for each particular clock when it is created, thus saving the need to create each window separately. The ability to use loops to undertake a repetitive series of instructions is another advantage of having *arrays* for related groups of variables.

There is no need to use the gUSE command in this program, since a window is automatically made *current* when it is created. As mentioned earlier, the clocks are displayed in the very top left corner of the current window: on initiation, the gBORDER command will 'overwrite' the edges of the clock and so will be complete. But when the clock is updated, which for the clocks used in this program is every second, the clock will 'overwrite' the border and clear a part of it in the process. So don't be surprised or think your Series 3a is cracking up!

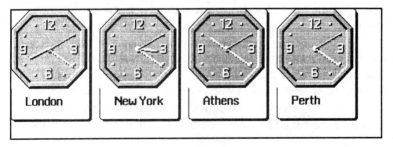

The Clocks program

CHAPTER 24
The status window

This Chapter discusses the Status window display. The OPL words covered are:
DIAMINIT, DIAMPOS, STATUSWIN, STATWININFO

About the status window

The status window is always available for temporary display in your programs, without you having to do anything: the PSION and MENU keys pressed together will bring up the display for a few moments. This brief display is 'on top' of all other windows, so that it can be seen. However, you may choose to have the status window available for permanent display, on demand by the user. Ideally, you would arrange for the same key combination to do this as other Series 3a applications: CONTROL and MENU.

Unlike the windows that you can create in your programs, the status window you generate has no 'reference' number, and unlike the temporary status window display, it *always* appears at the very 'back' of the screen. This means *any* of your windows that occupy the same area will cover it up: 'any' includes the text screen and the default graphics window (number 1).

It is therefore up to your program to ensure that, when and if the status window is called for, all windows (including the text and default graphics windows) are moved out of the way.

Your program can tackle this by using the gSETWIN and SCREEN commands which, you may recall, allow the size of the graphic and text windows to be changed as well as their positions. If only the default window is being used, you could use the FONT command (after the status window has been created) - which will automatically resize the default window so that the text displays will fit the new area. Using FONT -$3fff,0 will retain the current font and style whilst resizing (and clearing) the text and graphic window, so you don't have to work out anything at all.

When (and if) the status window is removed, you will probably want the windows to resume their original size. You could do this by using *actual* values in your program: all you need to do is keep check of the various locations that the windows can have.

However, in a program which allows the windows to be moved around by the user, and for making program changes, it is probably better to store the window location information in array variables, to be used when required. You can use the gINFO function to get all of the information about a current window display, and there is a similar function available to obtain information about the status window.

Any program can be made to have the status window appear.

What's in the status window?

By default, the status window displays the OPL program name (which you can change), the OPL 'running' icon (which also can be changed when you use an *OPA* type of program that has its own icon), a clock (digital or analogue, as selected in the system options), plus all of the other options that may have been selected in the STATUS WINDOW option of the Control menu item in the system screen. An *OPA* type of program is one that is installed as an application in the main system display, and consequently appears on the main system screen. The techniques for doing this are discussed in Part 3 of this book.

You can also choose to use the 'diamond' display in the status window - similar to that used, for example, in the Data or Diary applications - to switch between different parts of the program, different views, different modes, and so on. In some respects, the diamond display is akin to a special menu, with the options selected by the diamond key on the keyboard.

As previously mentioned, the status window is quite separate from the other windows, and is unaffected by many of the window controlling OPL language words - gRANK and gORDER, for example.

Creating a status window display

The command for creating a status window is STATUSWIN.

STATUSWIN ON, type%   This displays a 'narrow' status window (type%=1) - which has a small digital clock and abbreviated information, or the wider status window (type%=2). You can also use the command STATUSWIN

253

ON without the *type%* argument, to produce the wider window.

To get information about a status display's size and type, in order to set the position of other windows so that they don't cover it up, use the STATWININFO function.

STATWININFO(*type%*,*vinfo%()*) As a function, the format is

curtype%=STATWININFO(*type%*,*vinfo%()*)

You can use this function even if a status display hasn't been created: in such a case, the information it 'returns' will tell you the dimensions of a status window if it *were* to be created. After using the function:

curtype% holds the current *type* of status window being displayed - '1' for small, '2' for large, and '0' if a status window isn't being displayed.

type% must be given a value when the STATWININFO function is used. This should be '1' to return details about the small status display, '2' to return details about the large status display, and '-1' to return details about the *current* status window display. If you use '-1' for the *type%* value and there isn't a display, then the width information will be zero (as you'd expect for something which doesn't exist!), the height will be the full screen height (160 pixels), and the position of the 'non-existent' window will be 1 pixel to the right of the actual screen display. The reason for this will be evident when you see the information returned in the array *vinfo%()*. *type%* can also be given a value of '3': this specifies the status window used by a Series 3, should you be preparing a program that is to be compatible with a Series 3.

vinfo%() This four element array, which *must* have been declared, holds information about the status window display:

vinfo%(1)	The number of pixels from the left of the screen to the left edge of the status window.
vinfo%(2)	The number of pixels from the top of the screen to the status window.
vinfo%(3)	Status window width, in pixels
vinfo%(4)	Status window height, in pixels

Thus, to change the size of a current window so that it is clear of the status window display (or extends to the right of the screen after a status display has been removed), you could use program lines such as:

```
ct%=STATWININFO(-1,vinf%())
gSETWIN x%,y%,vinfo%(1),h%
```

where x% and y% are the horizontal and vertical positions, in pixels of the top left of the window, and h% is the window's height.

As mentioned previously, the text screen can be set to full height and full permissible width - allowing the status window to be displayed if it has been created - by using the command FONT -$3fff: whilst this clears anything that as in the screen, it retains the currently selected font and style for text.

To switch the status window off, use the command

STATUSWIN OFF

If you want the status window to be available 'on demand' by the user (rather than permanently on display throughout your program), then you should ideally use the same key combination as provided by other Series 3a applications (CONTROL and MENU together) to toggle the display on and off. The MENU key returns 290 (into a GET or KEY command), while the CONTROL keypress can be detected with a 'KMOD AND 4' instruction.

Creating a 'diamond' display

To set up a list of 'diamond' options in the status window, use the DIAMINIT command.

DIAMINIT *place%,str1$,str2$...* This command displays a list of items in the status window (replacing any existing list you may have created) as specified by *str1$*, *str2$* and so on, with the 'diamond' marker against the item that is in the *place%* position. The top position is '1' - and the items are displayed in the order that you list them. If *place%*=0 (or is not supplied), then the list is not displayed. If it is '-1', then the program icon is displayed (large status window) instead of the diamond list. If it is greater than the number of items in the list, then the last item in the list is displayed.

Remember that the status window display is of a fixed width (wide or narrow), and so if any *str$* item is too long, the end characters won't be seen.

You can subsequently change the position of the 'diamond' in the listing (as you will need to do if the DIAMOND key is pressed), by using the DIAMPOS command.

DIAMPOS *place%*   This simply sets the diamond marker to the *place%* position within the list. If *place%* = 0, then the diamond marker simply disappears. If it is greater than the number of items in the list created with DIAMINIT, then the diamond marker is positioned alongside the last item in the list.

If your program uses the diamond display within the status box, it will obviously need to detect when the diamond key has been pressed. To retain the Series 3a conventions, you should have your program move the pointer down to the next item when the DIAMOND key is pressed on its own, and moved back to the previous item if the DIAMOND and SHIFT keys are pressed together. Pressing the DIAMOND key when it is at the last item on the list should make it wrap round to the first item - and similarly, it should move from the first item to the last if the DIAMOND and SHIFT keys are pressed.

The code value returned (when using GET, for example), when the diamond key is pressed is 292: use KMOD to detect whether the SHIFT key has also been pressed (KMOD AND 2).

As well as shifting the diamond up or down, your program should also carry out the option selected by the diamond, of course!

If you wish to display the diamond symbol (♦) - in a menu, perhaps - the character code is '4' (thus PRINT CHR$(4) will display a diamond).

Here is a program which demonstrates the use of the status window and diamond displays. It creates two full screen windows (making three, with the default screen), and displays a simple message on each. The DIAMOND key is used to select a window and bring it to the top of the screen, irrespective of whether the status window is on display. Each press selects the next window: SHIFT and DIAMOND keys pressed together select the previous window. Pressing the E key allows you to make a simple edit to the message on display. Finally, pressing the CONTROL and MENU keys brings in the status window display - first the small window, then the larger window, then the status window is 'hidden' behind the other windows (rather than switching it off). A further press of CONTROL and MENU keys brings up the small window display again, and so on.

To quit the program, press the ESC key.

It is a fairly long program with a number of procedures, all of which must be entered - into the same file - before the program can be translated and run. Nevertheless, it will be well worthwhile entering and trying out (before removing it from your Series 3a), as it shows typical processes involved in creating the status window and diamond displays. Some particular points to note are given in the notes following the program. You don't have to enter any of the Remarks made in the program: they're there for guidance only.

```
PROC statdemo:
 LOCAL k%,d%,m%
 GLOBAL msg$(3,24),dia$(3,1)
 GLOBAL id%(3),dp%,sw%
 msg$(1)="This is Window A"
 msg$(2)="This is Window B"
 msg$(3)="This is Window C"
 dia$(1)="A"
 dia$(2)="B"
 dia$(3)="C"
 dp%=1
 creatwin:
 prmsgs:
 poswin:
 DIAMINIT dp%,dia$(1),dia$(2),dia$(3)

 DO                             REM Main Program loop
  k%=KEY
  m%=KMOD                       REM See Note 1
  IF (k%=290) AND (m%=4)        REM Menu+Control keys
   statwin:
  ELSEIF (k%=292) AND (m%=2)    REM Diamond+Shift keys
   diadisp:(-1)
```

```
  ELSEIF k%=292
   diadisp:(1)
  ELSEIF k%=%e OR k%=%E            REM for editing the message
   dINIT "Edit Window Text"
   dEDIT msg$(dp%),"Current:"
   DIALOG
   prmsgs:
  ENDIF
 UNTIL k%=27
ENDP

PROC creatwin:                    REM create 2 more windows
 id%(2)=gCREATE(0,0,480,160,1,1)
 id%(3)=gCREATE(0,0,480,160,1,1)
ENDP

PROC prmsgs:
 LOCAL c%
 DO
  c%=c%+1
  gUSE c%
  gAT 182,75
  gPRINTB msg$(c%),200,2
 UNTIL c%=3
ENDP

PROC statwin:
 LOCAL c%
 sw%=sw%+1
 IF sw%=3                         REM See Note 2
  sw%=0
 ENDIF
 IF sw%=0                         REM See Note 3
  resize:
 ELSE
  STATUSWIN ON,sw%
 ENDIF
 resize:
ENDP

PROC diadisp:(ud%)
 LOCAL c%
 dp%=dp%+ud%                      REM Update diamond position
 IF dp%=4
```

```
   dp%=1
ELSEIF dp%=0
   dp%=3
ENDIF
DIAMPOS dp%                         REM Renew diamond display
poswin:                             REM Put window on top
ENDP

PROC resize:                        REM Resize windows
 LOCAL st%,swinfo%(4)
  st%=STATWININFO(sw%,swinfo%())
  st%=1
  DO
   gUSE st%
   gCLS
   gSETWIN 0,0,swinfo%(1),160
   gBORDER 2
   prmsgs:
   st%=st%+1
  UNTIL st%=4
ENDP

PROC poswin:
 gORDER dp%,1
ENDP
```

Note 1   You may wonder why, the first 'IF' statement line doesn't read
`IF (k%=290) AND (KMOD=4)`
Once KMOD has 'shed' the value it has stored, it cannot be used again - and it is needed in a subsequent test. Hence the value is first stored in another variable, m%.

Note 2   There are three states for the status window, 0, 1 and 2. The state is incremented every time a status key combination is pressed: after the third press, it must be switched off and reset to zero.

Note 3   If the status window flag (sw%) is zero, it means 'switch off' the status display. You could use STATUSWIN OFF, followed by a 'resize' operation on the other windows. However, since the other windows will hide the status

259

window when resized to the full screen width, there is no need to switch it off.

Now for a brief explanation of each of the procedures.

PROC statdemo: This is the main controlling procedure, which 'drives' the other procedures. It starts by declaring all the variables and assigning the initial values, the 'calls' the creatwin procedure to create two windows, and the prmsgs procedure to print the messages on each screen so that you know which screen is which. The programming controlling loop is then entered - checking for the various key presses, and exiting when the ESC key is pressed. The appropriate procedures are called according to the key presses made: if an 'edit' operation is requested, a simple dialog box is set up. The current window will be on top, as a result of the rest of the program.

PROC creatwin: This simply creates two full screen windows.

PROC prmsgs: This uses a DO...UNTIL loop to print out the messages on each screen. Notice that the window to be 'written to' must first be specified with a gUSE command. gPRINTB is used since this command clears a box first: gPRINT on its own will simply overprint anything that's there.

PROC diadisp: This procedure adjusts the diamond position (if the status window is being displayed), by assigning the appropriate value to the diamond position variable dp%. The value to 'add' or subtract' is passed into the procedure as a parameter from the main program control loop in the first procedure. Having repositioned the diamond against the appropriate item - the selected window is positioned 'at the top' by a call to the poswin procedure.

PROC resize: This procedure is called whenever the status window keys are pressed. First, information is obtained about the current status window (stored in sw%, though you could use '-1' here). The variable st% is not required any further - the information required is in the array swinfo%() - and so it is used as a counter for the loop that resizes the three windows. When this procedure is called, it means a status window has been requested (or is being hidden), and so a border is drawn round the windows so that you can see what is happening. The screens must be cleared first - otherwise part of the border drawing is left during subsequent resizing operations - and since each window is cleared, it is necessary to re-display the messages by a call to the prmsgs procedure.

PROC poswin: This procedure simply positions the window selected by the diamond key operation to the top of the display: the window is identified by the value of the diamond position flag, dp%.

You'll no doubt have noticed that the window id array (id%) wasn't used in this program, apart from assigning to it the identification number for each window. It was included primarily to show how it is done: your programs may need to keep track of window id's, and this array can help in that task.

The techniques used in this program are by no means the only ones available to you, but they should give you an of how to prepare programs of a similar nature.

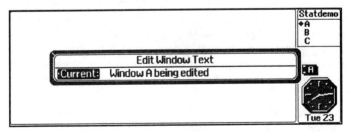

The Statdemo program in use

CHAPTER 25
Creating menus

*This Chapter discusses the process of creating menus
like those Series 3a uses, and introduces a different way
to call procedures. The OPL words covered are*
mCARD, MENU *and* mINIT.

What's on the menu?

The last Chapter showed how the DIAMOND key can be used to select
from a number of items, with the list of items in the status window
display. However, choice is on a rotation basis, and as you will be
aware, the Psion Series 3a has another way to show a variety of options
that can be selected - the menuing system.

Menus make choosing from a variety of functions and operations a
simple process. You can write menus with the same look and feel as
those provided by the Series 3a menus. You can make your menu
'active' as part of the natural running of a program, or arrange for it to
'pop up' when the MENU key is pressed. When a menu is displayed,
the options can be selected by using the arrow keys and pressing
ENTER. Alternatively an option can be selected by pressing a short-cut
key combination (which you must define). Your program can act on the
short-cut keys even when the menu isn't being displayed (just as the
DIAMOND key options are selected even though the status window
may not be displayed). Clearing a menu from the display without
selecting an option is achieved by pressing the ESC key.

Menu displays appear 'over the top' or in front of any other display
on the screen at the time. When they are cleared, the original display is
restored.

A menu comprises a list of main 'subject' headings across the top
of the screen, rather like the 'tabs' on a card filing system. Each tab has
its own 'drop-down' options, which appear when the tab is selected. In
fact it's all the same as the menus provided by Series 3a applications.

There are three steps to creating a menu:

a)   Get the Series 3a ready to receive a new menu operation, using the mINIT command. Only one menu 'set' can be used at a time.

b)   Define the menu options using mCARD commands: a separate command is needed for each 'subject' option you want at the top of the screen, and you can have up to eight.

c)   'Switch on' the menu display, using the MENU function.

Naturally, you would group associated options under one 'subject' heading at the top of the screen. The commands concerned are:

mINIT   Series 3a needs a section of memory devoted to the creation and display of menu items. You have to tell it to abandon the current menu information, and prepare for new information: mINIT is the command that does this. It cancels any existing menu, and prepares Series 3a to receive information about your new menu.

mCARD *head$, opt1$, key1%, opt2$, key2%...opt8$, key8%*

The first item, *head$*, is a string variable or literal that gives the name of *a single* menu option on the top line of the display. You need an mCARD command for each option you want displayed at the top of the screen. You can have as many mCARD commands as *head$* names will fit across the top of the screen, up to a maximum of eight: if the names you choose are, together, greater than the width of the screen, you will get an error when the program is run.

Number of options: You can have up to eight items named on the drop-down part of the menu, specified by the string variables or literals *opt1$, opt2$,* and so on. Each item *must* be associated with the *character code* for a short-cut key, defined by the variables *key1%* and so on.

Short cut keys: The short-cut key is the one that can be pressed, together with the PSION key, to select the particular menu option (without having to use the MENU key, if you program for it!).

Thus, if you want the short-cut key for the first item to be the lower case letter 'a', `key1%` would be '97'. You could also write this as ASC("a"), or, the easiest way of all, as %a, to save looking up the *character code*, and to make your program easier to understand when checking it through.

You should be aware that 'A' and 'a' are *not* the same as far as short-cut keys are concerned, *even though the capital letter* is shown along with the PSION key as the hot key combination in the menu display. The capital letter has the code '65' - but, as just mentioned, the easiest way to choose the capital letter 'A' is to use the '%A' construction. If a capital letter is used, then the SHIFT key must be pressed as well as the PSION and chosen letter keys, to select the particular option: the hot key display in the menu shows that SHIFT must also be pressed. This increases the range of hot keys you can use. You must avoid using exactly the same hot key twice, of course - not surprisingly, your program won't be able to differentiate between them, and only one of the two actions will be performed.

> **Note:** Unfortunately, techniques which make it easy to branch off to other procedures depending on the selected item *don't* differentiate between upper and lower case letters - so if you do use both, your program will have to cater for them in a rather long-winded manner.

Although almost the entire keyboard is available for use as short-cut keys, those that can be used with the PSION key to produce a character (indicated by the yellow letters or symbols above the keys) are best avoided.

Separating the options: You can have a greyed line under a group of options, by making the hot key assignment negative. Thus, to have a greyed line under an option `"Copy",%c`, you would write instead `"Copy",-%c`. This is useful for dividing a series of options into groups.

In most instances, you will be able to choose a short-cut key related to the function it selects. Thus, if the option is 'Edit', you would probably choose the short-cut key 'e' or 'E'.

MENU   This function 'switches' the menu display on. The format is

m%=menu

where m% holds the character code for the hot key associated with the item that is selected from the menu.

All of the 'subject' headings appear along the top of the screen, with the previously selected 'drop-down option' highlighted, or if it's the first time the menu has been used, the first option under the first heading will be highlighted. If your program uses two or more sets of menus, then the option highlighted will be in the same position as on the previous menu (if that position exists in the new menu). You can avoid this by using the construction

m%=menu(*vinit*%)

where *vinit*% is a variable that must have been previously declared, and which should be unique to the particular menu. When an option is selected, *vinit*% is given a value corresponding to the selected option. The next time the menu is called, the value of *vinit*% determines the option to be highlighted first. The top row of options (that is, the first item under a menu heading) have *vinit*% values ranging from 0 to the number of headings used. The second row of options have values ranging from 256 to the number of headings used - and so on, each option line increasing the value by 256. You could arrange for a particular item to be highlighted every time a menu is first called, by assigning the appropriate value to *vinit*%: if you assign a value for an option that doesn't exist, either the first option under the appropriate heading, or the first option under the first heading will be highlighted.

When the menu is displayed, *any* short-cut key + PSION key combination will clear the menu and return the code for the key pressed. In this instance, the value assigned to *vinit*%, if used, will be zero. If the short-cut key is pressed *without* the PSION key, then the code for that key is returned, as before, but this time the value of *vinit*% will correspond to the selected option.

Note that the short-cut key combinations won't select the actions for an option item when the menu is *not* being displayed unless you specifically program for it to happen.

A simple menu example

A menu can be the main core of your program. You can arrange for it to be displayed as soon the program starts to run: after performing the selected option, the menu would be redisplayed for further action. One of the menu options, of course, must be to quit the program.

This is the simplest way to use a menu: a more complex approach is to have the menu 'pop up' whenever the MENU key is pressed, and to arrange for your program to 'react' when the short-cut key combinations are pressed even though the menu *isn't* being displayed at the time. This approach will be dealt with later.

Here is an example of a simple menu program, which just multiplies or adds any two numbers that you care to input. It uses the form of MENU that allows the initial highlight to be set when the program is initiated. Enter all the procedures of the following program 'menu1' before translating and running it.

```
PROC MENU1:
 GLOBAL fn,sn,init%
 LOCAL k%
 init%=1
 FONT 10,1
 DO
  CLS
  AT 18,9
  PRINT "CHOOSE FROM THE MENU..."
  mINIT
  mCARD "Program","Run",%R,"Quit",%Q
  mCARD "Action","Multiply",%M,"Add",%A
  k%=MENU(init%)
  IF k%=%R
   PRINT "I'm running!"
  ELSEIF k%=%M
   mult:
  ELSEIF k%=%A
   add:
  ELSEIF k%=%Q
   PRINT "OK, I'll quit"
```

```
    GET
    STOP
   ENDIF
  UNTIL k%=%Q OR k%=0
ENDP

PROC add:
  CLS
  getnums:
  PRINT fn,"+",sn,"=",fn+sn
  GET
ENDP

PROC mult:
  CLS
  getnums:
  PRINT fn,"x",sn,"=",fn*sn
  GET
ENDP

PROC getnums:
  PRINT "Enter first number :",
  INPUT fn
  PRINT "Enter second number:",
  INPUT sn
ENDP
```

This program uses capitals for the short-cut keys, and is terminated by selecting 'Quit' from the 'Program' option list (if two items can be called a list!) or pressing SHIFT+PSION+Q: a 'quit' message is given - press enter to actually quit the program. If you press the ESC key whilst the menu is displayed, the 'returned' value is zero: in this instance the 'quit' message will not be displayed.

When you have entered the program and tested it out a few times, edit the line 'IF k%=%R' to read 'IF k%=%r', then translate and run the program again: you will find that, when you select the MENU 'Run' option, the action required *won't* be performed. This shows that it is important to keep your short-cut keys consistently the same throughout the program.

This program uses a series of IF statements to test which particular action has been selected. However, the Series 3a offers another way to call procedures, which can save having to use a whole string of IF statements.

Another way to call procedures

If your overall menu has a large number of options, then you will be faced with an equally large number of 'IF' statements in order to cater for the action required for each. Good programming practice would require that each IF statement would simply call a relevant procedure.

However, OPL allows you to call a procedure *whose name is stored in a string variable*. If the variable is called *procnam$*, and *procnam$* holds the string 'mult' - *without* a colon, note - then you can call it with a statement line such as

$$@(procnam\$):$$

The '@' sign is in effect saying "Call the procedure named in the following brackets". Notice that the colon comes *after* the brackets. It's as if you had written 'mult:' in your program. The advantage, of course, is that the string can be assigned a 'name' according to the operation of the program, *without* necessarily having to make a whole series of tests. We'll see how this works in a moment.

This technique can also be used for functions which 'return' values, and for passing values to the functions. The formats under these circumstances are as follows:

```
r%=@%(procnam$):( parameter list )
r&=@&(procnam$):( parameter list )
r$=@$(procnam$):( parameter list )
 r=@(procnam$):( parameter list )
```

Note the use of the 'identifier' following the '@' symbol in each case - as well as in the variable that will hold the 'returned' value. The identifier must *not* be included as part of the *procnam$* variable.

Obviously any variables used must have been declared as LOCALs or GLOBALs, and string variables must have been declared sufficiently large to hold any information they're likely to carry.

You may wonder how this technique can help: it looks fairly complicated at first sight, and let's face of it, one has to somehow or other create the 'contents' of the *procnam$* variable for each procedure that is likely to be called.

In practice, this is not as difficult as you might imagine. In the menu1 procedure, a test had to be made to discover which option had been selected, by examining the integer value returned: this is always the *character code* for the key press, remember, that is associated with the option. Thus, the IF statements tested for the codes of each character in the short-cut key list.

With the '@' technique, instead of testing for the *character code*, the returned value can be converted into a *character*, and the character can be then be used to call the required procedure. This way, one line can replace a whole range of IF statements.

However, you must remember that if a short-cut key combination that *hasn't* been catered for is used whilst the menu is on display, the code returned will be for a key which isn't associated with a procedure. You must allow for such cases, if you don't want a '**Procedure not found**' error to stop the program from running.

There are (at least) two ways to do this. One is to use the ONERR command to trap any error. The other is to ensure, *before* any 'option' procedure is called, that the returned character code is one that you have catered for. These two methods will be covered later in this Chapter.

Selecting options with short-cut keys

MENU1 program showed how to write a program where the menu is displayed automatically after a selected option has been executed.

However, it is probably better if you can arrange your program to act on short-cut key presses even when a menu isn't being displayed, and for the menu to 'pop-up', just as Series 3a menus, when the MENU key is pressed.

The programming necessary for this is a little bit more advanced: the approach can be demonstrated here easily enough, but for large programs you must arrange your 'flow-charts' very carefully, or allow short-cut key or MENU key operations only at specific points or times while the program is running, otherwise the actual flow of the program can get itself in a tangle.

Briefly, at the points in your program where you will 'allow' the menu to be selected, you need to have a test to see whether a key press has been made. You must then determine whether this key press is a short-cut key, the MENU key, or something else to do with the operation of the program.

There are two basic ways to test for a keypress. GET (or GET$), which actually *waits* for a key to be pressed, and KEY (or KEY$), which looks to see if a key has been pressed, but doesn't wait: program execution continues with the next statements. There is also another more advanced method (GETEVENT) which waits for an *event* to occur, of which a key press is one of the possible events. Only the basic methods are discussed here.

If you want your program to continue performing its function without waiting for a key press, then use the KEY command. A typical example could be a game involving movement of an object across the screen, where you may want one of the arrow keys to change the direction of the object's movement. Only when a key is pressed would you want to detect it and make the necessary changes accordingly.

Where the display is 'static', and nothing is expected to occur until a key has been pressed, then use the GET command. An example of this could be a 'conversion' program, where a key press calls up the menu offering different conversion options - or selects the option through short-cut keys, or allows new figures to be entered for the current conversion operation.

When using 'pop-up' menus, at least two tests need to be made: one to check whether the MENU key has been pressed, and one to check whether a short-cut key has been pressed. The MENU key button returns the value '290' in decimal (or $122 in hexadecimal). For short-cut key presses the PSION key (and possibly the SHIFT key) must be pressed. There are two ways to check this: you can use the KMOD function - which will have the '8' bit set for the PSION key, or you can simply see whether '512' (represented by $200 in hexadecimal) has been added to the returned value of the keypress. Either way, since '512' is always added to a key press combination involving the PSION key, this must be deducted from the returned value in order to get the character code for the 'other' key. To see whether the SHIFT key has also been pressed, test the '2' bit of KMOD. Thus, to see whether both the PSION and SHIFT keys are pressed, the test would be

```
IF KMOD AND 10
```

(10, in binary, is 1010 - the 'bits' representing 8 and 2 being 'set')

Where more than one test is to be made on the value of KMOD, it is important to assign its value to another variable first. The reason is, after one test (or assignment) has been made, KMOD reverts to zero. You can check this for yourself with the following short procedure: when translated, run it and press PSION, SHIFT and one of the letter keys simultaneously. Then run it with other key combinations.

```
PROC kmodtest:
 LOCAL k%
 k%=GET
 PRINT "k%=",k%,CHR$(k%)
 PRINT "KMOD first check:",KMOD
 PRINT "KMOD second check:",KMOD
 GET
ENDP
```

Note how '512' is added to the value of k% when the PSION key is pressed together with a letter or number key - and interestingly, how pressing the SHIFT key at the same time as the PSION key yields the *lower* case of the letter key pressed.

The order and the way that tests are made is also quite important. Consider the following sequence, for example.

```
 k%=KMOD
 IF k% AND 8
   do option A
 ELSEIF k% AND 10
   do option B
 ENDIF
```

With this sequence, even if both PSION and SHIFT keys are pressed, option B will never be performed, because the *first* test will prove to be true and, after option A has been executed, program flow will jump to the ENDIF statement. You must make sure that the sequence of tests is logically correct. You *could* use the 'equals' sign instead of AND in this particular construction, but if another modifier key has also been pressed inadvertently, none of the required options will be true.

Pop-up menu program examples

There now follows two examples of 'pop-up' menus, both using the '@' technique for calling procedures. The first uses the ONERR method for detecting invalid procedure names, and the second checks specifically for valid key presses

The ONERR method

With this technique, you must be aware that when ONERR is used, *any* error that occurs will be trapped. (the use of ONERR is a handy way to detect programming errors during the development stages). This demonstration program, which provides the same menu options as the menu1 program, uses the ERR$ and ERR commands to inform of the error that has occurred: if entered exactly as shown, the only error you should get when the program is run is '**Procedure not found**'. Enter all of the procedures in the program before translating and running it: don't enter the REMarks, shown in a different typeface - they're included just to help you understand how the program works. When you run the program, test it by pressing a variety of keys and key combinations, to see what happens.

```
PROC menu2:
 LOCAL c%,m%,msg$(14)
 GLOBAL fn,sn
 msg$="I'm working! "              REM note space after !
 FONT 10,1
 DO                                REM Main program loop
  AT 10,11
  PRINT "Press a key,short cut keys,MENU,or ESC"
  m%=KEY                           REM See if a key was pressed
  IF m%                            REM A key has been pressed
   IF m%=290 OR m% AND $200        REM It's Menu or shortcut key
    domenu:(m%)                    REM    ...so go do it
   ELSE                            REM Otherwise ...
    prmsg:(m%)                     REM ...display the pressed key
   ENDIF
  ENDIF
  c%=c%+1+12*(c%=14)               REM 'Rolling display'
  gAT 190,70
  gPRINTB MID$(msg$,c%,15-c%),120,2
  gAT 190++gTWIDTH(MID$(msg$,c%,15-c%)),70
  gPRINTB MID$(msg$,1,c%),120,2
  PAUSE 4
 UNTIL m%=27                       REM ESC key
 ENDP
```

```
PROC domenu:(m%)                        REM Menu/short-cut keys
 LOCAL k%
 ONERR noproc::                         REM Switch on error check
 IF m% AND $200                         REM $200=Psion key
  k%=m%-$200                            REM See Note 1
  @(CHR$(k%)):                          REM Go to it!
 ELSE                                   REM Must be MENU key
  mINIT                                 REM Display menu
  mCARD "Program","Run",%r,"Quit",%q
  mCARD "Action","Multiply",%m,"Add",%a
  k%=MENU
  IF k%                                 REM i.e. not ESC key
   @(CHR$(k%)):                         REM go to it!
  ELSE                                  REM Must be ESC key
   gAT 185,100
   gPRINTB "Escaped from menu",160,2
  ENDIF
 ENDIF
 RETURN                                 REM Miss out error stuff
noproc::                                REM An error occurred
 ONERR OFF                              REM Switch off checks
 gAT 185,100
 gPRINTB err$(err),160,2                REM and display error
 RETURN                                 REM then go back
ENDP

PROC a:                                 REM The ADD routine
 CLS
 getnums:
 PRINT fn,"+",sn,"=",fn+sn
 GET
 CLS
ENDP

PROC m:                                 REM The MULTIPLY routine
 CLS
 getnums:
 PRINT fn,"x",sn,"=",fn*sn
 GET
 CLS
ENDP

PROC r:
 CLS
```

273

```
PRINT "I'm running! (Press Enter to continue)"
GET
CLS
ENDP

PROC q:
STOP
ENDP

PROC getnums:
PRINT "Enter first number :",
INPUT fn
PRINT "Enter second number:",
INPUT sn
ENDP

PROC prmsg:(v%)
gAT 185,100
IF v%=27
  gPRINTB "You pressed ESCape",160,2
  PAUSE 5                    REM ...to see the message
ELSE
  gPRINTB "You pressed "+CHR$(v%),160,2
ENDIF
ENDP
```

Note 1:   Since m% is passed to the routine as a parameter, its value cannot be changed. Hence its value is assigned to another variable, k%.

Note how the 'rolling message' is achieved using MID$() to split the message, and gTWIDTH to determine where the next part should be printed.

You'll find that when using the short-cut keys, an option can be selected whether the SHIFT key is pressed or not: this is because the '@' command *acts on both the upper or lower case character, treating them as the same. This means that with the '@' method of selecting the procedure to call, you can't use the same letter as a capital and lower case for different options.*

If you use more than one menu in your program and choose to use the '@' method of calling procedures, you must ensure that none of the short-cut key options are duplicated. Alternatively, you can use the '*string concatenation*' technique to build the names up into something else, although the difference between the procedure names will always be in the one character. For example, for each menu you could use something like:

```
k$=CHR$(k%)+"job"
@(k$):
```

(where 'job' is unique to the menu) and the procedures named accordingly - PROC ajob, PROC mjob, and so on. Another menu within the same program would have a different string attached to the short-cut key character, so producing a different set of procedure names.

You will also notice that, if you use short cut keys for which there is no procedure, the error is 'trapped' and a message is displayed. Of course, you needn't display a message in your program - it was included here to show you that the error had been trapped.

The 'valid key press' method

Now here's the same procedure again, but this time using the 'test for a valid key press' technique: the program is identical except for the 'domenu' procedure. Alter domenu to read:

```
PROC domenu:(m%)
 LOCAL k%,t%,sck$(4)
 sck$="amrq"                    REM the vaild key list
 IF m% AND $200                 REM Psion key pressed?
   k%=m%-$200
   t%=LOC(sck$,CHR$(k%))        REM Valid key?
   IF t%                        REM ...yes, a match is found
     @(CHR$(k%)):               REM ...so do it
   ELSE
     RETURN                     REM otherwise, ignore it
   ENDIF
 ELSE
   mINIT
   mCARD "Program","Run",%r,"Quit",%q
   mCARD "Action","Multiply",%m,"Add",%a
   k%=MENU
   IF k%
     @(CHR$(k%)):
   ELSE
     gAT 185,100
     gPRINTB "Escaped from menu",160,2
   ENDIF
 ENDIF
ENDP
```

You'll notice that it's only necessary to check whether a valid key has been pressed if the short-cut key combination is used. This time, errors don't occur - if the key press isn't valid, program flow returns to the main routine.

These are just two techniques for ensuring the program doesn't stop running if an invalid key combination is used. There are undoubtedly other ways - and other ways to use these techniques. The ONERR method is perhaps a little less 'rigid' - since it will trap *any* program-stopping error that may occur in the procedures in which it is used. With the 'valid key' method you know what keys you're using and can test for them accordingly, but you have to be a little more careful if, at a later stage, you add options to your menu: you'll have to make changes at various points throughout the program - in the declared length of the string holding the key list and the key list itself, for example.

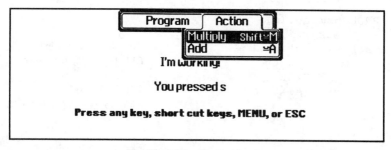

The Menu2 (or 3) program in use

CHAPTER 26
Animation and sprites

This Chapter deals with the movement of drawn objects across the screen. New OPL words covered are
APPENDSPRITE, CHANGESPRITE, CREATESPRITE,
CLOSESPRITE, DRAWSPRITE, POSSPRITE,
USESPRITE

Getting things moving

Previous chapters discussed how a window's position can be moved across the screen a step at a time. For drawn objects appearing within a window, a different process is required. First the object is drawn at its start position. Then, to give the appearance of movement, it has to be *cleared* from the screen, and drawn again in a new, close by position - and so on. The visual effect is that the object is moving. Alternatively, its shape can change, to give an animated appearance.

An easy way to clear a drawn object prior to re-drawing it is to simply draw it again, in the same position, with the gGMODE set to 1 or 2. Here's a very simple example: this program produces a pulsing box until a key is pressed. gGMODE 2 (invert) is used to alternately set and clear pixels and, to show the effect of inverting, another black box is positioned near to the pulsing box.

```
PROC move1:
 LOCAL x%,c%,d%
 d%=1
 x%=1
 c%=5
 gAT 120,70
 gFILL 30,30,0
 gAT 100,60
 DO
   gAT 100,60
   gGMODE 2
   gBOX c%,c%
   PAUSE 2
   gBOX c%,c%
   IF c%>30 OR c%<5
    d%=d%*(-1)
```

```
    ENDIF
    c%=c%+d%
  UNTIL KEY=27
ENDP
```

You could also use different windows to make the movement - writing the new position to the next window, then simply bringing that window to the top, or making the current window 'invisible' and the new window 'visible', and so on.

The 'inversion' method just demonstrated is fine where only one plane is being used, but can get a little more complicated when the background uses both grey and black planes.

For this and similar types of situation there is an alternative way to create animated and or moving objects. Sprites.

What is a sprite?

A sprite is a picture or drawing, which can be in black, grey and white, and which can be animated and moved around the screen without having to worry about 'what's underneath it'. However, it requires that the drawings involved in creating the sprite are first saved as files. This process need only be performed once of course (provided the created drawing files are not deleted). This gives you two options: within the program, you can either test for the existence of the files - and if they don't exist, create them using a separate procedure. Alternatively, you can create the drawings and save them to files with a separate program, deleting the program once you are happy with the files. The second method enables you to generate a series of animated pictures for use in *any* program

Up to 13 drawings or combinations of drawings can be used to produce one animated sprite, The drawings can be as small or as large as you choose - but it must be remembered that sprites can use a considerable amount of memory. If more than one drawing is used to create *one* of the animated parts of the sequence, then those drawings *must* be the same size.

You should also remember that the maximum size for a sprite is screen size (it would be difficult to imagine why you would want one larger): creating sprites larger than the screen will cause your machine to crash.

Generating sprites

Before generating sprites, you will need to create the necessary drawing or picture files. Once this has been done, the next step is to inform the Series 3a that a sprite is to be initiated, using the CREATESPRITE command, the format for which is simply:

spid%=**CREATESPRITE**

where spid% will be assigned the identification number of the sprite. (This is probably for future use, since the current Series 3a supports only one sprite)

The next step is to load the drawing files, in turn, into a *bitmap set* (which will then be added to the sprite). You will need to do this as many times as there are drawings for the sprite, so if your sprite is animated with 13 separate drawings, you'll have to define the *bitmap set* 13 times. With two drawings, you'll need only to define the bitmap set twice. The bitmap *set* is a string array of six elements: the required picture file or files are assigned to elements of the array according to how the drawing is to be displayed:

bm$ (1)	Sets the black pixels
bm$ (2)	Clears the black pixels
bm$ (3)	Inverts the black pixels
bm$ (4)	Sets the grey pixels
bm$ (5)	Clears the grey pixels
bm$ (6)	Inverts the grey pixels

For example, if you want a drawing in a file called 'Box.pic' to invert the black pixels, you would assign the file name to bm$ (3) of the set, (bm$ (3) ="Box"), and if you wanted it to clear the grey pixels, you would assign the file name to bm$ (5) of the set (bm$ (5) ="Box"). Note that the extension '.pic' is not required: Series 3a assumes, if no extension is given, that the 'pic' file is required.

You can assign drawing files to more than one element of the bitmap array, but you must remember three factors.

1. Black pixels are drawn 'on top' of grey pixels, so set or cleared *grey* pixels in the same position will be hidden.
2. Pixels of one colour (black or grey) in one bitmap of a set should not overlap those of the same colour in another bitmap of the same set. In other words, don't try to set ,clear or invert the same pixel in the same bitmap set.

3. The drawing files *must* be the same size within a bitmap set - that is, occupy the same area of the screen

Note that although up to thirteen bitmap *sets* can be used to define a sprite, you need declare only *one* bitmap array: the same array can be used for each bitmap *set*, as you will see later on.

After the elements of a bitmap set have been appropriately assigned, they are added to the sprite, and this is achieved with the APPENDSPRITE command.

APPENDSPRITE $t\%,\mathbf{v}bm\$()$,$x\%$,$y\%$ This command must be called *before* the sprite is actually displayed on the screen, otherwise an error will occur.

$t\%$ gives the duration, in tenths of a second, that the drawing will remain on the screen before the drawing in the *next* bitmap set is displayed.

$\mathbf{v}bm\$()$ is the string array which must have been declared as a LOCAL or GLOBAL array of six elements, and which must have had the required drawing or drawings assigned to the appropriate elements, as discussed..

$x\%$ and $y\%$ are optional, and give offsets in pixels from the sprite position, at which the drawings will be displayed. $x\%$ moves the top left corner of the bitmap drawing to the right or left (negative values) of the sprite location, while $y\%$ moves the top left corner of the bitmap drawing down or up (negative values).

You must assign each animated drawing or drawings to the sprite in turn, using the APPENDSPRITE command.

Before you create another sprite, you must *close* the current sprite with the command CLOSESPRITE.

CLOSESPRITE $sprid\%$ This closes the sprite with the identification number $sprid\%$.

Currently, the Series 3a can use only one sprite. When - and if - Series 3a can use more than one sprite, the USESPRITE command will enable you to select which one to use

USESPRITE *sprid%*   This will make the sprite with the identification number *sprid%* the current sprite, for display or further actions: ***currently, it is a superfluous command.***

Displaying, moving and changing sprites

Once a sprite has been fully defined, it can be displayed on the screen using the DRAWSPRITE command.

DRAWSPRITE *x%,y%*   This displays the sprite in the current window, with the top left corner at the pixel location defined by *x%* (horizontal) and *y%* (vertical)

To move a sprite around the screen, use the POSSPRITE command.

POSSPRITE *x%,y%*   This moves the *current* sprite to the window position determined by x% and y%, which are the horizontal and vertical pixel locations.

Once a sprite has been displayed on the screen - using DRAWSPRITE - the drawings that make up its animation can be changed, using the CHANGESPRITE command.

CHANGESPRITE *bm%,t%,***v***bm$(),dx%,dy%*   This is very similar to the APPENDSPRITE command. However in this instance, Series 3a must be informed which of the 13 possible bitmap drawings is to be changed - and this information is provided in the first argument, *bm%*. You will get an error, of course, if *bm%* is given a value higher than the number of bitmaps appended to the sprite. The other arguments are the same as for APPENDSPRITE: *t%* determines the duration of the bitmap, in tenths of a second, before the next one is displayed; ***v***bm$() is the bitmap array to which the drawing file has been assigned, and *dx%* and *dy%* are optional, providing an offset from the screen location of the sprite.

An example program

The capabilities of the sprite handling commands are very extensive: the potential inherent in the commands enables numerous effects to be achieved. Sprites can be of any size *up to screen size*: any larger and your machine will crash. The *sets* of bitmaps can be of different sizes -

281

but if more than one drawing is used *within* a bitmap set, for the grey and black planes for example, then the drawings used within that bitmap set *must* be of the same size. It is the 'saved area' that is important, not the area occupied by the actual drawing.

Here is a program - which you can use as a basis for experimentation to explore some of the capabilities.

The picture files are generated by a *separate* program, which *must* be entered and run before you can use the sprite program. The alternative would be to incorporate this picture generating program as a separate procedure within the sprite program, and to test for the existence of the picture files at the start - calling the procedure if they don't exist. Details of how this can be done are given after the `sprite` program listing.

```
PROC drawpics:
 LOCAL c%,d%
 DEFAULTWIN 1
 c%=6
 d%=1
 DO
  gCLS
  gGREY 0
  gAT 0,0
  gBOX c%,c%
  gSAVEBIT "Box"+num$(d%,2),40,40
  gCLS
  gAT 0,0
  gFILL c%,c%,0
  gSAVEBIT "Fill"+num$(d%,2),40,40
  gCLS
  gAT 14-(c%/2),14
  gLINEBY c%,0
  gAT 14,14-(C%/2)
  gLINEBY 0,c%
  gAT 0,0
  gSAVEBIT "Cross"+NUM$(d%,2),40,40
  c%=c%+2
  d%=d%+1
  UNTIL d%=7
ENDP
```

This creates three suites of drawings - six open boxes, six filled boxes, and six crosses, each increasing in size. The sprite program will use the six drawings in each suite twice - to show, for example, an open box increasing and decreasing in size.

Now here is the sprite program. To show you the effect of moving a sprite over various black and grey areas, it starts by generating a number of randomly sized, randomly positioned filled boxes of black or grey.

In use, the cursor keys will move the sprite around the screen, and the DIAMOND key will change the sprite to a different design. The ESC key quits the program. As before, don't enter the REMarks. They're included to help you understand how the program works.

```
PROC sprites:
 GLOBAL dk%,bm$(6,6),fn$(8)
 LOCAL c%,bc%,sx%,sy%
 DEFAULTWIN 1               REM Required for grey plane
 dk%=1                      REM Diamond key variable
 RANDOMIZE HOUR*SECOND
 DO                         REM create a background
  c%=c%+1
  gAT 1+int(rnd*400),1+int(rnd*120)
  gGREY INT(rnd*2)
  gFILL 10+INT(RND*70),10+INT(RND*50),2
 UNTIL C%=30

 CREATESPRITE              REM Initialise the sprite
 fn$="Box"                 REM Install the 'Box' pics...
 bc%=1                     REM   using a loop
 DO
   IF bc%>6                REM After 6, decrease sizes
     bm$(3)=fn$+NUM$(13-bc%,1)   REM Inverted black picture
     bm$(6)=fn$+NUM$(13-bc%,1)   REM Inverted grey picture
     APPENDSPRITE 2,bm$(),bc%,bc%
   ELSE
     bm$(3)=fn$+NUM$(bc%,1)      REM Up to 6, increase sizes
     bm$(6)=fn$+NUM$(bc%,1)
     APPENDSPRITE 2,bm$(),13-bc%,13-bc%
   ENDIF
   bc%=bc%+1
 UNTIL bc%=13              REM 12 pics added to sprite
 PRINT "DIAMOND KEY CHANGES SPRITE"
 PRINT "CURSOR KEYS MOVE IT"
```

283

```
 sx%=140                          REM Start locations
 sy%=80
 DRAWSPRITE sx%,sy%               REM Draw the sprite
 DO                               REM Get user input
  c%=GET
  IF c%=256                       REM Up key
   sy%=sy%-1
  ELSEIF c%=257                   REM Down key
   sy%=sy%+1
  ELSEIF c%=259                   REM Left key
   sx%=sx%-1
  ELSEIF c%=258                   REM Right key
   sx%=sx%+1
  ELSEIF c%=292                   REM Diamond key
   chsprite:                      REM Change sprite
  ENDIF
  POSSPRITE sx%,sy%               REM Reposition sprite
 UNTIL c%=27
ENDP

PROC chsprite:
 LOCAL bc%
 dk%=dk%+1                        REM DIAMOND key update
 IF dk%=4                         REM Only 1-3 allowed
  dk%=1
 ENDIF
 IF dk%=1                         REM Set the pic file names
  fn$="box"                       REM according to the value
 ELSEIF dk%=2                     REM of dk%
  fn$="fill"
 ELSEIF dk%=3
  fn$="cross"
 ENDIF
 bc%=1                            REM Change bitmap pics
 DO                               REM        using a loop
   IF bc%>6                       REM Decreasing size
    bm$(3)=fn$+NUM$(13-bc%,1)
    bm$(6)=fn$+NUM$(13-bc%,1)
    IF dk%<>3                     REM No offset for '3'
     CHANGESPRITE bc%,2,bm$(),bc%,bc%
    ELSE
     CHANGESPRITE bc%,2,bm$()
    ENDIF
   ELSE
```

```
    bm$(3)=fn$+NUM$(bc%,1)
    bm$(6)=fn$+NUM$(bc%,1)
    IF dk%<>3
      CHANGESPRITE bc%,2,bm$(),13-bc%,13-bc%
    ELSE
      CHANGESPRITE bc%,2,bm$()
    ENDIF
    ENDIF
    bc%=bc%+1
  UNTIL bc%=13
ENDP
```

Translate and run the program, and test it out by moving the sprite over various areas of the screen, and by selecting all three sprite shapes, before experimenting with your own ideas and perhaps pictures.

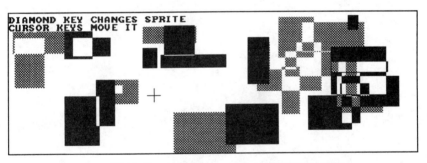

The Sprite program in use, showing the 'Cross' sprite.

Including the drawing program

If you wish to combine the procedure that creates the sprite drawings (drawpics) with the sprite program, then add it, as listed *to the end* of the sprites program: you can delete the DEFAULTWIN 1 line from the drawpics procedure - it isn't needed in this instance.

Then, immediately after the DEFAULTWIN 1 line in the sprites procedure, add the following lines:

```
IF NOT EXIST("Box1.pic")
  drawpics:
ENDIF
```

This will test for the existence of just *one* of the drawings in one of the three suites of drawings needed for the sprite program to operate: under normal circumstances, this test should be sufficient. However, you must remember not to delete any of the picture files (which will be located in the OPD directory of your Psion Series 3a), otherwise errors will occur.

PART 3

Files and data handling

This Part of the Book deals with the extensive file handling capabilities of OPL, enabling you to manage files and create databases to suit your own needs.

CHAPTER 27
All about files

This Chapter takes a preliminary look at files, directories, paths and file names, to help you understand file handling processes.

What is a computer 'file'?

In essence, anything saved in memory is saved as a computer file of some kind. However, as you may by now have realised, files can contain different types of information or data. For example, the programs you write are saved as pure text files, whilst when they are translated into a form the Psion Series 3a can understand, they are saved as binary files of machine coding. The picture files are saved in a different form again - with data about the picture. Word processor files are saved with special codes to reflect the formatting of the document, database files are saved in a special form that allows access to individual items of data - and so on.

Each of these is different, and generally speaking, can be used only for the purpose it was created for. Obviously you wouldn't expect to run your Address database as a 'program': it is a listing of records.

Nevertheless, *all* files have one or two things in common: the way their *names* are constructed, and the way their type can be 'identified'. The naming convention or format used is the same as that for your office computer or PC. This feature gives a degree of compatibility between Psion Series 3a files and the files on desk-top machines using different operating systems. However, your *programs* will not run on a desk top machine (unless you have an 'emulator'), because the *operating system* is different - and so too is the screen size and so on. But your Series 3a document files and databases can be transferred to and copied from PCs. Furthermore, it is possible, with special 'converter' programs, to change for example a Psion Series 3a Spreadsheet file to a file that can be read by a PC spreadsheet program.

The way files are named and the way they can be stored is fairly important when creating programs involving files and file-handling (such as Databases).

Paths and directories

Just as you would keep related documents in one drawer of a filing cabinet, so it makes sense to keep files of a related nature in one 'area' of a computer.

The RAM memory inside your Series 3a has an area allocated for saving data. You can also have SSDs fitted, specifically for saving data. Like a filing cabinet, this area is effectively divided up into 'drawers' - only instead of being called drawers, they are called *directories*. A *directory* is really like a 'heading', under which files of a related nature are saved. All of your database files, for example, are saved under a heading called 'DAT', your Agenda files are saved under a heading called 'AGN', and your word processor files are saved under a heading called 'WRD'.

These names are the *directories*, and each *directory* can have a 'sub-directory' - which in turn can have sub-sub directories. This is exactly the same as in office computers, lap-tops and so on: it is the standard practice, to keep your files organised and easy to locate.

Your SSDs can have directories, just as floppy disks can have directories. In fact, your SSDs will often have the same directory names as inside the Series 3a. You may ask "How does the Series 3a know the difference between a directory on an SSD and a directory of the same name stored in the Series 3a's RAM area?" The answer is that each *location* is also identified individually.

Each *location* is identified by a letter: locations are usually referred to as *drives*, this term being derived from the floppy drives that are associated with desk top machines. You will be aware that your Series 3a has two slots for SSDs, referred to as 'A' and 'B'. This is the identification letter for that particular slot or drive, and serves to differentiate similar directories stored on them. The internal memory area of Series 3a that is reserved for saving files is referred to as 'drive' 'M' - which stands for 'Memory'.

PCs too can have drives labelled 'A' and 'B'. So the next question is, if you're transferring files to a drive on a PC, how do you differentiate between directories on the 'A' drive of Series 3a and directories of the same name on the 'A' drive of a PC? The answer is there is another 'location' identifier - 'LOC' (Local) for drives that are associated with the Series 3a, and 'REM' (Remote) for the files that are associated with any externally connected computer.

These elements are combined together, to construct or define the *path* to a file that may be wanted. First of all, the *computer* location is written as the identifier followed by *two* colons. Thus

> LOC:: for files on any drive inside the Series 3a
> REM:: for files on any drive on an external computer

Don't confuse these two identifiers with the two OPL words REM and LOC! If you are dealing only with the Series 3a, then these identifiers are not needed: the 'default' location is taken as, or is assumed to be, 'LOC::'.

Next, the drive location letter must be specified, and this is done by following the identifying letter with a *single* colon. This is exactly the same practice as is used on PCs. Thus, an SSD in slot A of the Series 3a is identified as

> A:

If you are accessing drive 'A' on an external computer, then it would be identified as

> REM::A:

If a drive is *not* specified when using your Series 3a, it is assumed to be drive 'M' - the internal memory drive. So for files saved in the internal RAM area of Series 3a, you do not need to specify the ''LOC::M:' part at all.

This now takes us to the directory to be used. All directories are identified by a *backslash* - '\'. And all drives have a main or *root* directory, so the 'root' or basic directory at any location is identified by '\'.

If you want to store files in this particular place - rather than under a *directory name*, then the backslash can be ignored. However, it is unlikely that you will want to save files in such a haphazard way on your Series 3a.

Following the 'root directory' backslash comes the name of the directory, which must also be followed by a backslash. The directory where your source code files for your program modules are kept is

'OPL', so to identify any file in this directory on the Series 3a's internal memory, you would use

\OPL*filename*

The same file in a directory on an SSD (any SSD) in slot or drive A would be referred to as

A:\OPL*filename*

and on drive A of an externally connected computer as

REM::A:\OPL*filename*

You could have a sub-directory of the OPL directory - perhaps for program 'Library' modules - which could be called '\LIB\'. To access such a directory (if it existed) on Series 3a's internal memory, you would refer to it as

\OPL\LIB*filename*

and on an SSD in the A drive as

A:\OPL\LIB*filename*

This *route* to the required filename is called the **path**, and enables you to identify the files at specific locations.

It is very important to note that directories have to be created: *you cannot specify a directory in a path if the directory doesn't exist.*

Your Series 3a has a number of directories that it uses for storing files. It stores them automatically in the correct directory for the application you're using, without you having to specify the *path*: it is only when you are writing your own programs, or wish to store information in a directory of your own choice, that you need to specify the path. As we shall see later on, you can create your own directories and sub-directories, and you can delete them, all under program control.

You *could* in some instances load a file used by one type of application into a different application -for example, you could load a spreadsheet file into the Series 3a word processor, but it would look an absolute mess of symbols. To prove this for yourself (if you have a spreadsheet file saved), on the system screen position the cursor highlight on a file name under the word processor icon, then press the TAB key. You will see a list of the word processor files that have been saved (if any), in the \WRD\ directory. Using the 'up' arrow key, position the highlight on the '\' symbol above the \WRD\ line, and press

ENTER. You will now see a list of all the *directories* that are on your Series 3a. Again using the cursor keys, move the highlight to the '\SPR\' directory, press ENTER, then select one of the files listed in that directory. The word processor application will be opened, showing the spreadsheet data. Gibberish.

To exit from this, press the system button, then, with the highlight on the spreadsheet file name under the *word processor* icon, press the DELETE key. You won't delete the file - merely stop the word processor application from running with it.

Here is a list of the directories that Series 3a uses as a *default* for storing files created using it's *own* applications:

Directory Name	Type of File stored
\AGN\	Agenda files.
\APP\	System screen lists, programs and groups
\DAT\	Database files.
\OPD\	Bitmap files, picture files and so on.
\OPL\	OPL *source* code files.
\OPO\	OPL programs that can be run.
\SPR\	Spreadsheet files
\WDR\	Word template files and printer drivers
\WLD\	World application files
\WRD\	Word processor files
\WVE\	Sound files

The Series 3a knows the directory in which to automatically save a file by the default *extension* to the file's name - discussed later.

Three final points about path names. First, they can be in upper or lower case letters - all are the same as far as Series 3a (or other computers) are concerned.

Thus, 'A:\OPL\' is the same path as 'a:\opL\'.

Secondly, when you create a new directory you must not use the name of an existing directory on the same device.

Thirdly, when you save or copy a file to an SSD, Series 3a automatically creates the appropriate 'default' directory for it.

Naming files

We now come to the business of naming files. The Series 3a system is identical to that used on PCs. Normally, when you decide to save a file or when you create a 'new' file (such as a new OPL program), you just give it a name of up to eight characters.

However, file names comprise *two* parts: the actual *name* - such as the one that you give it when creating a new document - and an *extension*.

The *name* part must comprise no more than a total of eight characters and numbers.

The *extension* is separated from the name by a full point, and comprises (up to) three letters or numbers.

Series 3a automatically adds extensions to your file names, as well as placing the files in the correct directory for storage. So normally you don't have to worry about such things. But when dealing with files on other computers, or creating your own directory or filing system, then you must start adding extension names yourself.

Extensions are used to identify the *type* of file being stored: this is not quite the same as the directory in which it is stored. For example, in your the word processor directory, which will hold all 'word' documents, Series 3a will automatically save files with the extension '.WRD'. When you specify the file name - either when you create it or when you 'SAVE AS', you *can* add an extension to distinguish it - perhaps '.LET' for letters, or '.REP' for reports. However, since such files will not have the *default* extension for the directory in which they are saved, they will not appear on the main *system* display: you will have to use the 'OPEN FILE' and TAB key facilities to find them.

The complete file name for an OPL source code file called 'Myprog' would be 'Myprog.OPL'. This would be saved in the '\OPL\' directory. The corresponding 'program' file, when 'Myprog' is translated, will be 'Myprog.OPO' - and this will be saved in the \OPO\ directory.

Some of the default file extensions automatically added by Series 3a when you create a new file are:

.AGN	For Agenda files.
.DBF	For Database files.
.OPD	For bitmap and picture files.
.OPL	For OPL source code files.
.OPO	For translated OPL code files.
.PIC	Bitmap picture files.
.SPR	Spreadsheet files.
.WRD	Word processor files.

Many of these are the same as the *directory* in which they are kept.

Wildcards

When specifying a filename for a *search* operation - when looking for a particular file to 'open' for example, you can use *wildcards* in either the *name* part or the *extension*.

A *wildcard* is a way of saying 'any letter or letters'. The wildcards are

         *   Meaning 'match any number of letters'.

         ?   Meaning match just *one* letter in this position.

Thus, in a file search, '*.OPL' would mean 'find *all* the files with the extension 'OPL'. Similarly, '*.OP?' would mean 'find *all* the files that have an extension starting with the two letters 'OP'.

Wildcards can only be used for *file* names, not directory names.

You'll find wildcards useful when writing file handling programs, for selecting specific groups of file names, or for searching records.

CHAPTER 28
Database principles

*This Chapter discusses the concept of a database, and
why you might need to create one for your own use.*

What is a Database?

In simple terms, a database is a computer file that contains records,
each of which relates to someone or something. The files listed under
the Data icon of your Series 3a System screen are databases. If used for
addresses, each record contains information about one particular person
or company: the name, telephone numbers, address, and any notes you
may have included. Each piece of information is stored in a 'field',
which has - or can have - a title or label to identify it. The Series 3a
database allows you to add or change the 'labels' that precede each item
of a record, to add, change and delete records, and so on.

Each record can be likened to a card in a card-index system, where
all the information related to one 'subject' is kept on one card. In an
address card index system, the 'subject' is the person concerned. Each
card holds all the information about that person.

There is, however, a fundamental difference between a computer
database and a card-index system - a difference that gives computer
databases a clear advantage. (This is particularly true where your Series
3a is concerned). With a card-index system, the order of the cards is
determined by the prime search requirement. For example, cards
holding names and addresses are most likely to be maintained in
alphabetical order, based on the person's name: it's not much fun
having to search through every card to find Joe Blogg's telephone
number, if the cards aren't arranged alphabetically.

With a computer, the order is completely irrelevant (unless you
want to print out all of the records). The time it takes a computer to find
a particular record is insignificant - faster than the bat of an eyelid.

This difference is particularly valuable when *other* criteria form the
search requirement. For example, if you have a card-index system
arranged alphabetically by people's names, you'd spend some time
finding all those who lived in a particular town. To a computer like

Series 3a, this makes no difference: it's just as fast and as easy as finding a person by name.

Computer files have fields

Let us take the card-index analogy a little further. If you were to use cards to keep names, addresses and other relevant information about individuals or companies, you would undoubtedly organise each record card so that you knew exactly where to look on it for a particular item of information. In a system for keeping details of family and friends, for example, each individual record card may look like this:

```
Name: .......................................
Phone No: ................................
Address: ..................................
Wedding Anniversary: ..............
Birthday: .................................
```

Each of these lines, in computer terms, is called a *field*. On record cards, you could add other fields to some of the records, if you wanted, to meet particular needs. For computer databases it is generally necessary to specify the number of fields for *all* of the records at the outset.

On a card-index record you can determine what fields you want, and have different fields on each record. On the databases you create with a program, you must determine at the outset what fields you want, and stick with them: they may not be allocated any data, but they have to be there.

Why do you need to create databases?

You may well wonder, since there is a perfectly good database system in the Series 3a, why you need to create your own database management system.

Basically, it is because the database built into Series 3a is such that calculations based on the contents of one or more of the fields are difficult to achieve. If you needed, for example, a stock control database - where each record held the name of an item, its part number, how many are in stock, the minimum permissible stock level, the buying and selling price of each item, and perhaps even the VAT element, then the Series 3a's built in database would be pretty inadequate. With your own database management program, you could have Series 3a *automatically* give you a warning if an item's stock level is reduced below a permitted or acceptable minimum. You can also arrange for your program to give you the value of each item in stock, the total value of all the stock, how much it will cost to bring all the stock up to the minimum level, and so on. All under 'Menu' control, and using Dialogs for ease of entry.

The types of database that you can create to do specific types of work are limitless: you could have a program to look after your bank account for you, automatically 'transferring' funds or deducting standing orders at the beginning of each month, to save you from having to do it (to your records). You could have a club membership database, telling you 'at the touch of a button' who owes what. And so on.

In other words, if you need to extract information and make calculations based on the records you keep, then it is well worth writing your own database manager.

However, there is a down side: database management programs tend to be fairly lengthy, if they are going to be useful. So they must be very carefully planned.

What a database program should include

Whatever other functions you want a database management program to perform, there are certain facilities that should be included every time. These are

1) The ability to open an existing or create a new Database file, and possibly to delete unwanted files (although deletion can be achieved using the Series 3a file handling system).
2) The ability to add, change (update) and delete a record.
3) The ability to search for specific records on a given clue (like 'Find' in your Series 3a databases).

In addition to these, you will also want routines to extract and or manipulate data according to your requirements, and perhaps to provide a print-out onto a connected printer.

This makes for a lot of 'procedures' to build into your program. If you intend to have two or more database management programs - say one for stock control, and one for bank account management - then it can make sense to have some standard routines that are common to both placed in a Library module, which can be loaded and used as and when required by such programs.

The next Chapter details the OPL commands available to you, with a 'shell' database manager program, to demonstrate as far as is practical how such commands can be used.

As a general guide, the approach to adopt is to write the program as simply as possible to start with, using just the basic elements required, then add and change those elements to 'improve' and enhance the way the program operates, and the way it can be used.

In this respect, 'breaking' the program up into small discrete procedures will help considerably when the time comes to enhance it: all you need to do is replace individual procedures, and test it thoroughly again before proceeding with the next step.

CHAPTER 29
Database management

This Chapter discusses how to create and manage a database to meet your own specific requirements. The OPL words covered are
APPEND, BACK, CLOSE, COUNT, CREATE, EOF, ERASE, FIND, FINDFIELD, FIRST, LAST, NEXT, OPEN, OPENR, POS, POSITION, RECSIZE, UPDATE, USE.

Planning your database
When you decide that it is time to create your own database, the very first step to take is to set down, very clearly, everything that you want it to do. This way, you can structure the program to cater for all of your needs - even if you don't implement them all to start with.

As a typical example, if you wanted to have a stock control database, your requirement list might look something like this:

1) Item names and stock numbers
2) Current stock level
3) Minimum permissible stock level
4) Buying and selling prices
5) Value of each stock item
6) Total value of the stock

In addition to these requirements to satisfy the *purpose* of your database, there are the basic needs that every database should have - as detailed in the previous Chapter (the ability to add, change and delete records, for example).

Having ascertained your needs, examine them to see exactly what each record should actually contain. In the stock control list, for example, items (1) to (4) could be data provided by each record, but (5) and (6) needn't be a part of any actual record: they can be calculated by Series 3a for display whenever you want, thus saving record (and storage) space.

You might decide that you want to keep one type of stock separate from another - perishable goods in one database *file* and non-perishables in another, for example. This is the same concept as keeping your business and personal addresses separate in the Series 3a's built in database: you simply open a new record file for each type of record you wish to keep, all of them being under the control of the one database management program.

Remember, your database management program *controls* the database *files*.

The file handling process

The sequence of events for a database management program would, generally speaking, be as follows.

1) Open (or create) the database file. A file must be 'opened' before you can work on it.
2) Perform the necessary file handling operations. These include finding files, adding records, extracting information and so on - in fact, performing the tasks you wanted to achieve with your database. With Series 3a, this can be achieved very easily by using the menu system available, so that you can go straight to the operation that you want to perform once a file has been opened.
3) Close the file (or files). When you leave a program that has been handling files, those files are normally closed automatically. However, it is good programming practice to ensure that such files are closed automatically.

It is possible to have more than one file open at a time - in fact, you can have up to four files open at once. You may wish to transfer information from one file to another, for example: all of this is possible, provided that you write the program accordingly.

A 'shell' database manager

Before examining the many OPL words available for database management, it will be helpful to create a 'shell' or 'start-up' program to handle some of the operations you are likely to need. The following program uses the Series 3a menu system, which you will be able to adapt to suit your own needs. So that you can test this 'shell' out without having to write the entire database first, 'dummy' procedures are used: these will be expanded later as the programming language associated with databases is explored. An error handling procedure is also used, to cater for some of the things that can go wrong when the program is running.

Please note that this 'shell' program is only a guide: it will give you an idea of how to prepare your own database management program. It is by no means complete, and will undoubtedly need modifying and expanding to suit your own requirements.

```
PROC datman:
 LOCAL m%
  DO
AGAIN::                          REM For error trapping
   ONERR noproc::
    mINIT
    mCARD "Files","Create",%c,"Open",%o,"Read",
same line continued                %r,"Close",%k
    mCARD "Manage","Add",%a,"Update",%u,
same line continued               "Delete",%d
    mCARD "Analyse","Browse",%b,"Find",%f,
same line continued               "IValue",%i,"SValue",%s
    mCARD "Quit","Quit",%q
    m%=MENU
    IF m%
       @(CHR$(m%)):
    ENDIF
  UNTIL m%=%q
    STOP                         REM The program stops here
Noproc::                         REM 'No procedure' handler
 ONERR OFF
 showerr:(err$(err))
 GOTO AGAIN::
ENDP


PROC a:
 notimp:
ENDP
```

IMPORTANT: Datman must be the first procedure in the File. *Repeat the* PROC a *procedure above for* PROC b, PROC c, PROC d, PROC f, PROC i, PROC k, PROC o, PROC q, PROC r, PROC s, and PROC u. (You can use the copy text editing commands, and simply change the procedure name appropriately. Make sure they are *all* entered as they are needed in order to test datman). **Then enter,** *in the same File:*

```
PROC notimp:
 BUSY "Not implemented yet"
 GIPRINT "Press a key"
 GET
 BUSY OFF
ENDP

PROC showerr:(msg$)
 dINIT "ERROR"
 dTEXT "",msg$,2
 DIALOG
ENDP
```

The 'notimp' procedure displays a message for all of the procedures that haven't been fully written yet. Once they have *all* been implemented, this procedure can be deleted. The 'showerr:' procedure displays all (or most) of the errors that can occur when the program is running - without stopping it from running: at the moment, only incorrect 'short-cut key' combinations are 'trapped' by the error handling routine.

The process just adopted will enable you to test your database as it is written, piece by piece, without known potential errors stopping the program from running.

Before continuing, test the program out thoroughly, to make sure it works properly: if it doesn't work now, it won't work when all of the procedures are completed!

Creating a database file

Before your program can handle a database file, it must be opened. And before you can open a database file, it must have been created. Thus, the very first time you use the program (for real), you must *create* the file you want to use. The command to use is

CREATE *file$,lfi,field1,field2...field32* This is not to be confused with gCREATE, which is used to create a window. As you can see, this command requires a number of *arguments*. Here's what they mean:

file$ This is the name of the file that you want to create, and where you want it to be stored. It can be just the *name* (obeying the rules for file names), with or without the *extension*, or it can include the full *path*, with the directories, to where you want the file to be saved. If you omit the *extension*, the default extension (.ODB) is used. If you omit the *path*, a path to the \OPD\ directory is used. In most instances, this will be perfectly adequate for your needs. If, however, you choose to save the database file in a directory of your own choosing, and with your own extension, then you must be sure to use the same path to the directory and the same file extension when you subsequently open the file again - otherwise it won't be found.

Note that the maximum permissible length for *file$*, including the path and so on, is 128 characters.

lfi It has been mentioned that you can have up to four database files opened at a time. Series 3a needs to know, when you use a file, which of the four you intend to use (in much the same way it needs to know which window or bitmap file you want to use). In order to do that, each of the four files has to be identified, and that's done by giving each file that you create or open a *logical file identifier*. The identifier is just a single letter - 'A', 'B', 'C' or 'D' - without quotes, and as you will see later on, is used when *accessing* a file and any information it contains. If, when you create the file, you give it the *identifier* 'A', then that is how the file will be referenced whilst the program is running. Note that, when a file is created, it is automatically 'opened for business'.

field1...field32 The previous Chapter discussed how each record in a database has *fields* where the relevant information is stored. You have to identify the fields that you want to use when you *create* the file, and that is done with the *field?* arguments. You can have up to 32 different fields in every record of your file, but of course you will only specify as many as you need. Irrespective of the number of *fields* you have, the maximum length any file record can have in your database is 1022 characters, which should be more than adequate for your needs. The *fields* are, in effect, global variables of a special kind: you specify them in the

CREATE command (or in one of the OPEN commands, as we shall see later), and they are then available to *all* of the procedures in your program module.

As variables, *field* names must obey the rules of all variables: the *type* of information they are to store must be signified by an identifier symbol at the end, and they must not be more than eight characters long, including the identifier. Thus, if a field is to store integer numbers, the field might be called 'number%'. There is an important difference, however, as far as fields holding *string* information are concerned: the number of characters that they will hold does *not* have to be specified. The record will hold as many characters in a string field as are assigned to it.

When, in your program, you wish to use or assign a value to one of the field variables, you do so by prefixing it with the *logical file identifier* letter and a full point. Thus, a field named 'number%' in a file created (or 'OPENed') as file 'a' is subsequently identified as

```
a.number%
```

This differentiates that particular variable from a similar variable in, say, a file created or opened as logical file 'b', which would be identified as

```
b.number%
```

Series 3a will not allow you to create a file with the same name as another at the same storage location. If you try to do this, then a program stopping error will usually occur. You could use the DIALOG function's dFILE own facility for trapping 'existing file name' errors. There is another way: the 'EXIST' function.

EXIST(*file$*) This checks to see whether the file, specified by *file$* (which *can* include the path and extension, as before) exists at the specified (or default) location. If it *does* exist, then *true* (-1) is returned. Otherwise, *not true* ('0') is returned. The general format is

```
e%=EXIST(file$)
```

As a function, EXIST can of course be used as part of another statement.

For the demonstration program datman, a 'mini stock-control' data file that has three fields - *item$*, *number%* and *cost* - will be created. *item$* is a string field to hold the name of the stock item, *number%* an integer field to hold the number of items in stock, and *cost* is a floating point field to hold the price of each item. Notice how the variables are *identified* by the type of information they are to store. The dialog dFILE function is used to get the file name: but notice that we also provide our own error trapping routine.

Now, go into the 'datman' file, and edit 'PROC c:' to read as follows:

```
PROC c:                     REM The 'Create' procedure
  LOCAL fn$(128)
  dINIT "Create New File"
  dFILE fn$,"File ",9
  IF DIALOG                 REM ie, not ESC key
   IF NOT EXIST(fn$)
    CREATE fn$,A,item$,number%,cost
   ELSE
    dINIT fn$+" already exists"
    dBUTTONS "Continue",13
    DIALOG
   ENDIF
  ENDIF
ENDP
```

When you have edited PROC c: in the 'Datman' file, translate and run it again: this time, you will be able to use the 'Create' option to create a database file. If you try to create the same file name twice, you will get an error message dialog box appear. Note that, if you don't enter the path for the file name, it is automatically provided by Series 3a (as you'll see if you try to enter the same name twice): the default directory for the files created is \OPD\, and the default extension is '.odb'.

Tip: If you want to delete a database file that you have created - perhaps because in your experimentation you have created a number of files which you don't need - follow the following steps *carefully*:

1) Press the 'System' button to enter the main system display of your Series 3a.

2) Press the PSION and ' D ' keys together (or select 'Delete file' from the 'File' menu option).

3) A dialog will appear: *do not press* **ENTER**: press instead the TAB key.

4) Use the up arrow key to highlight the backslash ('\') at the top left of the screen, then press ENTER. (If you have saved to an SSD, use the left/right arrow keys to select it first).

5) Use the up/down arrow keys to select '\OPD\' (or the directory in which you saved your datafiles if you entered your own directory), then press ENTER.

6) Use the up/down arrow keys to select the file you wish to delete: unless you specified otherwise, it will have the extension '.odb'. (You can select a number of files for deletion by pressing the ⊞ key - which will place a tick by each file's name). Then press ENTER.

7) The 'Delete file' dialog will now be displayed: check that the file you wish to delete is displayed on the 'File name' line, then press ENTER.

8) A new dialog will ask you to confirm the deletion: press ' Y ' to delete, ' N ' to abort the deletion.

You can use this process to delete *any* file you no longer need. A similar process can be used should you want to *copy* a database file from one location to another: in this case, the main System Menu option to choose is 'File - Copy' (PSION and ' C ' keys). But be warned - once deleted, files cannot be restored, so do *not* delete files unless you are sure they are no longer required!

Opening and closing files

When you *create* a new file, it is automatically made ready for use. It is said to be 'opened'. However, next time you come to use the program, the file(s) that you have created will be lying dormant in memory 'closed'. Like a filing cabinet, a file has to be *opened* before it can be used.

Opening a database file simply means telling Series 3a you wish to perform some operations on it, perhaps adding records, or changing them. Two commands are available for opening files: one allows you to modify the file in some way, the other provides 'read-only' access. That means you can examine the contents of the file, but you can't change them.

OPEN *file$,lfn,field1,field2...field32*   You'll notice that, apart from the OPL word OPEN, this command is identical to CREATE. All the *arguments* that the command takes are the same - and as far as the fields are concerned, these *must* be of the same number and *type* as those used when the file was created, and though they need not necessarily have the same names, it makes sense to retain the same names. If you think about it, it is logical to have the same number of fields and field types when you open a file as when it was created: the records, after all, are for the same purpose, and have the same number and types of field.

OPENR *file$,lfn,field1,field2...field32*   This is identical to the OPEN command, except for the fact that the opened file can only be *read*, it cannot be altered or added to. A database file opened in this way could be accessed by other programs running at the same time as your database manager program.

When your database manager program ends, all the files are closed automatically. However, it is good practice for your program to close the files. If you want to access *more* than four files during the running of your program, then you will have to close some files down so that there are never more than four opened at a time - the maximum allowed.

Should this be one of your requirements, then you will also need to keep track of the *logical file identifiers*. Note that these are not *variables* and not *strings*, but simply a letter, without quotes. Most often, you will have different *types* of database file open at the same time. For example, in a bank-account managing program, you may have one file holding records about your current bank account, and another holding records concerning standing order payments (how much, how many, who to, and so on). You can arrange that one type is always opened as, say, the 'a' *logical file*, and the other as the 'b' *logical file*. You will also need to CLOSE a database file that has been opened for 'Read-only' and re-open it with the OPEN command, if you subsequently decide you wish to make changes to it.

CLOSE This command closes the *current* file (not to be confused with gCLOSE, which closes a window). The current file is the last one to be created or opened, or the one that has been selected to be current by the USE command.

When you close a file, memory is recovered from records that have been *deleted* - provided the file has been saved in the internal RAM of Series 3a, or on a RAM SSD. Flash SSD memory is not restored until you *re-format* the SSD - which wipes all the memory clean. For this reason, it is probably better to save database files which are subject to a lot of record *changes* in a RAM memory area.

The 'shell' database manager program, datman, can now be edited to cater for opening a database file for adding or changing records, for read-only, and to close database files. Since the action needed to open a file for alteration or read-only is almost identical, one procedure can be used to handle both cases, and that procedure called from 'PROC o:' and 'PROC r:' with an appropriate 'flag'. First of all, edit these two procedures as follows:

```
PROC o:
      openfile:(0)                REM That's a zero
ENDP

PROC r:
      openfile:(1)                REM and that's a 'one'
ENDP
```

Now, *add* the following 'openfile:' procedure to the 'datman' file: notice how the parameter passed from PROC o and PROC r determines the required dialog display and action.

```
PROC openfile:(m%)
 LOCAL fn$(128),msg$(12)
 fn$="*.odb"                    REM The default extension
 IF m%                         REM 1 means 'Read-only'
  msg$="Reading Only"
 ELSE
  msg$="Updating"
 ENDIF
 dINIT "Open for "+msg$
 dFILE fn$,"File ",72          REM 72=file choice list
 IF DIALOG
  IF m%
   OPENR fn$,A,item$,number%,cost
  ELSE
   OPEN fn$,A,item$,number%,cost
  ENDIF
 ENDIF
ENDP
```

By keeping both of the 'open' file actions in one procedure, it is easy to check and amend should the need ever arise.

If you choose to use your own extension rather than the default (.odb), then you must change the line `fn$="*.odb"` accordingly.

Now, to allow you to close a file that has been opened for, say 'Read-only' (for re-opening in order to make changes to it), and to give the program a clean ending, edit the 'PROC q' and PROC k procedures as follows (note the use of TRAP to detect if a file hasn't been opened):

```
PROC k:
 q:
ENDP

PROC q:
 TRAP CLOSE
 IF ERR
  GIPRINT ERR$(ERR)
 ELSE
  GIPRINT "File Closed"
 ENDIF
ENDP
```

The procedure PROC k simply calls the quit procedure, PROC q, which actually closes the file: PROC q is called when you exit the program - the actual exit is dealt with in the main loop of datman.

Adding records to the file

Without exception, you will want to be able to add records to your file. You do this by first making the required *file* the *current* file (if more than one is opened) with the USE command. If only one file has been opened, then it will automatically be the current file.

USE *lfi*   This selects the data file previously created or opened with the logical identifier *lfi* - a, b, c or d - as the current file, making it ready for further actions.

To add a record to a file, you must assign values to the field variables. You don't have to assign them all: those you don't assign will be 'blanks' in the database file, or will retain existing values.

You must remember that field variables have to be prefixed by the *logical file identifying* letter (you can use either a small or capital letter). Thus, in the database example file, the variables are identified as

```
a.item$
a.number%
a.cost
```

This distinguishes them from similar variables in other database files that may have been opened. The prefix, in fact, forms part of the variable's name, so you could, for example, assign information to 'a.item$' by a statement such as

```
INPUT a.item$
```

This would take information straight from the keyboard and assign it directly to the variable. More 'user friendly' would be to use a dialog. However, these field variables *cannot be used for data assignments in dialogs*, and so LOCAL variables have to be used, and the values given to the LOCAL variables re-assigned to the field variables.

APPEND   This command adds the information *currently* in all of the field variables to the database file as a *new* record. The new record is 'appended' to the end of the file, and is then made *the current record.* Unassigned fields are given zero values or, for strings, 'null' values in the new record.

A file must be opened before values can be assigned to its field variables or any new records APPENDed to it, otherwise a program-stopping error will occur.

The 'Add' procedure (PROC a:) of datman can now be completed. Edit 'PROC a:' of datman to read as follows:

```
PROC a:
 LOCAL d%,item$(16),number&,cost
 ONERR filerr::
 DO
  dINIT "Adding a Record"
  dEDIT item$,"Item:",16
  dLONG number&,"How many: ",0,10000
  dFLOAT cost,"Each costs: £",0,10000
  dBUTTONS "Add & End",13, "Add & More",
```
same line continued   `9,"Cancel",27`
```
  d%=DIALOG
  IF d%
   a.item$=item$
   a.number%=number&
   a.cost=cost
   APPEND
   item$=""                    REM Reset variables
   number&=0
   cost=0
  ENDIF
 UNTIL d%=13 or d%=0
 RETURN
filerr::
 ONERR OFF
 showerr:(ERR$(ERR))
ENDP
```

The Series 3a error messaging system will report *any* type of error that occurs in the procedure. Notice how the 'buttons' are used to enable another record to be added, just the current record, or to cancel the operation altogether. Strictly speaking, the 'Cancel' option isn't necessary: the ESC key will always exit a dialog, with DIALOG returning a zero. But to help when using the program, it is a good idea to show all the options available if possible.

When you have entered this procedure, test it out by adding a few dummy records to your database file: test the error routine as well, by trying to add records without first opening a file.

Browsing through the records

One of the important features that must be built into any database manager is the ability to browse records: when you want to change a record, for example, you will need some way of finding the one you want to change. You will also undoubtedly want to examine the records as well: one 'set' of 'search' procedures can be used for all these and related tasks.

OPL has a number of commands that enable you to flip backwards and forwards through your records, or to find records on a specific clue - just as in the built-in Series 3a database.

When a file has been opened, Series 3a keeps track of which record is the *current* record in that file, for action or viewing. This is much the same as the way it keeps track of the screen positions for the next graphic or text action. Usually it doesn't matter where a record is, but there are occasions when you do need to know the precise *position* of a record: for example, in a *sort* routine, where the records are being sorted into some order. You can find the position with the POS function.

POS   The format for this function is simply

$$p\%=POS$$

After it has been executed, *p%* will hold the number of the current record in the file, the first record being number 1. A file on Series 3a can have a maximum of 65534 records: as an integer variable, *p%* can only hold values between -32768 and 32767. Consequently, record numbers *above* 32767 are shown as negative values, ranging from -32768 (for record number 32768) down to -2 for record number 65534. If you wish to actually display the record number (rather than just use it in the file management process), then if *p%* has a negative value, 65536 needs to be added to it, to get the correct number. Thus, if you anticipate having more than a paltry 32767 records and you wish to display the record number for some reason, you will need a section of code something like this: (*don't enter this into Datman!*)

313

```
IF POS<0
     PRINT POS+65535
ELSE
     PRINT POS
ENDIF
```

As well as being able to determine the *number* of the current record, you can also make any record in the file the current record. This is like positioning the cursor on the screen display, with the gAT or AT commands.

POSITION *x*% This command makes the record number *x%* the *current* record. If *x%* is greater than the number of records in the file, then the record 'pointer' will be *one* past the last record in the file - a 'blank' record since it doesn't exist yet - and an 'End Of File' function (EOF, discussed a little later) will be *true*.

There are times when it can be necessary to know exactly how many records there are in a database file. In a stock control program, for example, the number of records in the file is an indication of how many *types* of item have been recorded.

COUNT The format is

$$c\%=\text{COUNT}$$

After this function has been executed, *c%* will hold the number of records in the file, or zero if there are no records.

There are many file management operations that you'll want to tackle, which will entail searching through *every* record and acting on the data each contains. You could perform this operation by using COUNT to determine the number of records, then constructing a loop with a 'loop counter' that will run through the required number of times. There is, however, an easier way.

EOF This function, which stands for 'End Of File', tests the current position of the record pointer. The general format is

$$e\%=\text{EOF}$$

If an attempt is made to 'push the pointer past the last record in the file', then EOF returns *true* (-1). Otherwise, it returns *not true* (0). The examining loop can therefore be simply

```
DO
    act on each record in turn
UNTIL EOF
```

There's a little group of commands that enable you to move backwards and forwards from record to record. These are now discussed:

FIRST This command makes the first record in the file the current record.

LAST This command makes the last record in the file the current record.

NEXT This command makes the next record in the file the current record. If the current record is already the last record in the file, then a 'null' record is returned, and the EOF function, if used, will return a *true* condition.

BACK This command makes the previous record in the file the current record. If the current record is the first record in the file, then this command has no effect.

Finally, there are two functions to search through the entire file for a match to a specified *string* clue.

FIND The format for this function is

```
f%=FIND(clue$)
```

FIND starts with the *current* record (it's important to remember that) and searches through all of the *string* fields in the data file (it's important to remember that, too), until it reaches a match for clue$. The record with the match is then made the *current* record. Note that numeric fields are *not* searched.

Unlike the clues that you use in the Series 3a Database system, the clue that you give for *clue$* must cover the *complete* field. If you want to give only a part of the field as a clue, then you *must* use wildcards.

315

For example, suppose the contents of a field in one of your records is 'APPLES and PEARS'. A clue of 'APPLES' will *not* find this record. The wildcards are:

*   To match any consecutive *group* of letters

?   To match any *single* letter

So, to find the 'APPLES and PEARS' record, your clue must be something like 'APP*'. You can mix the wildcards in the clue. Thus '?PP*' will also find the 'APPLES and PEARS' record - and any other record that has *one* character before 'PP', and any number of characters after it.

Your clue can consist of upper or lower case letters: with FIND, Series 3a treats them as the same for search purposes. Thus '*pple*' will find a record with 'APPLES and PEARS' as one of its string fields.

FINDFIELD(*clue$,start%,no%,flag%*)   This is a more sophisticated version of the FIND function. The format is

 f%=FINDFIELD(*clue$,start%,no%,flag%*)

Like FIND, this function finds a specified string, starting from the *current* record, and makes the first record with a match the current record. The arguments are

clue$ is the string to look for - and can include 'wildcard' symbols, as for FIND.

start% is the number of the field to start looking in - the first field being '1'.

no% is the number of fields in each record to examine, starting with the field specified by start%.

flag% holds the sum of two values that determine how the search should be made. The first value can be 0, 1, 2, or 3:

0	searches *backwards* from the *current* record.
1	searches *forwards* from the *current* record.
2	searches *backwards* from the *end* of the file.
3	searches *forwards* from the *start* of the file.

The second value can be 0 or 16:

0   for case independent searches (capitals and lower case letters will match).

16   for case dependent searches (capitals and lower case letters match exactly)

Thus, to search forwards from the start of the file for a case dependent match, flag% should have a value of 19 (3+16).

Note: Early versions of the Programming Manual supplied for the Psion Series 3a *incorrectly* describe this function, stating that it is the *search direction* that should be multiplied by 16, rather than the case dependency.

Adding 'browse' to 'datman'

Using the commands discussed in the previous pages, you can now complete more procedures in the 'datman' program, to deal with browsing through the records (PROC b, and some new ones). These procedures will also be needed to find a record for updating and for deleting. The 'browsing' operation is actually handled in three procedures: one for simple back and forth viewing of records, one for *finding* a record on a given clue, and since the contents of a record must be displayed to see if it is the one required, one to display a found record's contents. You should also allow for some errors that can occur - such as trying to search for a record in a file that hasn't been opened!

First of all, edit 'PROC b:' to read as follows:

```
PROC b:                         REM Browse thru' records
 LOCAL b%
ONERR filerr::
 FIRST
showrec:                        REM Show first record
 dINIT "To Search Records"      REM User friendly stuff
 dTEXT "","Use left/right arrow keys",2
 dTEXT "","for previous/next record",2
 dTEXT "","Up/down arrow keys for",2
 dTEXT "","first/last records",2
 dTEXT "","F=Find, ESC or ENTER=Quit",$202
 dTEXT "","PRESS ENTER TO CONTINUE",$102
 dPOSITION 1,1                  REM Put Dialog in a corner
 DIALOG
```

```
DO                                  REM Here's the action...
  BUSY "Use SEARCH keys now",3
  b%=GET
  IF b%=256                         REM Up=First record
   FIRST
   ELSEIF b%=257                    REM Down=Last record
   LAST
ELSEIF b%=259                       REM Left=Previous record
   BACK
  ELSEIF b%=258                     REM Right=Next record
   NEXT                             REM But don't go past
   IF EOF                          REM  the last record!
    LAST
   ENDIF
  ELSEIF b%=%f OR b%=%F             REM Means 'Find'
   BUSY OFF                        REM Clear 'Busy' message
   dofind:                         REM  and call 'Find'
   b%=27                           REM Exit when record found
  ENDIF
  CLS                               REM Keep things tidy
  showrec:                          REM Show the record!
 UNTIL b%=27 OR b%=13               REM Until done
 CLS                                REM Then tidy up
 BUSY OFF
 RETURN 1                           REM '1' for other routines
filerr::                            REM  The error handler
 ONERR OFF
 showerr:(ERR$(ERR))
ENDP
```

'1' is returned from this procedure, to indicate a successful search to the procedures that call it. Now you need to enter the 'dofind:' and 'showrec:' procedures into the file (these are new):

```
PROC dofind:
 LOCAL f%,x%,p%,f$(36)              REM 36 character clues
 FIRST                              REM Search from the start!
 dINIT "Find"                       REM Dialog for the clue
 dEDIT f$,"Enter clue:",8
 IF DIALOG
 DO                                 REM A loop, to allow for
  f%=FIND(f$)                       REM   repeat searches
  IF f%                            REM Means record found
```

```
       CLS
       showrec:                          REM  so show it!
       p%=POS                            REM Hold the record number
       dINIT "Find Next?"                REM see if more are wanted
       dPOSITION 1,1
       dBUTTONS "Yes",%y,"No",%n
       x%=DIALOG
       IF x%=%y                          REM 'y'=another to find
         NEXT                            REM Else finds same record!
       ENDIF
      ELSE                               REM f%=0 = past last record!
       GIPRINT "No more found"
       POSITION p%                       REM Re-select last found*
       x%=0                              REM Prepare to exit
      ENDIF
     UNTIL x%=%n OR x%=0
   ENDIF
 ENDP

PROC showrec:
 AT 1,3
 PRINT "ITEM      :",a.item$
 PRINT "QUANTITY :",a.number%
 PRINT "COST EACH: £";a.cost
 PRINT
 PRINT "Record No.",POS,"of",COUNT
 ENDP
```

You should now be able to run your program to create and open files, add records, and examine the records, either by using the arrow keys, or by the 'FIND' function. Remember when using FIND to locate a record you must either enter all of the field string, using wildcards if you wish when asked for a clue. You could avoid this by adding the 'group of characters' wildcard (*) before and after the entered clue, by re-assigning the clue variable with the following line

$$f\$="*"+f\$+"*"$$

entered immediately after the IF DIALOG statement in the dofind procedure. With this addition to the program, the find operation will work much the same as in the Series 3a's own database system.

Finding a record

The browse procedure allows you to move back and forth through the records, and to find a specific record using the FIND command. However, you may wish to locate a record directly from the main menu - without having to go through the browsing' operation. To demonstrate the use of the FINDFIELD command, a find option has been included on the main menu, which will call PROC f when selected.

Edit the current PROC f procedure to read as follows:

```
PROC f:
 LOCAL str$(32),field&,no&,flag%,cd%,borf%,d%
 LOCAL x%
 DO
   dINIT "Search for..."
   dEDIT str$,"Clue"
   dLONG field&,"Field to search:",1,5
   dLONG no&,"Number of rec fields to search",1,3
   dCHOICE cd%,"Case dependent?","No,Yes"
   dCHOICE borf%,"Which way?","Back from current,
same line continued      Forward from current,
same line continued      Back from end,Forward from start"
   d%=DIALOG
   IF d%
    cd%=(cd%-1)*16
    borf%=borf%-1
    IF borf%=0            REM Otherwise finds same record
     BACK
    ELSEIF borf%=1
     NEXT
    ENDIF
    flag%=cd%+borf%
    x%=FINDFIELD(str$,field&,no&,flag%)
    IF x%
     showrec:
    ELSE
     gAT 1,3
     PRINT "NONE FOUND"
    ENDIF
    GET
    CLS
   ENDIF
  UNTIL d%=0
ENDP
```

When using the 'Find' option from the menu, you can enter wildcards for the search clue, just as for the FIND option when browsing the records. The procedure PROC f allows for a specific field to be selected for the search: however, in the current program, only one field is a string field, and searches, remember, are made only through string fields.

Updating records

Updating records is a fairly similar process to adding a record. However, this time the record needs to be found and its contents displayed ready for updating. Remember that the field variables hold the contents of the *current* record in the *current* database file.

UPDATE This command *deletes* the current record from the file, then *appends* the data held in the field variables as a new record *at the end of the file*. This newly updated record - now the last one in the file - is made the *current* record.

You will perhaps appreciate, from the action of this command, that 'sorting' out the records into some kind of order can be a little futile for general purposes: the order will change as soon as you alter the contents of one of the records. For print-outs, you may wish to sort the records of course.

Each record in a data file is limited to a total of 1022 characters. You can test the size of an individual record with the RECSIZE function.

RECSIZE The format is

$$r\%=RECSIZE$$

This returns the number of characters used by the current record. If you think that the records in your file may exceed the 1022 limit, then before an 'APPEND' or 'UPDATE' command, you should have a section of code which checks the size of the record first.

Adding an 'update' routine to 'datman'

You can now add an update routine to the Database Manager program: edit 'PROC u:' to read as follows:

```
PROC u:
 LOCAL d%,t%,item$(16),number&,cost
 t%=b:                          REM First find the record!
 IF t%                          REM Found - see PROC b:
  item$=a.item$                 REM Assign the variables
  number&=a.number%             REM Watch the identifiers!
  cost=a.cost
  dINIT "Changing a Record"
  dEDIT item$,"Item:",16
  dLONG number&,"How many:",0,10000
  dFLOAT cost,"Each Costs: £",0,10000
  dBUTTONS "Change",13,"Cancel",27
  d%=DIALOG
  IF d%
   a.item$=item$                REM Assign field variables
   a.number%=number&
   a.cost=cost
   UPDATE
  ENDIF
 ENDIF
ENDP
```

As you can see, the 'browse' procedure (PROC b) is used to find the required record: when it is found, you simply press ENTER or ESC and '1' will be returned into t%. in this procedure. (The PROC f procedure could have been used, but the browse procedure makes it easier to search through the file).

The 'Update' dialog is then displayed, ready for your amendment(s). If a data file hasn't been opened, then the 'browse' routine will detect it - and '1' will not be returned into t%: this procedure will then just terminate, the error message having already been displayed via the 'browse' routine.

Deleting a record

To delete a record, first of all you need to locate the record you wish to delete (the 'browse' function will do nicely again), confirm the deletion (just in case), then do it.

ERASE This command deletes the *current* record from the *current* file. When the record is deleted, the next one is made the *current* record. However, if you delete the last record in the file, the *next* record is a 'null' (it theoretically doesn't exist yet), and the EOF function will return *true*. Your programs should cater for this eventuality: in datman, the FIRST record is always chosen to start any record searches, so erasing the last record will not present any problems when displaying records.

Adding a 'delete' routine to 'datman'

You can now complete PROC d. Edit it to read as follows:

```
PROC d:
 LOCAL t%
 t%=b:                          REM Find record
 IF t%                          REM Is the file open?
  showrec:                      REM Yes: carry on
  dINIT "Delete Record?"        REM Confirm deletion
  dPOSITION 1,1
  dBUTTONS "Yes",%y,"Cancel",27
  IF DIALOG                     REM If not cancelled
   ERASE                        REM Yes, it's that easy!
   CLS                          REM Tidy up
   GIPRINT "It's deleted, oh master",0
  ENDIF
 ENDIF
ENDP
```

Tailor your database

That completes all of the basic database handling functions: as you can see, it takes a considerable amount of programming just to get a simple database into action.

The good news is that most of the 'donkey work' has been done when you reach this stage: for your own database, you will need to arrange for the *fields* that you want, and adjust the field variables throughout accordingly.

When displaying dialogs involving the contents of field variables, remember that a dialog box can have only nine lines altogether, including the title and buttons. The alternative is to use the text screen commands (such as PRINT and INPUT).

You can of course adapt the record fields (and the number of them), and dialog messages to suit your own particular database requirements. The basic (*very* basic) datman program should give you a good starting point, but do be careful when you change it to examine *all* the routines that the changes may affect!

It is extremely unlikely that you would want to produce a database in which you can perform just the basic functions: it would be better to use the Series 3a database. You will probably want to extract specific information based on the data that's stored in each of the records, to produce analytical data that you may need. Read on...

Analysing the records

This is the area where you have to write the program procedures to suit your specific needs. To demonstrate the processes that can be involved, the so-far unused procedures 'PROC i' and 'PROC s' will be used to provide analytical routines.

As datman has been written as a mini-stock control program, the chances are one would want to find the cost of the stock of one particular item - and the cost of all the stock added together. These two possibilities are chosen since one involves selecting a record, and making a calculation, and the other involves going through *all* the records: two of the most common requirements in database management programs.

The total value of a specified stock item is dealt with first. For this, the particular item needs to be selected (good old 'browse' again), and then the calculation made. As before, the 'browse' routine will take care of unopened files: you just need to make sure before any calculations are performed that there hasn't been an error - in other words, 'PROC b:' returned a '1'. For this demonstration procedure, the information is displayed using the text screen. You could choose to use a graphics window, in order to embolden or italicise certain parts of the display: remember to close the window at the end of the procedure though (gCLOSE), otherwise it will mask out the other displays.

Here's the procedure: edit PROC i to read as follows.

```
PROC i:
 LOCAL t%,tc
 t%=b:                          REM Find required record
 IF t%
  tc=a.number%*a.cost
  AT 1,1
  PRINT "Item           : ",a.item$
  PRINT "Number in stock: ",a.number%
```

```
   PRINT "Each costs    : £";a.cost
   PRINT "TOTAL VALUE   : £";tc
   GET
   CLS
  ENDIF
ENDP
```

To analyse every record in the file, you need a simple loop so that each record is examined in turn and the necessary calculations made. To find the total value of all the items in stock, the individual values are added to a running total. Here's a simple procedure to tackle the job: edit 'PROC s' as follows.

```
PROC s:
 LOCAL total,ic%
ONERR notopen::
 FIRST
 DO
  total=total+a.number%*a.cost
  ic%=ic%+a.number%
  NEXT
 UNTIL EOF
 AT 1,1
 PRINT "Total Items in Stock =",ic%
 PRINT "Total stock Value =    £";total
 GET
 CLS
 RETURN
notopen::
 ONERR OFF
 showerr:(err$(err))
ENDP
```

When you're happy with your datman program, and you have 'filled in' all of the procedures, you can delete the procedure 'notimp'. You can leave the error handling routines in the datman procedure itself, if you wish, as these will trap any other errors that may crop up.

Remember though that, by having your own error trapping routine, you prevent Series 3a from locating the error for you. If you want to prevent this, 'switch off' the error handling routines by preceding the 'ONERR' statements with 'REM' and a space.

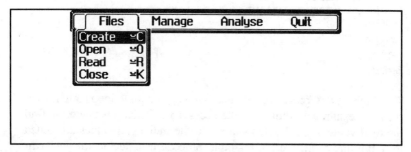

The Datman program menu

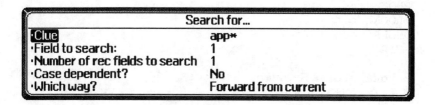

Using the 'Find' option to locate a record item

Chapter 30
Handling files

This Chapter shows you how to manage files. The OPL words covered are
SPACE, MKDIR, RMDIR, SETPATH, DIR$, COMPRESS, COPY, RENAME, DELETE, LOPEN, LPRINT, LCLOSE.

Looking after the files

Whilst the Series 3a has excellent facilities for creating and removing directories and for file handling in general, you may wish to have your own file handling program. OPL will certainly allow you to do this, with a range of commands and functions specifically designed for the purpose.

When you first start using your Series 3a, looking after the files is not much of a problem. Like Topsy, however, they have a habit of growing (in number), until one day you'll find you have long lists of files stored in various directories. Being able to handle the files - moving them around, deleting and generally keeping them organised - is good 'computer housekeeping'.

With the commands discussed in this Chapter - and all of the others available to you, you can create a File Handling program along the same lines as the Database Manager built-up in the previous Chapter. To do this, construct a 'shell' procedure to start with, using a Menu system with all of the options you wish to have. Then, for each of the individual routines, set up a 'dummy' procedure (as you did for the Database manager), so that you can test your 'shell' program as you go along.

Alternatively, you may wish to incorporate all or some of the facilities into your Database Manager program, by adding additional options to the Menu with corresponding handling procedures.

How much memory is left?

Although you can quickly look at how much memory you have used through the Series 3a's system menus, it may be necessary for your *programs* to know. For example, when adding records to a file, there could well come a point when the file is then too long to fit in the memory area allocated to it.

327

SPACE   This command returns the number of free *bytes* (or 'characters') available in the memory area *currently* being used by a file. With SSDs, the amount of space available can be as much as 2 megabytes (2 million characters) - and so the value returned is a *long* integer. The format is

s&=SPACE

You could use this function to simply report the number of bytes available on the current 'drive' at any time, with a statement line such as

```
PRINT SPACE
```

or you can use it in, say, a record APPENDing routine, with statement lines such as:

```
...
IF RECSIZE>SPACE
 PRINT "Disk full"
 GET
ELSE
 APPEND
ENDIF
...
```

The message can be displayed in a variety of ways, of course, using dialogs or the BUSY command and so on, to suit your program.

Creating and removing directories

To save leaving your program in order to create or remove a directory, you can incorporate appropriate routines in your program. Remember that a directory is simply a 'heading' under which files are stored. It can have sub-directories which in turn can have sub-sub directories - and so on, as requirements demand. A directory does not allocate or specify any particular amount of memory: one directory can be crammed with files, another virtually empty. As long as there is space on the 'drive', files can be added to any directory.

Series 3a maintains a number of 'default' directories for its own operations, automatically creating them if they don't exist. For example, if you decide to save a program source code file to an SSD which has just been formatted, then without any effort on your part, the appropriate default directory is created for that program.

MKDIR *name$*   This creates a new directory with the path and name specified by *name$*. The details of paths and names were given in Chapter 27. For example, to create a sub-directory of the word processor directory 'WRD', called 'LETTERS', you could use a program statement such as

```
MKDIR "\WRD\LETTERS"
```

To create the same directory on an SSD fitted into drive 'A', the command would be

```
MKDIR "A:\WDR\LETTERS"
```

If the directory 'WRD' isn't already present on the SSD, then that would also be created. The directory names must always be preceded by a 'backslash' ('\').

You could of course use the INPUT or the dFILE dialog function to get the name in from the keyboard: if using the dFILE function, remember that you can set the type of input that can be accepted to 'Directories only'.

RMDIR *name$*   This command simply removes an *empty* directory specified by *name$*, and is used in the same way as the MKDIR command. If the directory specified doesn't exist, or there are files contained in it, an error will be reported.

SETPATH *name$*   This sets the path and directory to be used for data files to that specified by *name$*: it doesn't affect the directory used by the currently running program - or the directory used for a LOADM command (to load a file of procedures into the current program).

What's in a directory?

There may be occasions when you need to obtain a listing of what is in a particular directory. This can be achieved with the DIR$ function.

DIR$(***spec$*)**   This function has two formats. The very first time it is used, *spec$* must contain the path and 'specification' of the type of files you wish to see. The *first* file matching

329

that specification is then returned. To find the *subsequent* matching files, the second format is used, with *spec$* made a 'null' string. When no files match the specification originally set by *spec$*, then a null string is returned. Thus, the formats are

```
d$=DIR$(spec$)        REM First time used
d$=DIR$("")           REM Subsequent use
```

The variable d$ must have been declared to hold at least 128 characters. The *filename* part of *spec$* can contain wildcards, so that you could, for example, examine all the files of a specific type in a particular directory, or examine all the files in a directory - with the filename specified by wildcards only - '*.*'. Here is an example procedure.

```
PROC files:
 LOCAL spec$(128),d$(128),c%,y%
 dINIT "Examine Files"
 dFILE spec$,"Path and ",3        REM dFIlE adds 'name'
 IF DIALOG
  d$=DIR$(spec$)
  WHILE d$<>""                    REM If no file, don't bother
   IF c%<15
     PRINT d$
     d$=DIR$("")
     c%=c%+1                      REM Line counter
    ELSEIF c%<31                  REM Screen filled?
     AT 35,y%+1                   REM Second column
     PRINT d$
     d$=DIR$("")
     c%=c%+1
     y%=y%+1
    ELSE
     BUSY "More...",3             REM Well, you never know...
     GET
     CLS                          REM Ready for next lot
     c%=0                         REM Reset the counter
     y%=0                         REM Reset line position
    ENDIF
  ENDWH
  BUSY "All Done",3
  GET
  BUSY OFF
```

```
ENDIF
ENDP
```

This procedure will let you examine the files meeting your path and name specification: if more than a screen full of files are to be displayed, then the program waits for you to press a key. Notice how the *full* path to the file is listed during the display: for files stored in the Series 3a itself, you need only enter the directory and file specification. For example, to produce a list of all of the opl source code programs you have, for the 'Path and Name' you would enter

\opl*.opl

Copying files

Two commands are available for you to make a copy of a file at a different location, or to make a copy with a different name in the same directory. The commands are COPY and COMPRESS. The 'rules' for each are fairly similar, but COMPRESS is used only for *data* files: it doesn't copy any *deleted* records to the new location (whereas COPY does).

COPY *source$,dest$*   This copies the file or files specified by the directory path and filename *source$* to the directory and filename specified by *dest$*.

If there is already a file of the same name at the *dest$* specification, then *that file is deleted.*

The *source$* filename and extension can, if you wish, include wildcards, so that you could copy a whole group of files. However, if you do this, then *only* the *directory* path must be specified for the *dest$* (remember to use the closing backslash after the last directory name): all the files matching your 'wildcard' specification will be copied to the specified destination, deleting any files with the same names that may already exist there. If you choose to copy more than one file, then the extension *must* be specified for *source$*:

either the full extension, or the wildcard '*' for all extension names.

Thus, to copy all of your OPO program files (the translated versions) from internal memory to an '\OPO\' directory on an SSD fitted to drive (slot) 'A', you would use the statement line:

```
COPY "M:\OPO\*.OPO","A:\OPO\"
```

The destination directory must, of course exist, otherwise you'll get an error: if it doesn't, you can create it with the MKDIR command. You could also copy your '.OPO' files to, say, an \OPO\ directory on the 'C:' drive of connected PC, with the statement:

```
COPY "M:\OPO\*.OPO","REM::C:\OPO\"
```

'M:' is the internal memory area of the Series 3a. Provided that you don't use wildcards in the *source$* specification, you can also change the name when you copy the file to a new location. For example, if you have a database file called 'STOCK95.ODB' in the Internal '\ODB\' directory, you could copy it to an SSD in drive 'A' with the new name 'OLD92.ODB' with the line

```
COPY "M:\ODB\STOCK95.ODB","A:\ODB\OLD95.ODB"
```

COMPRESS *source$,dest$*   When you have a data file saved on a *flash* SSD, each time a record is deleted the space it occupies is not 'restored' for use again. If you use the COPY command to copy such files to another location, the 'deleted' records are also copied. The COMPRESS command avoids this: when it performs the copy operation, it ignores any records that have been deleted. (Note that the space occupied by deleted records in files saved in Series 3a's internal memory or on a RAM SSD is automatically 'recovered' for further use). COMPRESS can be used *only* on data files.

The *source$* and *dest$* specifications are as described for the COPY command. However, with COMPRESS, if a file of the same name as that being copied already exists at the destination, then the file being copied doesn't replace (or 'overwrite') the existing one, but is instead *appended* to it. If you don't want this to happen - you want the file being copied to replace any existing file - then before the COMPRESS statement you need to delete the existing file first. To save worrying about whether or not the file exists before you try to delete it, you can use the statement

TRAP DELETE dest$

This prevents Series 3a from stopping the program to report an error if the file doesn't exist. Since you won't be worried whether it exists or not - you just want the new file to be copied - no further action need be taken.

Renaming and deleting files

You can, from within a program, rename or delete any file at any location.

RENAME *oldname$,newname$* *oldname$* is the directory path and name of the file being renamed, and *newname$* is the directory path and new name for the file.

If you specify a different location (directory path) for *newname$*, then the original file is 'deleted', and copied to the newly specified destination with the new name. This provides an easy way to transfer or *move* any type of file from one location to another, and, if you wish, change its name in the process.

You *cannot* use wildcards in either the *oldname$* or *newname$* specifications.

DELETE *fname$* This command deletes the file specified by *fname$*, which should include the directory path. With this command you can use wildcards to delete a whole range of files. For example, if you wish to delete *all* of your '.OPO' files from the '\OPO\' directory in internal RAM, then the command would be

```
DELETE "M:\OPO\*.OPO"
```

You should note that, once a file has been deleted, it is irretrievable. You should be particularly careful, therefore, when deleting your *source* code files: the program-running files can always be re-created from a source file, by 'translating' them again. But there is no way back to a source file, short of re-writing it.

Printing data files

Three commands are involved in printing a data file to a connected printer, or to a file.

LOPEN *device$*   Before any data file can be printed, the *route* or *device* must be identified to the Series 3a. If a printer is being used, then one of the two following options are available:

```
LOPEN "PAR:A"    REM For a printer connected to the parallel port
LOPEN "TTY:A"    REM For a printer connected to the Serial port
```

If you want to copy file data into another file - either in the Series 3a or on an externally connected computer, then *device$* becomes the directory path and file name of the file concerned. Thus, for externally connected computers, you could have commands such as

```
LOPEN "REM::C:\WORD\DATA.DBF"    REM For PCs
LOPEN "REM::WORD:DATA:MINE"      REM For Apple Macs™
```

When writing to computer files, whether internal or external, any existing file of the same name will be overwritten.

You can have only one device open at a time: if you wish to use another and one is already opened, the opened one must be closed first.

LCLOSE   This command closes the device opened by LOPEN: The device is automatically closed when the program ends, but it is good programming practice to close a previously opened device within the program.

LPRINT *expression list*   This is exactly the same as the PRINT command, with the only difference that the 'print-out' is directed to the opened device, usually a printer. A route to the destination for the print-out must have been opened (using LOPEN), otherwise an error will occur.

Printing to a parallel port is fairly straightforward. However, you should be aware that your data is not being formatted by any of the built in drivers: your program must incorporate all the printer commands that you wish to use - including new lines and tabs. If you simply direct a data file's output to the printer, you may or may not get a formatted display. You will need to check with your printer manual for the codes it needs to produce formatted print.

As a *guide only* to the type of programming sequence you *might* have, here is a section of a program which could send a data file to a parallel connected printer (it is assumed that a file with the logical identifier 'A' has been opened):

```
LOPEN "PAR:A"
FIRST
WHILE NOT EOF
  PRINT "ITEM :";CHR$(9);a.item$
  PRINT "QUANTITY :";CHR$(9);a.number%
  PRINT "COST EACH:";CHR$(9);a.cost
ENDW
```

The 'CHR$(9)', on most printers, issues a 'TAB' command.

Printing to a Serial port can be a little trickier: it all depends whether the default characteristics match the connected device. Full details of how to set the transmission characteristics are given in your Series 3a Programming Manual, together with a straightforward routine (rsset:) which will set the required values for you. You will be able to obtain the values you need from your Printer manual.

Sorted print-outs

However careful you may be to enter data into a file in some kind of order, as soon as you start to change that data, the order also changes. This makes any print-out a little random - the records are printed in order of their position within the file.

There is a variety of different techniques for sorting individual items or complete records into some kind of required order. These techniques enjoy wondrous names such as Bubble Sort, Shell Sort, Insertion Sort, Heap Sort, Quick Sort, Radix Sort ... and so on. Complete books have been written about sorting techniques alone. Each technique has advantages and disadvantages, although it must be said that, whatever the application, some sorting techniques are considerably faster (by a factor of ten or more) than others.

To produce a program for Series 3a that sorts records into order is almost a waste of time and memory storage space, for the order will be changed as soon as the file is updated again. However, it is recognised that, if you have a series of records to be printed out, it would be more practical for the print-out to be in some kind of order.

Here is a very (*very*) crude way to achieve this objective. It takes a file, and, before printing out any record, it goes through the file to find the 'first' record that should appear in the list, and prints it. That record is then 'tagged' (using an array dimensioned large enough to cope with all of the records) so that it isn't selected again. The process is then repeated to find the next record that should be printed, and when found, that too is printed and tagged. It sounds a long-winded process, but is in fact fairly quick - tagged records are ignored, so the searches speed up as printing continues.

This program assumes that you have a file in which the field on which the listing is to be based is *item$*, and that other fields for print-out are *number%* and *cost*: you must use the appropriate field names when adapting the program to your own needs. For demonstration purposes, the program prints to the screen: it is written as separate procedures, so that you can easily adapt it to provide for your own printer. It would make a useful addition to the datman program given in Chapter 29 - adding suitable items to the menu (Print to Screen, and Print to Printer, perhaps). The destination for the print-out - screen or printer- can be controlled by the use of an LOPEN command before the sorted printout procedures are called, with tests to determine where the print-output should be directed (e.g. IF LOPEN=....)

```
PROC prntsort:
 LOCAL fn$(128),d%
 dINIT "Sort and Print"
 dFILE fn$,"File",3
 IF DIALOG
  OPENR fn$,A,item$,number%,cost        REM See Note 1
  sortit:
 ENDIF
ENDP

PROC sortit:
 LOCAL r%,c%,t%(2000),rec$(36)          REM See Note 2
 FIRST
 DO
  WHILE t%(POS)=1                       REM See Note 3
   NEXT
  ENDWH
  rec$=a.item$                          REM See Note 4
  r%=POS
  DO
   NEXT                                 REM Note 5
   IF UPPER$(a.item$)<UPPER$(rec$) AND t%(POS)=0
    rec$=a.item$
    r%=POS
   ENDIF
  UNTIL EOF
  t%(r%)=1                              REM Note 6
  doprint:(r%)
  c%=c%+1                               REM Note 7
  FIRST                                 REM Do it again
 UNTIL c%=COUNT+1                       REM for all records
 GET                                    REM Note 8
ENDP

PROC doprint:(recno%)
 POSITION recno%                        REM Note 9
 IF NOT EOF                             REM Note 10
  PRINT a.item$;CHR$(9);                REM Note 11
  PRINT a.number%;CHR$(9);
  PRINT "£";a.cost
 ENDIF
ENDP
```

Note 1: Open the file (for read-only, preferably) with the field names you used for *your* database file.

Note 2: Set `t%()` so that it is large enough to hold all of the records in your data file, *plus at least one*: too few will cause an error when the program is run. The string `rec$` is for storing the information that is going to be used to determine the order. Dimension it large enough to hold the longest string. If you want the print-out to be ordered on, say, the *cost*, then this must be a *float* type of variable, and you will compare the *cost* fields rather than the *item* fields.

Note 3: Things can be speeded up a bit by not bothering with records that have already been tagged: this little routine short-cuts to the first *untagged* record.

Note 4: The information in the field that you want your print-out based on is stored ready for the comparison test. The program also needs to know *which record* this is, so the record number (`POS`) is also saved.

Note 5: Each of the following records is selected in turn, to see if the comparison record should come before it, or after it. If the next record should come first *and* it hasn't already been tagged, the 'comparison' variable is updated *as well as* the corresponding record number. This becomes the new comparison record.

Note 6: When the End Of the File has been reached, `rec$` will be holding the next *item* to print (or whichever field you have chosen), and its *record number* or *position* will be saved in r%. As this record is about to be printed, it is assigned a value ('tagged') in the tag array `t%()`, so that it isn't selected again.

Note 7: The end of the file has been reached, and the whole process needs to be repeated for the next record that should be printed out. Each time round, one record number is tagged (who knows which? Only Series 3a!). The 'file pointer' needs to be reset back to the first record, the print routine called, and a count kept of the number of records printed out.

The program continues until all records are printed (UNTIL c%=COUNT+1).

Note 8: This is for the screen print-out - you won't see the list without this!

Note 9: In the print-out routine, the right record must be selected - passed into the routine via recno%.

Note 10: When EOF is *true* in the previous routine, the program is actually looking at the blank record beyond the end of the file (it will usually be the very first one that's found, as it contains nothing and, in a sort, 'nothing' comes first). It will in fact have a record number one higher than the number of records in the data file: that's why the *minimum* value that the t%() array should be dimensioned is the number of records plus one. You don't want this one printed, so it is ignored.

Note 11: Here ordinary PRINT statements have been used to send the display of records to the screen: for a printer, you would use LPRINT statements, *remembering that you must have first used the* LOPEN *command*. Normally this is best located in the very first procedure (PROC prntsort:). The CHR$(9) produces a 'TAB' on the screen and on most printers: you must provide all the formatting that you want in this part of the program, using the printer codes for your printer. Individual characters can be sent using the CHR$() format. To send two or more characters, say 'ESC' followed by the letter 'A', you can use CHR$(27);"A", the semi-colon being important. Alternatively, you can set up a 'constant' variable. For example, if to embolden print on your printer requires a code of 'ESC E', you can set up a variable as follows

```
bold$=CHR$(27);"E"
```

and use 'bold$' whenever you want the next bit to be printed in bold letters. You must also, of course, send the code to clear or cancel bold printing when bold is no longer required.

Finally, any other information you want printed out - such as totals and so forth, you can tackle in a separate procedure called after the 'sortit:' procedure. Simply perform the analysis (as was demonstrated in the datman program), then print out the results formatted as you wish.

```
apples   40      10
bananas  30      30
beans    58      35
fish     50      31
grapes   20      40
meat     12      32
peaches  10      35
pears    30      15
plums    45      22
```

A file of random records created with the Datman program, displayed in alphabetic order using Prntsort

PART 4

Advanced topics

This Part of the Book introduces some of the more advanced programming capabilities provided by OPL.

CHAPTER 31
Creating applications

*This Chapter discusses the ways you can turn a program
into an 'application' to be run from an icon on the system
screen. OPL words covered are*
APP, TYPE, PATH, EXT, ICON, CMD$, GETCMD$,
TESTEVENT, GETEVENT, LOCK

What is an application?

So far, to run the programs discussed in this book from the *system*
screen, you had to select the program name from beneath the second
OPL icon (known as the RunOpl icon). But you may wish to have your
program 'installed' as an *application*, just like the other Series 3a
applications (Word processor, Spreadsheet, World, and so on). You
could achieve this when you write your program, by simply preceding
the program code with a few new instructions, not yet discussed.

However, creating an application properly can involve far more
than just adding these few lines of code. First of all, applications on the
system screen are identified by an icon, and whilst you don't actually
have to have a suitable icon saved (as a '.pic' file) for your application,
it is better that you do since without one, Series 3a will simply display a
standard box-shaped icon.

Secondly, the application program must (ideally) cater for *system
events* - that is, operations that occur externally to your program from,
say, the system screen. For example, you should be able to run the
application with a particular file (as when running the Spreadsheet or
Word processor), or to delete a file from the system screen in the usual
manner (PSION and ⌷ keys). Catering for system events adds
considerably to the code as well as making it more complex, and
requires a little better understanding of the way that the Series 3a
operates. In fact, creating an application requires a slightly different
approach when creating programs to that discussed so far in this book.

To give an example, the datman program described in the File
Handling Chapters allows files to be created or opened only while the
program is being run, and doesn't allow for their deletion: as a proper
application, it should be possible to create, open and delete files from
the *system* screen. The program should ideally cater for these actions.

You *could* simply convert the datman program by adding the necessary few lines of code at the beginning, allowing all file handling to be within the program itself. But then you wouldn't get the file names listed under the datman application icon - simply the program name.

A *translated* application program (an .OPA file rather than an .OPO file), is saved in the \APP\ directory within the Series 3a - *not* the \OPO\ directory, and it has to be *installed* on the system screen like any other application you may add (the INSTALL item from the APPS menu option). Once installed, any .OPO files created during program development can, of course, be deleted.

Full details about creating applications are beyond the scope of this book. Given in this Chapter is a comprehensive outline of what is involved, with details of the necessary OPL language words, to enable you to construct simple applications.

Types of application

You may not have appreciated it, but there are various *types* of application on your Series 3a, according to the *file handling* requirements. The Calculator application, for example, doesn't use files at all, the World application uses files, but only one can be opened at a time, the Word, Spreadsheet and Agenda applications uses files - and you can either have just one in use at a time or, by using SHIFT and ENTER keys on a new file name (from the system screen) you can have two or more files opened at a time (shown in bold on the system screen). With this last type, when you start the application by opening a second file, the application actually 'runs again' - so two (or more) versions of the application will be running. As you will appreciate, this can be memory consuming.

Finally, there is the type of application that *always* runs the application again when you select a new file (by simply pressing ENTER on the file's name from the system screen). The translated OPL programs under the RunOpl icon (the rightmost of the two OPL icons) are like this: for these, of course, each file is an actual program. You can, therefore, have a number of OPL programs running at the same time.

In all, there are five different types of application. They are as follows:

TYPE 0   The application uses no files. (like the calculator)

TYPE 1   Only one data file is used. This is effectively the same as a TYPE 0 application - the difference is the application will be using a file that has the same name as the application.

TYPE 2   Can use more than one data file, but only one can be in use at a time: in other words, you can only run one version of the application at a time. (Like World)

TYPE 3   Can use more than one file, and any number can be in use at a time. If a file had previously been opened (shown in bold on the system screen) and you select another then press ENTER, then the application will simply switch files: if you press SHIFT and ENTER, then another version of the application starts running, using the selected file. (The Word processor, Spreadsheet and Agenda applications are examples of this type)

TYPE 4   This is just like TYPE 3, except that pressing ENTER on a file name *always* starts the application with that file. The OPL programs under the RunOpl icon are of this type - whichever one you select runs that particular program. You can have as many of your OPL programs running as memory will permit (leaving them running by simply pressing the SYSTEM button).

Application Types 2, 3 and 4 will allow you to create new file names to add to the list under the icon, by selecting 'New File' from the Files menu option on the system screen (provided that the application programs you write cater for this!).

You can stop any application from running by selecting its (bold) name on the system screen, and pressing the DELETE key: again any application you write should cater for this. Note that this is achieved for you with translated OPL programs: try it - run a program that you have entered, then press the SYSTEM button to switch to the system screen. Select the highlighted program and press the DELETE key - you will be able to quit the program. On the other hand, if you try to create a new file whilst an OPL program is highlighted on the system screen, you will get the message that that's not possible.

Defining an application

To create an application, your program needs a few lines of code at the very start. Instead of the usual PROC, the first line must be the word

'APP' followed by a name, and the following lines can be any or all of the keywords PATH, EXT, ICON and TYPE. The final line of the application definition must be ENDA. Thus, a typical application using all of the optional keywords might look like this:

```
APP Datman
  TYPE 3
  PATH "\OPD"
  EXT "DAT"
  ICON "\OPD\datman.pic"
ENDA
```

The keywords are as follows:

APP   Just as PROC tells Series 3a that a new procedure is about to be defined, so APP tells Series 3a that an application is being defined. It must be followed by a name which *must* begin with a letter, and be no longer than 8 letters and numbers long. The name does *not* have quotation marks round it.

TYPE   This optional keyword is followed by an integer number (*not* a variable, *nor* an expression) representing the type of application you want to create (as discussed in the previous paragraphs). **For Series 3a applications that have their own 48x48 pixel black *and* grey icons, you must add the hex value $1000 to the type number.** Series *3* applications use icons sized 24x24 pixels and are in black only.

There are also three other hex values you can add to the TYPE value, as follows:

$8000   This prevents new files from being created by using the system screen menu's 'New File' option (as the RunOpl files)

$4000   This prevents the application from being closed from the system screen (as the Time application). Do not use this one unless it is absolutely necessary!

$100   This enables the application to be terminated from the system screen *without* sending a system message to the application that 'exit' has been requested (as the RunOpl files). You should *not* use this one if your application uses files: the program will terminate without the files being saved properly, with a potential loss of data.

Remember that the value following TYPE must *not* be a variable or an expression. TYPE $1000+3, for example, will cause an error: instead you must write TYPE $1003

If you do not use this keyword, then the application will be TYPE 0 by default.

PATH   If you are using files, then you can, with this keyword, identify the directory where you will be saving files in your program. The path simply consists of the directory name, in quotes - do not include the drive (for an SSD, for example). The maximum length, including the 'backslash', is 19 characters.

If you do not use this keyword, then the directory will be considered to be \OPD by default.

EXT   This gives the *extension* you are going to give to file names in your program - the extension is the three characters that follow the full point after the file name. This does *not* define the file type - that's governed by your program.

> **Note:** The PATH and EXT keywords provide information for the system screen, and don't actually determine *where* the files will be saved or the extension they will be given. Your program does that. The information provided by these two keywords enables Series 3a to list the files you create under the application's icon.

ICON   This keyword is followed by the directory and name of the bitmap '.pic' file to be used for the application's icon: the bitmap must have been created *before* the application is installed (that is to say, it must already be in existence as a file). If $1000 is added to the TYPE value, then a Series 3a icon is expected - a 48x48 pixel black bitmap followed by a 48x48 grey bitmap. If you created the icon and used gSAVEBIT to save it, then the black and grey bitmaps will be in the correct order.

ENDA   This ends the application header details.

All of the arguments to any of the keywords *must* be actual values, and not variables or expressions (you can't use 'TYPE 1+$1000', for example - you must use 'TYPE $1001').

Catering for system events

The multitasking capabilities of the Series 3a mean that a number of things are going on at the same time. You may have a number of applications and programs running (shown in bold on the system screen), and from the system screen, select a new file to use, close an application, delete a file, choose to start an application with a new file, and so on. These and similar actions are known as *events*. They are communicated to an application by a *system message*.

Your application must cater for such messages - it must check whether an event has occurred, and find out what the event is.

Determining the file to use

The first thing an application that can use more than one file (Types 2, 3 and 4) must do is find out which file the application is to use - and whether it is an existing file to be opened, or a new one to be created. The command to achieve this is CMD$, which passes information to the application when it is started, as follows.

CMD$ (1) This is the full path name used to run the application.

CMD$ (2) This gives the full path name for the file to be used by the application.

CMD$ (3) This will be "C" (upper case) to *create* a new file - which will be the case the very first time the application is used, or whenever 'New File' has been selected from the system screen to start the application with a new file. Otherwise, it will be "O", to open an existing file.

CMD$ (4) need not concern you.

CMD$ (5) This gives the application's name, as declared with APP.

Thus, the two CMD$ () values that provide the required information are CMD$ (2), which gives the name of the file to use, and CMD$ (3), which says whether it should be created or opened. Your program can handle the requirement with code something like this:

```
fname$=CMD$ (2)          REM Get the file name
IF  CMD$ (3) ="C"        REM A new file is wanted
   docreate: (fname$)    REM Call a file creation procedure
ELSE
   doopen: (fname$)      REM Call a file opening procedure
ENDIF
```

The file creation (especially) and the file opening procedures should have error trapping routines (TRAP CREATE and TRAP OPEN, for example), in case an unacceptable name is used.

Testing for events

Two commands are available. They are TESTEVENT and GETEVENT. *All* types of OPA application should use these keywords to test for key-presses and system messages. Some keyboard commands - such as EDIT, GET, INPUT, PAUSE, MENU and DIALOG - cause system messages to be ignored. So before using such keywords, you should ensure that Series 3a is prevented from sending such messages by use of the instruction 'LOCK' (described later).

TESTEVENT   simply checks whether an event has occurred - but does nothing about it: the program continues immediately with the next instruction. TESTEVENT returns zero if an event hasn't occurred, and non-zero if an event has occurred. If an event *has* occurred, it can be 'read' by the GETEVENT function.

GETEVENT ve%() Unlike TESTEVENT, this command *waits* for an event to happen or, if an event has occurred - as detected by TESTEVENT - then it will acquire the event information. The information is saved in an integer array ve%(), which must have been previously declared with six elements - although currently, only the first two are used.

The contents of the ve%() array depend on the type of event that has occurred, and are as follows.

If the event is a keypress:

ve%(1)   ve%(1) AND $400 is zero, and the value stored by ve%(1) is the key code for the pressed key (as for GET).

ve%(2)   ve%(1) AND $ff gives the code for any modifier key that may have been pressed (as for KMOD). If GETEVENT is used, the modifier will *not* be returned by KMOD.

ve%(2)/256 gives the auto-repeat count (a value ignored by the GET command).

If the event is *not* a keypress:

ve%(1) ve%(1) AND $400 is non-zero, and the values of ve%(1) then have the following meanings:

$401 The program has moved into the 'foreground' (on screen)

$402 The program has moved into the 'background'.

$403 The machine has been switched on.

$404 A request has been made from the system screen to change files, or exit.

$405 The date has changed.

Of particular interest for applications that operate on files is the non-key event $404 - which means that a change of file has been selected from the system screen. On such an event, your program must ascertain the name of the file to be used, and the operation - open an existing file, create a new one, or exit the application running with the current file.

Getting in a new file name

The OPL function available for this is GETCMD$.

**GETCMD$** Whereas CMD$() returns the name of the file to use when starting an application, GETCMD$ returns the name of a new file after a 'change the file' or a 'quit the application' event has occurred from the system screen. That is to say, if the application is running (one of the file names under its icon is bold) and, from the system screen, you select another file to use, or select the emboldened file name and press the DELETE key to quit the application. The format is

fd$=GETCMD$

The *first* character of string fd$ is either "C", "O", or "X" - always upper case. These have the following meanings.

"C" means *close down the currently opened file*, and *create* a new one with the name specified by the remaining contents of fd$.

"O" means *close down the currently opened file*, and *open* the file specified by the remaining contents of fd$.

> **"X"** means *close down the current file - if one is opened*, and *quit* the application. In this instance, fd$ will not contain a file name.

Thus, an application program that uses files (a Type 3, for example) could have a portion of code that looks something like this (it is assumed all variables have been properly declared and the procedures named actually exist!):

```
IF TESTEVENT            REM An event has occurred
 GETEVENT ve%()         REM What is it?
 IF ve%(1)=$404         REM System file instruction
  fd$=GETCMD$           REM What is it?
  a$=LEFT$(fd$,1)       REM Strip off first letter
  fd$=MID$(fd$,2,127)   REM Get file name in fd$
  IF a$="X"             REM Quit application
   quitapp:             REM So go do it
  ELSEIF a$="C"         REM Create a new file, so
   docreate:(fd$)       REM go and create new one
  ELSEIF a$="O"         REM Open another file
   doopen:(fd$)         REM so go and open it
  ENDIF
  SETNAME fd$           REM If using a statuswindow
 ENDIF
ENDIF
```

Note that if your application allows only one file to be opened at a time then before creating a new file or opening an existing file, the current file should be closed. You should also use the TRAP command (followed by IF ERR code segments) to catch any errors that may occur during the closing/creating/opening processes.

As you will be aware, when you create a new file from the system screen, you can specify the location and device where the file is to be saved. Thus, you can create a file that is to be saved to a new directory on an SSD. It is important of course that your program is aware of this and, whenever creating a file, an application *should*, ideally, determine the location: it may be necessary, for example, to create the directory if it doesn't exist. An OPL word is available to determine the full path -

PARSE$** *(fn$,loc$,*__vos__*%())* This will return the full file and path specification of the file named by *fn$*. The variable loc$ contains any path information that is known (in case files of a similar name exist elsewhere), whilst **vos%() is an integer array of at least six elements that has been previously declared. The format is

```
path$=PARSE$(fn$,loc$,vos%())
```

After use, path$ will contain the full path and file name, and **vos%()** will hold offsets from the start of the full path name to various elements of the path, as follows.

vos%(1) This is always '1'. Ignore it.

vos%(2) This gives the position in path$ of the *device* letter (i.e. **vos%(2)** will have a value of 6 if path$ is "LOC::**M**:\DAT\STOCK.DBF".

vos%(3) This gives the position in path$ of the first character of the actual directory path (i.e., if path$ is as shown above, **vos%(3)** will have a value of 8, representing the position of the first '\').

vos%(4) This gives the position in path$ of the actual file name (i.e. using the above example for path$ again, **vos%(4)** will have a value of 13, representing the position of the 'S')

vos%(5) This gives the position of the file extension 'dot' (i.e., in the above example, **vos%(5)** will have a value of 18)

vos%(6) This holds a value representing any wildcards appearing in the full path, as follows

0	no wildcards
1	wildcard in the file name
2	wildcard in the file extension
3	wildcard in filename and extension

Thus, you could use TRAP MKDIR to ensure that the correct directory will be created if it doesn't exist - if it does exist, the TRAP command will ensure that the application doesn't stop to report the error, and everything will continue as required. The name for the *directory path* can be extracted from path$ using the offset positions given by $vos\%(3)$ and $vos\%(4)$, thus:

d$=MID$(path$,vos%(3),vos%(4)-vos%(3))

Inhibiting system events

It was mentioned earlier that some keywords cause system messages to be discarded. Before using these words, and on those occasions when your application goes into a long processing task, you should inhibit system messages from being passed to the application by *locking* it.

LOCK ON This command should be used *immediately* prior to the keywords EDIT, GET, KEY, INPUT, PAUSE, MENU and DIALOG, to prevent system messages from being passed to the application. When the LOCK ON is used and the application is, say, waiting for an input as a result of a GET command, if from the system screen an attempt is made to exit the application (by pressing the DELETE key with the application file name highlighted), a message will inform you that the application cannot close down at that moment.

It would also be good practice to use LOCK ON immediately before an application becomes busy for a length of time - perhaps calculating data within a loop - or at points where a 'clean exit' from the application is not possible.

LOCK OFF This command should be used as soon as possible after LOCK ON - for example, immediately after a DIALOG construction has been completed - to enable system messages to be passed to the application.

Installing the application

Once you have translated an application, it is stored in the \APP\ directory of the Series 3a. Instead of the usual "Run Program" request, you will get a dialog message informing you "Translation Complete", and you clear the dialog by pressing the ESC key.

Your application program has now been saved in the \APP\ directory of the Series 3a. To install it as an application:

1. Press the system button, to get to the system screen
2. Using the arrow keys, position the highlight to the point on the display where you want your application installed.

3. Press the PSION and ⊡ keys simultaneously, *or* select the 'Install' option from the 'Apps' menu item.

4. Your application should appear as the 'File Name': if it doesn't, use the left and right arrow keys to select it, then press ENTER.

5. Your application will be installed on the system screen. You can now run it just like any other application of the same type (provided, of course, that your application has catered for the necessary system events).

You can uninstall the application by selecting the 'Remove' option from 'Apps' menu item. Note that the application is only removed from the system screen - not from memory. To delete the translated file:

1. From the system screen press the TAB key.

2. Using the arrow keys, move to the '\' symbol below the line across the top and press ENTER.

3. Select the '\APP\' directory and press ENTER.

4. Select the application you wish to delete, and press the PSION and ⊡ keys, *or* select the 'Delete file' option from the 'File' menu item.

Generally speaking, once the application has been installed, any changes you make to the source code will be effective when you next run the application from the system screen - after translating the source code, of course: the application should *not* be running when you translate the source code again, otherwise you will get a message that the file (application) is in use.

Quick icon generator

This short routine allows you to create very simple icon '.pic' files: if you like the icon, press ENTER and it will be saved in the \OPD\ directory. If you don't, press ESC and experiment with the code...

```
PROC kwikicon:
  LOCAL c%
  gCREATE (0,0,48,48,1)     REM Grey included, but not used
  gBORDER $203              REM Choose your own
  gFONT 9                  REM Choose your own
  gAT 10,24                REM Will need adjusting
  gPRINT "MyApp"           REM Your application name
  c%=GET
  IF c%<>27                REM If not ESC, save it as .pic file
    gSAVEBIT "MyApp"        REM Your application name
  ENDIF
ENDP
```

Chapter 32
Caching

This Chapter gives a method for making your programs run faster. The OPL words covered are
CACHE, CACHETIDY

How programs run

When you run a program on your Series 3a, what actually happens is each procedure is loaded, as it is 'called' or used, into a special part of memory. When a procedure has finished its job it is removed from that special part of memory. The next time it is called, it is loaded back into the special part of memory again. This takes time.

As discussed in Chapter 4 (in the section dealing with the scope of GLOBAL variables, page 35), it is possible for a group of procedures to be 'loaded' at the same time - for example, when one procedure calls another, which in turn calls yet another, and so on.

The time taken to load in all of these procedures each time program flow runs through such a loop can slow down the running of the program. The cure can be to provide a *cache*.

With a cache, loaded procedures remain loaded, and so the time taken to unload and re-load them is eliminated - and program execution can be as much as ten times faster! Even when programs do not need to load and unload a number of procedures, they *could* be made to run faster by using a cache, since the way the program is assembled is 'different'

However, care has to be taken in deciding the *size* of the cache. There is also a possibility that 'bugs' that go undetected without caching will surface when caching is used.

For example, without caching, the memory reserved for the variables of each procedure is immediately followed by the actual program code. If more data is saved to a variable than is allowed for (as could happen with the OPL word gPEEKLINE), then actual code could be overwritten and corrupted. Provided that piece of code is not again used whilst the procedure is loaded, the problem will go unnoticed - when the procedure is removed from memory on its completion, the corrupted code is also removed, so the next time the procedure is

355

loaded, it will be as the original uncorrupted code. With caching, the program code does not immediately follow the memory area reserved for variables - so any overwriting would be in an unknown part of code - which may well result in the program crashing.

The way a cache works

When you create a cache you specify the initial amount of memory to be used, and the maximum that the Series 3a will be permitted to use. Called procedures are then loaded into this area - which is allowed to 'grow' up to the maximum specified. Should further procedures need to be cached and there is no space available, then the least used procedure is removed from the cache. You can prevent this unloading of procedures, if you wish (cache off), and you can remove unused procedures from the cache to make room for others (cachetidy).

When a library file is loaded (LOADM), the procedures in that, too, will be cached. When the library is unloaded, (UNLOADM), library procedures still in use in the cache remain there until they are no longer in use - then they are removed. However, unloading library files while procedures are still in use is not advisable.

Note: If a procedure has been translated for the Series 3, rather than the Series 3a (as may be the case for a library file of procedures), it cannot be cached.

Creating a cache

The OPL word that allows you to create a cache is ... CACHE.

CACHE *initial%, max%*   This allows you to create a cache memory with an initial size as determined by *initial%*, and a maximum size as determined by *max%*.

initial%   The minimum value for a cache is 2000 (2000 bytes). If you specify less than this, then the default will be 2000. Ideally speaking, you will select an initial cache size that will be large enough to hold all of the procedures that are to be cached.

max%   The maximum size that a cache can grow to is, to a large extent, governed by the amount of free memory available when the program is running. If you know the maximum size that the program will be when cached, then you will most often choose the same value for the initial and the maximum permitted size.

The maximum value *max%* can have is theoretically 32,767. However, you can exceed this figure if you really need to by using hex notation ($A000 for example): using this technique, the maximum cache size is $FFFF (64k).

If you wish to ensure that procedures are *not* removed from the cache at certain points in your program (before a procedure loop, for example), then use the command CACHE OFF.

CACHE OFF/ON CACHE OFF prevents any further caching of procedures - the cache will still be searched for any procedures that have already been cached. To re-enable caching, use CACHE ON.

To be absolutely sure that sufficient memory is available to create the cache, you should use the TRAP command -

        TRAP CACHE initial%,max%.

Naturally the CACHE ON/OFF commands can be used only after the initial CACHE instruction, and equally, there can be only one CACHE command in a program.

If you specify a maximum cache size and sufficient memory is not available, when the maximum possible has been reached procedures will be removed to make room for new ones: if there still isn't room for the new procedures, they will be loaded and run in the usual manner, and removed from memory when finished.

CACHETIDY You can clear a cache of all procedures that are not in current use (that is, have completed their task and have returned program flow to the procedure that called them) with the CACHETIDY command. If there are a lot of procedures in a cache, then using this command to remove them can speed up program flow by reducing the time needed to search through the cache for required procedures.

It also saves the time needed to remove them one at a time should the space be required for new procedures.

Unfortunately, there can be no set 'formula' for evaluating the best size for a cache to produce maximum speed: it really depends on the number of procedures in the program and how they are called.

For experienced and professional programmers, there are two advanced cache commands - used during program development only - which provide 'header' information about the cache (its size, the number of procedures currently cached, the number of bytes used by procedures not in use and which can consequently be removed, and so on), and 'records' of the actual procedures (the size and location of the less recently and most recently used cached procedures, and so on).

CHAPTER 33
Accessing the system

This Chapter briefly discusses some of the OPL words available for accessing the Series 3a system itself.

Be careful!

The OPL functions and commands provided throughout this book will enable you to write programs to suit virtually almost any requirement. They represent the *high level* elements of the OPL language. However, there is also an extensive range of OPL words which provide *low level* access to the Series 3a - that is, they operate at 'near' machine code level: in the main, they directly access the ROM or RAM areas of Series 3a, and demand a sound knowledge of 'machine coding' and of the Series 3a's operating system. Full details on the use of these OPL words is beyond the scope of this book: indeed, to cover them fully would take another book *three or four times* the size of this one!

Whilst some of the OPL words concerned are fairly harmless, others can cause serious problems if used rashly or without a thorough understanding of what they do and how they work.

They are included in OPL for the benefit of experienced and professional program developers. Unquestionably, they enable shorter, faster, more flexible and more sophisticated programs to be written - enabling otherwise 'unreachable' features to be accessed - such as the built-in digital sound system for recording or playback. Such programs are best developed *externally* to the Series 3a, using one of the special Developer's Kits available from Psion, and enabling thorough checking before being downloaded to the Series 3a.

In view of the potentially disastrous problems that can arise, it is not proposed to discuss these 'low level access' OPL words in any great detail: until you have the necessary background knowledge and experience to use them properly, it is probably advisable to ignore them. Nevertheless, you will want to be aware of their existence and what they do. For your information therefore, *some* of the words concerned, their purpose and their 'safety factor' are outlined in this Chapter. Please remember that the descriptions are not complete, and that the information given is for guidance only.

Examining memory contents

A number of words are available for examining the contents or accessing the contents of the Series 3a's memory. To locate where in memory a variable is stored, use ADDR.

ADDR (`variable` **)** This function returns the memory address in the Series 3a where the specified `variable` is stored. As it simply returns an address, it is fairly safe to use. The variable can be of any type - integer, long integer, string or float, and it can be an array. ADDR returns the first address used to store the variable. This information can be useful for those who wish to access the particular variable directly: knowledge of how each type of variable is stored is required. The format is

$$a\%=ADDR(variable)$$

You can add (or subtract) values to get an 'offset' from an address. However it is important to note that an integer address can be anywhere between 0 and 65535 - whereas 'integer arithmetic' works on values from -32768 to +32767. If you do need to add or subtract an offset from a memory address, you *must* use the OPL words UADD or USUB.

UADD (`val1%,val2%` **)** This adds the values of `val1%` and `val2%` as if they were *unsigned* integers - that is, have values from 0 to 65535. Thus, when dealing with memory addresses, you must use, for example,

a%=UADD(ADDR(text%),5)

instead of

a%= ADDR(text%)+5

USUB (`val1%,val2%` **)** This subtracts `val2%` from `val1%` as if they are *unsigned* integers - that is, can have values from 0 to 65535.

To examine the contents of a specific memory area in the Series 3a, you can use one of the five PEEK functions. These functions should do no harm to your Series 3a even if used incorrectly, since they merely 'peek' into a specified memory area, and return what is found there.

p%=**PEEKB**(*address*%)   This examines the contents of the *byte* at the specified *address*%, and stores the value found there in p%. Bytes are used to store *single characters*, such as the code for the letter 'A'.

p%=**PEEKW**(*address*%)   This examines the contents of *two bytes* (known as a '*word*') starting at the address specified by *address*%, and stores the value of whatever is found in those two bytes in p%. Integer *variables* comprise two bytes, the *least* significant byte being stored first. The following short program demonstrates this: when run, you'll notice that the *decimal* value of the least significant *byte* value returned by PEEKB seems to bear no resemblance to the value saved in the two bytes of the integer variable: if you examine the *hexadecimal* values, however, you'll see that the first byte of the integer variable test% (as returned by PEEKB) is, indeed, the *least* significant part of the value. The *decimal* value shown simply represents that hexadecimal value.

```
PROC peekit:
    LOCAL x%,p%,test%
    FONT 11,0
    test%=6789              REM Try your own numbers
    PRINT "Test%=",test%
    PRINT "     in Hex =",HEX$(test%)
    PRINT
    p%=PEEKB(ADDR(test%))
    PRINT "PEEKB Test%=",p%
    PRINT "     in Hex =",HEX$(p%)
    PRINT
    p%=PEEKW(ADDR(test%))
    PRINT "PEEKW Test%=",p%
    PRINT "     in Hex =",HEX$(p%)
    GET
ENDP
```

p&=**PEEKL**(*address*%)   This examines *four bytes* starting at the address specified by *address*%, and returns what is found there as a *long integer* in p&. Long integers are stored in four bytes of memory, with the *least* significant byte stored first and the *most* significant byte stored last.

p=**PEEKF**(*address*%)   This examines *eight bytes*, starting at the address specified by *address*%, and returns whatever is found there as a *floating point* value in p. Floating point values are stored in eight bytes of memory, using a special kind of format. PEEKF converts whatever is found at the eight addresses to the corresponding floating point value.

p$=**PEEK$**(*address*%)   This examines the address specified by *address*%, and whatever value is found there, then returns the contents of that number of following addresses as a *string*. With string variables, the very first memory byte gives the *length* of the string. The rest of the memory stores the string as *character codes*:

As you will have seen from the peekit procedure given on the previous page, with all of these functions, ADDR can be used to specify the address of a variable. Thus,

```
p$=PEEK$(ADDR(var$))
```

will return in p$ the contents of the string variable var$, since ADDR points to the first byte where that string is stored.

The values stored in each element of an array can be found in a similar way. For example, to use a PEEK function to find the value stored in the *third* element of an array 'array%()':

```
p%=PEEKW(ADDR(array%(3)))
```

It must be pointed out that, taking this last case as example, this is the same as

```
p%=array%(3)
```

The difference is, with PEEK and ADDR, you are accessing the variables at the 'machine level'.

Changing memory contents

Just as you can PEEK the contents of specific areas of memory to find out what's there, so you can also POKE data into specific areas of memory. *Since POKE commands overwrite what already exists in memory, their use is potentially dangerous: an error in specifying the address, for example, can mean overwriting valuable data, possibly corrupting files or other programs. Use* POKE *commands with great care!*

There are five POKE commands.

POKEB *address%,c%*　　This stores the *single* byte value (less than 256) of *c%* at the address defined by *address%*.

POKEW *address%,v%*　　This stores the two bytes of the integer value of *v%*, starting at the address defined by *address%*. The two bytes are stored in the conventional manner - that is to say, the least significant byte is 'poked' into the address given by *address%*, and the most significant byte is stored at the next consecutive memory address.

POKEL *address%,v&*　　This stores the four bytes of the ` integer *v&*, starting with the least significant byte at the address defined by *address%*.

POKEF *address%,v*　　This stores the eight byte value of floating point variable *v*, starting at the address defined by *address%*.

**POKE$** *address%,y$*　　This stores the *length* of the string *y$* at the address defined by *address%*, followed by the actual string in the next consecutive memory addresses.

It must be stated again that careless 'poking' in memory can create all kinds of problem, with a potential loss of valuable data and even causing the Series 3a to 'crash'.

Here is a program to demonstrate the use of PEEKing and POKEing. It allows you to enter a text string and a new series of characters to insert within that string together at a specified starting position. Poking the new string using POKE$ will not have the desired effect, since the first byte in the string, which determines its length will also be 'poked' at the new location. The individual characters are PEEKed and POKEd within a loop.

Some error trapping is incorporated, to prevent memory beyond the original string from being corrupted.

The program runs within a loop - press the ESC key while the main dialog is on display to quit.

```
PROC testin:
 LOCAL orig$(20),new$(20),x&,x%,d%
 FONT 11,16
 DO
  dINIT "Text changes"
  dEDIT orig$,"Enter text"
  dEDIT new$,"Enter amendment"
  dLONG x&,"Starting position",0,19
  d%=DIALOG
  IF d%
   x%=x&
   PRINT "Original text    ="
   PRINT orig$
   PRINT
   PRINT "New text         =",new$
   PRINT "Starting at character ";x%
   PRINT
   orig$=insert$:(orig$,new$,x%)
   PRINT "It has changed to:"
   PRINT orig$
   GET
   CLS
  ENDIF
 UNTIL d%=0
ENDP

PROC insert$:(o$,n$,posit%)
 LOCAL oa%,na%,p%,c%,ot$(20),nt$(20)
 nt$=n$
 ot$=o$
 IF LEN(nt$)>LEN(ot$)
  error:("New text too long")
  RETURN
 ELSEIF posit%+LEN(nt$)>LEN(ot$)
  error:("Bad position for new text")
  RETURN
 ENDIF
 oa%=ADDR(ot$)
 na%=UADD(ADDR(nt$),1)          REM Avoid 'length' byte
 c%=0
 DO
  p%=PEEKB(UADD(na%,c%))
  POKEB UADD(oa%,c%+posit%),p%
  c%=c%+1
```

```
  UNTIL c%=LEN(nt$)
  RETURN ot$
ENDP

PROC error:(msg$)
 ALERT(msg$)
ENDP
```

A couple of points to note about this program. First, remember that parameters passed to another procedure cannot be altered - hence the need to re-assign the values, and to return the required amended string to the calling procedure.

Second, when PEEKing the new string, it is important to start at the address after the length descriptor byte - hence the address of the new string is incremented by one. Since the first byte is counted as 'zero', it's not necessary to do this for the original text string's address - you'll count the characters along the string starting with '1' for the first actual character, and so the location will be correctly defined by the position you select.

For this particular example, it must be pointed out that the program could have been written using the 'high level' commands available. To demonstrate, the insert$ procedure could be re-written as follows:

```
PROC insert$:(o$,n$,posit%)
 LOCAL temp$(20)
 IF LEN(n$)>LEN(o$)
   error:("New text too long")
   RETURN
 ELSEIF posit%+LEN(n$)>LEN(o$)
   error:("Bad position for new text")
   RETURN
 ENDIF
temp$=LEFT$(o$,posit%-1)+n$
temp$=temp$+RIGHT$(o$,LEN(o$)-(posit%-1+LEN(n$)))
RETURN temp$
ENDP
```

```
                        Text changes
Enter text         The quick brown fox
·Enter amendment   green
·Starting position 11
```

The insert program dialog...

365

```
Original text    =
The quick brown fox

New text         = green
Starting at character 11

It has changed to:
The quick green fox
```

The result of the insert program

Input and output statements

There is an extensive range of functions and commands, all starting with IO..., which provide direct 'Input/Output' access to files, sound and screen drivers, the keyboard, and so on. Since use of these functions - and an understanding if what they do - demands a knowledge of the operating system, they will not be discussed.

Machine code instructions

A number of instructions are available to access system code. They are all potentially dangerous to use: outline details only of some of the instructions are given here.

USR/USR$ These functions pass *register* values to the central processor unit, and run a machine code program from a specified address: the machine code program must exist in memory or have been written using *Assembly language*, which cannot be achieved on the Series 3a directly without difficulty: such programs require additional programming facilities for their creation.

CALL This passes data to the *registers* of the central processing unit, and 'calls' one of the functions built into the Series 3a's operating system via an *interrupt*: considerable knowledge is required of interrupts, registers and the Series 3a operating system before use of this command can even be contemplated.

OS This function is a more comprehensive variation of CALL, allowing values to be passed to the registers of the central processor unit, and storing the values returned by the registers.

Appendices

Appendix 1

Related keywords

This Appendix groups OPL keywords according to what they do, to help you find the right word for the task in hand, and shows the general format for using the keyword where applicable.

Program control
Controlling flow

USE	TO
BREAK	*Leave a loop and execute the line following the* UNTIL *or* ENDWH *statement*
CONTINUE	*Leave a loop and repeat the test for the loop - either at* UNTIL *or* WHILE.
DO...UNTIL	*Repeat a series of instructions within a loop* until *a condition is met*
ENDP	*Finish the instruction list for a procedure*
ESCAPE ESCAPE ON/OFF	*Disable or enable the stopping of a program from running*
GOTO GOTO *label*::	*Jump to specified label*
IF...ELSEIF... **ELSE...ENDIF**	*Perform instructions provided specified conditions are met*
PAUSE PAUSE *time%*	*Stop the program running for a specified period of time*
PROC PROC *name*: PROC *name*:(*paras*)	*To start a new procedure or function.*
RETURN RETURN RETURN *value*	*Leave a procedure and return to the procedure that called it, returning an integer, floating point or string value.*

`STOP`	*End the program*
`VECTOR...ENDV`	*Jump to one of a list of labels*
`WHILE...ENDWH`	*Repeat a series of instructions within a loop while a condition is met*

Handling memory

USE	TO

`CACHE`
  `CACHE init%,max%`
  `CACHE ON/OFF`
	Prevent procedures from being unloaded from memory when their task is done

`CACHETIDY`	*Remove non-running procedures from cache memory*
`GLOBAL` `GLOBAL` *variable list*	*Declare variables that can be used by called procedures*
`LOADM` `LOADM libfile$`	*Load a translated library module of procedures*
`LOCAL` `LOCAL` *variable list*	*Declare variables unique to the procedure.*
`SPACE` `s%=SPACE`	*Find out how much memory is free on a device that has an opened file.*
`UNLOADM` `UNLOADM libfile$`	*Remove loaded library modules*

Handling errors

USE	TO
`ERR` `e%=ERR`	*Determine an error number*
`ERR$` `e$=ERR$(x%)`	*Display the error message for a given error number*
`ONERR` `ONERR label::`	*Inform the program where to jump to if an error occurs*

RAISE RAISE e%	Generate a specified error condition
REM REM *remark*	Insert a comment in the program
TRAP TRAP *command*	Catch an error that may occur when certain OPL words are used

Text screen display and keyboard inputs

USE	TO
AT AT x%, y%	Position the text cursor
CLS	Clear the text screen
CURSOR CURSOR ON/OFF	Hide or display the cursor. (See also the graphics cursor)
EDIT EDIT a$	Display and edit a string
FONT FONT *fontid%,style%*	Set the text screen font and style.
GET GET g%=GET	Wait for a key to be pressed, and return the code for that key.
GET$ g$=GET	Wait for a key to be pressed, and return the character for that key
INPUT INPUT *variable*	Get an integer, floating point or string value from the keyboard
KEY k%=KEY	Find out if a key has been pressed, and if so, return its code
KEY$ k$=KEY$	Find out if a key has been pressed, and if so, return the character
KMOD k%=KMOD	Find out what combination of modifier keys has been pressed
PRINT PRINT *expression list*	Display text and numbers

SCREEN SCREEN w%,h% SCREEN w%,h%,x%,y%	Set the size and position of the text screen
SCREENINFO SCREENINFO vi%()	Get information about the text window into a declared array
STYLE STYLE style%	Set the font style for the text screen

Numbers

Basic functions

USE	TO
EVAL d=EVAL(str$)	Evaluate the value of a string expression
EXP v=EXP(x)	Raise e to a power
LN a=LN(x)	Get the logarithm of a number to the base e.
LOG a=LOG(x)	Get the logarithm of a number to the base 10.
PI p=pi	Use the value of π.
RANDOMIZE RANDOMIZE x&	Set the 'seed' value for a sequnce of random numbers.
RND r=RND	Get a random number.
SQR s=SQR(x)	For the square root of a number.
x**p	Raise a value x to a power p

Trigonometrical functions

USE	TO
ACOS a=ACOS(x)	*Find the arc cosine (inverse cosine), in radians, of a number between -1 and +1.*
ASIN a=ASIN(x)	*Find the arc sine (or inverse sine), in radians, of a number between -1 and +1.*
ATAN a=ATAN(x)	*Find the arc tangent (or inverse tangent), in radians.*
COS c=COS(radians)	*Find the cosine of an angle given in radians*
DEG d=DEG(radians)	*Convert an angle from radians to degrees*
RAD r=RAD(degrees)	*Convert an angle from degrees to radians*
SIN s=SIN(radians)	*Find the sine of an angle given in radians*
TAN t=TAN(radians)	*Find the tangent of an angle given in radians*

Number lists

USE	TO
MAX m=MAX(n1,n2,n3...) m=MAX(array(),numels)	*Find the largest number in a list*
MEAN m=MEAN(n1,n2,n3...) m=MEAN(array(),numels)	*Find the average of a list*

MIN	Find the smallest number in a list
m=MIN(*n1,n2,n3...*) m=MIN(*array()*,*numels*)	
STD	Find the standard deviation of a list
s=STD(*n1,n2,n3...*) s=STD(*array()*,*numels*)	
SUM	Add all the numbers in a list
s=SUM(*n1,n2,n3...*) s=SUM(*array()*,*numels*)	
VAR	Find the variance of a list
v=VAR(*n1,n2,n3...*) v=VAR(*array()*,*numels*)	

Changing number formats

USE	TO
ABS a=ABS(*x*)	Get the absolute (positive) value of a floating point number
EVAL d=EVAL(*str$*)	Evaluate the value of a string expression
**FIX$** f$=FIX$(*x,dp%,sl%*)	Convert a floating point value to a string of specified length, with a specified number of decimal places.
FLT f=FLT(*x&*)	Convert an integer value to floating point format.
**GEN$** g$=GEN$(*x,dp%*)	Convert a floating point value to a string, with a specified number of decimal places.
**HEX$** h$=HEX$(*x&*)	Convert an integer number into a hexadecimal number, as a string.
IABS i&=IABS(*x&*)	Get the absolute (positive) value of an integer or long integer number.
INT i&=INT(*x*) i%=INT(*x*)	Get the integer part of a floating point number or expression.

INTF `i=INTF(x)`	*Get the integer part of a floating point number, with the result in floating point format.*
NUM$ `n$=NUM$(x,sl%)`	*Convert the integer part of a floating point value to a string of specified length.*
SCI$ `s$=SCI$(x,dp%,sl%)`	*Convert a floating point value to a string of specified length, with a specified number of decimal places, using scientific format*
VAL `v=VAL(numstr$)`	*Convert a string number to numeric format*

Handling strings

USE	TO
ASC `a%=ASC(a$)`	*Find the character code for the first character in a string.*
CHR$ `a$=CHR$(x%)`	*Get the character with a specified character code*
EVAL `d=EVAL(str$)`	*Evaluate the value of a string expression*
LEFT$ `s$=LEFT$(a$,n%)`	*Copy a specified number of characters from the start of a string.*
LEN `a%=LEN(str$)`	*Find the length of a string.*
LOC `p%=LOC(s$,f$)`	*Find the position of a specified string within a larger string.*
LOWER$ `a$=LOWER$(str$)`	*Make a string all lower case.*

**MID$** m$=MID$(s$,f%,n%)	*Copy a specified number of characters from a specified position within a string.*
**REPT$** r$=REPT$(s$,n%)	*Repeat a specified string a specified number of times.*
**RIGHT$** r$=RIGHT$(s$,n%)	*Copy a specified number of characters from the end of a string.*
**UPPER$** u$=UPPER$(str$)	*Make a string all upper case.*
VAL v=VAL(numstr$)	*Convert a string number to numeric format*

The graphics screen

Displaying graphics text (and numbers)

USE	TO

BUSY
  BUSY msg$
  BUSY msg$,p%
  BUSY msg$,p%,delay%
	Display a short, flashing message

gAT gAT x%,y%	*Set the pixel location for the next gPRINT*
gFONT gFONT fontid%	*Set the graphics font*

GIPRINT
  GIPRINT msg$
  GIPRINT msg$,p%
	Display a message for a few seconds

gPRINT gPRINT expression list	*Display graphic text (and numbers)*

gPRINTB
  gPRINTB t$,w%
  gPRINTB t$,w%,a%
  gPRINTB t$,w%,a%,tp%
  gPRINTB t$,w%,a%,tp%,bt%
  gPRINTB t$,w%,a%,tp%,bt%,m%
	Display graphic text (and numbers) in a cleared box of a specified size

gPRINTCLIP w%=gPRINTCLIP(text$,width%)	*Display graphic text clipped to length*
gTMODE gTMODE mode%	*Set whether graphics text should set, clear or invert pixels*
gTWIDTH width%=gTWIDTH(text$)	*Find width required by graphic text*
gXPRINT gXPRINT str$,flags%	*Display graphic text underlined and or highlighted*

Setting graphic styles

USE	TO
gFONT gFONT fontid%	*Set the graphics font*
gGMODE gGMODE mode%	*Set whether graphics should set, clear or invert pixels*
gSTYLE gSTYLE style%	*Set format for graphics text to bold, underline, inverse, double height, monspace, italic*
gTMODE gTMODE mode%	*Set whether graphics text should set, clear or invert pixels*

Managing windows and bitmaps

USE	TO
DEFAULTWIN DEFAULTWIN 1	Allow the default window (1) to have a grey plane
gCLOSE gCLOSE id%	Close the specified window or bitmap
gCLS	Clear a window or bitmap
gCOPY gCOPY id%,x%,y%,w%,h%,mode%	Copy a a specified area from one window or bitmap to another
gCREATE id%=gCREATE(x%,y%,w%,h%,v%,g%)	Create a new window
gCREATEBIT id%=gCREATEBIT(w%,h%)	Create a bitmap in memory
gGREY gGEY mode%	Set which planes of the current window are to be used
gHEIGHT h%=gHEIGHT	Find the height of the current window or bitmap
gIDENTITY id%=gIDENTITY	Find the id number of the current window or bitmap
gINFO gINFO vinfo%()	Get information about the current bitmap and cursor
gLOADBIT id%=gLOADBIT(n$) id%=gLOADBIT(n$,wr%) id%=gLOADBIT(n$,wr%,i%)	Load a bitmap from a file
gORDER gORDER id%,level%	Set the level of a specified window

gORIGINX `x%=gORIGINX`	*Find the distance in pixels between the left of the screen and the left of a window*
gORIGINY `y%=gORIGINY`	*Find the distance in pixels between the top of the screen and the top of a window*
gPATT `gPATT id%,w%,h%,mode%`	*Fill a rectangle of specified size with repetitions of a selected window or bitmap*
gPEEKLINE `gPEEKLINE id%,x%,y%,d%(),ln%`	*Read pixel data from a horizontal line in a window or bitmap*
gRANK `r%=gRANK`	*Find the level of a specified window*

gSAVEBIT
    `gSAVEBIT n$`
    `gSAVEBIT n$,w%,h%`
	Save a window or bitmap

gSETWIN
    `gSETWIN x%,y%`
    `gSETWIN x%,y%,w%,h%`
	Size and/or position a window

gUSE `gUSE id%`	*Specify which window or bitmap to use*
gVISIBLE `gVISIBLE ON/OFF`	*Make a window visible or invisible*
gWIDTH `w%=gWIDTH`	*Find the width of the current window or bitmap*

Creating drawings

USE	TO

CURSOR
`CURSOR id%`
`CURSOR id%,asc%,w%,h%`
`CURSOR id%,asc%,w%,h%,t%`
	Switch on the graphics cursor, and specify its shape and position.

gAT `gAT x%,y%`	*Directly set the pixel location for the next drawing action*

gBORDER
`gBORDER flags%`
`gBORDER flags%,w%,h%`
	Draw a specified type of border round the current window - or a special border type box within a window

gBOX `gBOX w%,h%`	*Draw a box of specified height and width from the current pixel location*
gBUTTON `gBUTTON t$,t%,w%,h%,s%`	*Draw a 3-D button with text on it*

gCLOCK
`gCLOCK ON/OFF`
`gCLOCK ON,m%`
`gCLOCK ON,m%,os%`
`gCLOCK ON,m%,os%,f$`
`gCLOCK ON m%,os%,f$,f%`
`gCLOCK ON,m%,os%,f$,f%,s%`
	Display a digital or analogue clock in one of a wide variety of types and sizes

gDRAWOBJECT `gDRAWOBJECT t%,f%,w%,h%`	*Draw a 'lozenge' of specified size*
gFILL `gFILL w%,h%,mode%`	*Set, clear or invert a rectangle of specified size*
gINVERT `gINVERT w%,h%`	*Invert the state of the pixels in a specified rectangle*
gLINEBY `gLINEBY dx%,dy%`	*Draw a line from the current pixel location to a point a specified distance away*

gLINETO `gLINETO x%,y%`	*Draw a line from the current pixel location to a location specified in absolute terms*
gMOVE `gMOVE dx%,dy%`	*Set the pixel location for the next drawing action, relative to its current position*
gPATT `gPATT id%,w%,h%,mode%`	*Fill a rectangle of specified size with repetitions of a selected window or bitmap*
gPOLY `gPOLY a%()`	*Draw a sequence of lines*

gSCROLL
`gSCROLL dx%,dy%`
`gSCROLL dx%,dy%,x%,y%,w%,h%`
	Scroll a specified rectangle

gUPDATE
`gUPDATE`
`gUPDATE ON/OFF`
	Change the way the sceen is updated

gX `x%=gX`	*Get the current graphics horizontal pixel location*

gXBORDER
`gXBORDER t%,f%`
`gXBORDER t%,f%,w%,h%`
	Draw a specified type of border round the current window - or a box with a specified type of border type within a window - with shadows in grey

gY `y%=gY`	*Get the current graphics vertical pixel location*

Handling sprites

USE	TO
APPENDSPRITE APPENDSPRITE `t%,vbm$()` APPENDSPRITE `t%,vbm$(),dx%,dy%`	*Add a single bitmap to the current sprite*
CHANGESPRITE CHANGESPRITE `bs%,t%,vbm$()` CHANGESPRITE `bs%,t%,vbm$(),dx%,dy%`	*Change a set of bitmaps in the current sprite*
CLOSESPRITE CLOSESPRITE `spid%`	*Close a sprite*
CREATESPRITE `spid%=CREATESPRITE`	*Create a sprite*
DRAWSPRITE DRAWSPRITE `x%,y%`	*Draw the current sprite at a specified location*
POSSPRITE POSSPRITE `x%,y%`	*Re-position a sprite to a specified location*

Handling the status window

USE	TO
DIAMINIT DIAMINIT `pos%,str1$,str2$...`	*Initialise a Diamond list for display in the status window*
DIAMPOS DIAMPOS `p%`	*Position the Diamond against an item in the diamond list*
SETNAME SETNAME `name$`	*Set the name of the program for display in the status window*
STATUSWIN STATUSWIN ON/OFF STATUSWIN ON,`type%`	*Display or hide the staus window*
STATWININFO `t%=STATWININFO(type%,vxy%)`	*Get information about the status window*

Time and date

USE	TO
DATETOSECS `s&=DATETOSECS(y%,m%,d%,h%,mn%,sc%)`	*Get the number of seconds between 1st January 1970 and a specified date and time.*
DATIM$ `d$=DATIM$`	*Get the current day, date and time from the system clock, as a string.*
DAY `d%=DAY`	*Get the current day of the month from the system clock.*
DAYNAME$ `d$=DAYNAME$(x%)`	*Get the day name from a specified day number.*
DAYS `d&=DAYS(day%,month%,year%)`	*Get the number of days from 1st Jan 1900 to a specified date.*
DOW `d%=DOW(day%,month%,year%)`	*Get the day of the week, as a number, for a specified date.*
HOUR `h%=HOUR`	*Get the hour from the system clock.*
MINUTE `m%=MINUTE`	*Get the current minute from the system clock.*
MONTH `m%=MONTH`	*Get the current month number from the system clock.*
MONTH$ `m$=MONTH$(x%)`	*Get the month name from a specified month number.*

SECOND `s%=SECOND`	*Get the current second from the system clock.*

SECSTODATE
`SECSTODATE s&,vy%,vm%,vd%,`
`        vh%,vmn%,vsec%,vyd%`
	Convert a number of seconds from 1st January 1970 to a date and time.

WEEK `w%=WEEK(day%,month%,year%)`	*Get the week number within a year in which a specified date falls.*
YEAR `y%=YEAR`	*Get the current year from the system clock.*

Handling Dialogs

USE	TO

ALERT
`r%=ALERT(m1$)`
`r%=ALERT(m1$,m2$)`
`r%=ALERT(m1$,m2$,b1$)`
`r%=ALERT(m1$,m2$,b1$,b2$)`
`r%=ALERT(m1$,m2$,b1$,b2$,b3$)`
	Display a simple 'alert' dialog

dBUTTONS
`dBUTTONS p1$,k1%`
`dBUTTONS p1$,k1%,p2$,k2$`
`dBUTTONS p1$,k1%,p2$,k2$,p3$,k3$`
	Define exit buttons for use in a dialog

dCHOICE `dCHOICE vch%,p$,list$`	*Define a list of options for selection.*
dDATE `dDATE vd&,p$,min&,max&`	*Define an edit box for the entry of a date.*

dEDIT
`dEDIT vstr$,p$`
`dEDIT vstr$,p$,len%`
	Define a text edit box.

dFILE dFILE *vstr$*,*p$*,*fn%*	*Define a file name edit box.*
dFLOAT dFLOAT *vf*,*p$*,*min*,*max*	*Define an edit box for the entry of floating point numbers*
DIALOG d%=DIALOG	*Display the dialog and wait for the appropriate keypress(es)*
dINIT dINIT *title$*	*Start a new dialog.*
dLONG dLONG *vl&*,*p$*,*min&*,*max&*	*Define an edit box for the entry of integers.*
dPOSITION dPOSITION *x%*,*y%*	*Position the dialog on the screen.*
dTEXT dTEXT *p$*,*text$* dTEXT *p$*,*text$*,*effect%*	*Display a line of text in a dialog.*
dTIME dTIME *vl&*,*p$*,*t%*,*min&*,*max&*	*Define an edit box for the entry of time information.*
dXINPUT dXINPUT *vstr$*,*p$*	*Define an edit box for the entry of 'secret' information.*

Handling Menus

USE	TO
mINIT	*Start a new menu set.*
mCARD mCARD *t$*,*nl$*,*k1%*...*nn$*,*kn%*	*Define a pull-down menu set.*
MENU v%=MENU v%=MENU(*vinit%*)	*Display the menu.*

File management
General

USE	TO
COPY `COPY source$,dest$`	*Copy a file to another place.*
DELETE `DELETE file$`	*Delete a file.*
DIR$ `d$=DIR$(path$),` *then* `d$=DIR$("")`	*Find out what files exist in a directory.*
EXIST `e%=EXIST(file$)`	*Check whether a file exists.*
MKDIR `MKDIR dirname$`	*Create a new directory.*
RENAME `RENAME old$,new$`	*Rename and/or move a file to a new destination.*
RMDIR `RMDIR dirname$`	*Delete a directory*
SETPATH `SETPATH path$`	*Set the directory to be used for file access.*

Handling data files

USE	TO
CLOSE	*Close the current data file*
COMPRESS `COMPRESS source$,dest$`	*Copy a data file or append it to another data file, removing deleted records,*
CREATE `CREATE fname$,log,f1...fn`	*Create a new data file.*
OPEN `OPEN fname$,log,f1...fn`	*Open a data file for read/write operations.*

OPENR	Open a data file for read-only operations.
`OPENR fname$,log,f1...fn`	
USE	Select an open file for subsequent actions.
`USE logical id`	

Handling data file records

USE	TO
APPEND	Add a new record to the currently opened file
BACK	Select the previous rfecord in a currently opened data file
COUNT `c%=COUNT`	Find out how many records there are in the currently opened data file.
EOF `e%=EOF`	Test whether the end of the file has been reached.
ERASE	Delete the current record from the current file.
FIND `f%=FIND(str$)`	Search records for a specified string
FINDFIELD `f%=FINDFIELD(str$,st%,no%,f%)`	Search specified fields for a specified string.
FIRST	Select the first record in the currently opened file
LAST	Select the last record in the currently opened data file.

NEXT	*Select the next record in the currently opened data file.*
POS `p%=POS`	*Determine the current record number.*
POSITION `POSITION recno%`	*Select a specified record number in the currently opened data file.*
RECSIZE `r%=RECSIZE`	*Determine the number of bytes used by the current record.*
UPDATE	*Change the current record's details to the current assignments.*

Sound

USE	TO
BEEP `BEEP time%,pitch%`	*Sound the internal buzzer*

Creating Applications

USE	TO
APP `APP` *name*	*Initialise the definition for an application.*
ENDA	*Complete the application description*
EXT `EXT` *extension*	*Specify the extension for files*
ICON `ICON` *path and filename*	*Specify the icon file*

PATH PATH *path*	*Specify a path for files*
TYPE TYPE *value*	*Define the type of the application.*

System level instructions

USE	TO
ADDR a%=ADDR (*variable*)	*Find the address of a variable in memory*
CMD$ c$=CMD$ (*x%*)	*Get the command line arguments when starting an application*
GETCMD$ w$=GETCMD$	*Get the new command arguments when an appliaction is running*
GETEVENT GETEVENT **va**%*()*	*Get a system event*
LOCK LOCK ON/OFF	*Prevent system events from affecting an application*
PARSE$ p$=PARSE$(*f$,pth$,***voff**%*())*	*Get the full file path specification*
PEEK$ p$=PEEK$(*addr%*)	*Get the string, the length of which is at the specified address*
PEEKB p%=PEEKB(*addr%*)	*Get the byte at the specified address.*
PEEKF p=PEEKF(*addr%*)	*Get the floating point value, saved in the eight bytes starting at the specified address*
PEEKL p&=PEEKL(*addr%*)	*Get the four-byte long integer starting at the specified address.*

PEEKW `p%=PEEKW(addr%)`	*Get the two-byte integer starting at the specified address*
POKE\$ * `POKE$ addr%,str$`	*Write a string, starting at the specified address*
POKEB * `POKEB addr%,b%`	*Write a byte at the specified address.*
POKEF * `POKEF% addr%,v`	*Write an eight-byte floating point value, starting at the specified address*
POKEL * `POKEL addr%,v&`	*Write a four-byte long integer starting at the specified address.*
POKEW * `POKEW addr%,x%`	*Write a two-byte integer starting at the specified address*
TESTEVENT `t%=TESTEVENT`	*Find out if a system event has occured*
UADD `addr%=UADD(val1%,val2%)`	*Add two unsigned integers - for adding an offset to an address*
USUB `addr%=(val1%-val2%)`	*Subtract two unsigned integers - for subtracting an offset from an address*

* USE THESE COMMANDS WITH EXTREME CAUTION!

Note: Variables shown with a leading bold 'v' (eg `vinfo()`) receive data from the function, and must have been declared.

Writing for the Series 3

You may wish to prepare a program that will run on a Psion Series 3 - using the optional 'S3 Translate' facility (Prog Menu of the Program editor). Series 3 programs will run correctly on a Series 3a in compatibility mode, but to create programs for a Series 3 on a Series 3a, you must be aware of the following differences between the two machines.

General differences

	Series 3	Series 3a
Diamond key display	Not available	Yes - can be programmed for status window use.
Grey plane	No: programming words and parameters associated with the grey plane are not available	Yes - and catered for by many graphics commands.
Screen size	240 x 80 pixels For Series 3 programs running on a Series 3a, each pixel occupies a block of 4x4 pixels.	480 x 160 pixels.
Sprites	Not available	Yes
Status window	50 pixels wide only	64 pixels wide, 32 pixels wide, or 50 pixels wide for Series 3 compatability

Menus

	Series 3	Series 3a
Menu Options	*Six*	*Eight*
Initial Highlight	*No*	*Yes - using* v%=MENU(**v**init%)
Case dependent hot keys	*No*	*Yes*

Dialogs

	Series 3	Series 3a
Number of lines	*Six*	*Eight*

Program language differences

Series 3a words indicated by 'New' are not available on the Series 3, and obviously shouldn't be used if writing programs to be translated for the Series 3.

	Series 3a
BEEP	*Cannot play notes as high as those on the Series 3*
CACHE CACHETIDY	*New -to allow procedure cacheing for extra speed*
CURSOR	*Can display new types of graphic cursor*
DIAMINIT	*New: initialises diamond display in status window*
DIAMPOS	*New - positions diamond in status window.*
FINDFIELD	*New - searches for a specified string in specified fields (*FIND *searches all fields)*

FONT	New - sets font and style for text displayed on the text screen.
gBUTTON	New - draws 3D buttons shown raised, normal or depressed.
gCLOCK	Supports Series 3 type clock displays, plus many new ones
gDRAWOBJECT	New - draws a lozenge shape
gFONT	Accesses more fonts as well as Series 3 compatible fonts
gINFO	Returns additional data about the cursor
gPEEKLINE	On the Series 3a, can read the whole screen, not just a window.
gXBORDER	New - draws bordered boxes like those used for dialogs
SPRITE commands	All new.
STATUSWIN	Allows different types of status window to be displayed.
STATWININFO	New - returns data aboput the status window
STYLE	New - sets a style for text displayed on the text screen
TYPE	Supports new actions and larger black and grey icons, and allows different icons to be specified for Series 3 and 3a
UADD	New, for address pointer arithmetic avoiding integer overflow errors
USUB	New, for address pointer arithmetic avoiding integer overflow errors

Series 3a compatibility mode

Programs written on a Psion Series 3 will run on the Series 3a in 'compatibility mode'. That means the screen will emulate the screen of a Psion Series 3 - where every Series 3 screen pixel is represented by a block of four pixels (2x2) on the Series 3a. All the keywords that specify a screen position (such as AT, gAT, gMOVE and so on) are automatically rescaled.

There is a slightly different set of symbols with character codes between 0 and 31 on the Series 3a: however, when in the 'compatibility mode', the Series 3a uses the Series 3 fonts.

Similarly, programs written on a Psion Series 3a and translated using the 'S3 Translate' option will run on the Series 3a in compatibility mode.

When writing programs for the Series 3 using the Series 3a, you must obviously remember not to use the language words and fonts available only to the Series 3a.

Error messages

Error messages have an error number (negative) as indicated in this Appendix. This number can be used to produce a specific error in your program (using RAISE number%*), so that, with appropriate handling routines, you can catch potential errors. For example, if a zero is input as divisor, you could use* RAISE -2 *(*Invalid *arguments) as a warning, but remember that your program must have an error trapping routine (such as* ONERR*) to deal with the 'error' so created.*

Note that some of the errors listed are significant only to professional programmers, and are given here for completeness.

Error Number	Error Message
General errors	
-1	General failure
-2	Invalid arguments (*for example, if an integer variable is used where a string variable is expected in an argument sequence*)
-3	O/S error
-4	Service not supported
-5	Underflow (*a number is too small*)
-6	Overflow (*a number is too large*)
-7	Out of range (*an array subscript, for example*)
-8	Divide by zero
-9	In use (*a port, for example, currently being used by another program*)
-10	No system memory
-11	Segment table full.
-12	Semaphore table full

-13	Process table full (*too many processes are running*)
-14	Resource already open
-15	Resource not open
-16	Invalid image or device file
-17	No receiver
-18	Device table full
-19	File system not found (*for example, if the connection to a remote computer is broken*)
-20	Failed to start
-21	Font not loaded (*for user defined fonts*)
-22	Too wide (*for example, a string for a dialog has too many characters*)
-23	Too many items (*in a dialog*)
-24	Batteries too low for digital audio
-25	Batteries too low to write to Flash
-26 to -31	*Currently not in use*

File and device errors

-32	File already exists (*for example, when trying to save a file with an identical name to another*)
-33	File does not exist (*for example, when trying to open a non-existant file*)
-34	Write failed
-35	Read failed
-36	End of file
-37	Disk full
-38	Invalid name
-39	Access denied (*for example, to a locked or protected file on a remote computer*)
-40	File or device in use
-41	Device does not exist (*trying to save to an SSD that has been removed, for example*)

-42	Directory does not exist
-43	Record too large (*it's over the 1022 characters maximum allowed for a record*)
-44	Read only file (*when trying to write data to a file that has been opened for read only*)
-45	Invalid I/O request
-46	I/O operation pending
-47	Invalid volume (*usually means a corrupted disk*)
-48	I/O cancelled
-49	*Currently not used*
-50	Disconnected
-51	Connected
-52	Too many retries
-53	Line failure
-54	Inactivity timeout
-55	Incorrect parity
-56	Serial frame
-57	Serial overrun
-58	Cannot connect to remote modem
-59	Remote modem busy
-60	No answer from remote modem
-61	Number is black listed
-62	Not ready
-63	Unknown media (*corrupt SSD*)
-64	Root directory full (*the maximum amount of memory available for a root directory - on a given device - has been reached*)
-65	Write protected
-66	Media is corrupt
-67	User abandoned
-68	Erase pack failure
-69	Wrong file type

Translator errors

-70	Missing "" (*the leading or trailing quotes have been omitted*)
-71	String too long
-72	Unexpected name
-73	Name too long (*files, procedures and variable names have a maximum length of eight characters*)
-74	Logical device must be A-D (*for example, assigning a logical device letter of 'F' when creating a new file*)
-75	Bad field name
-76	Bad number
-77	Syntax error
-78	Illegal character (*for example, using a backslash or a comma in a file name*)
-79	Function argument error
-80	Type mismatch (*for example, if a string is being assigned to an integer variable*)
-81	Missing label
-82	Duplicate name
-83	Declaration error (*for example, a string is declared without specifiying the number of characters*)
-84	Bad array size
-85	Structure fault (*for example, a missing* ENDIF, ENDWH *or* UNTIL *statement*)
-86	Missing ENDP
-87	Syntax error
-88	Mismatched (or)
-89	Bad field list
-90	Too complex
-91	Missing ,
-92	Variables too large

-93	Bad assignment
-94	Bad array index
-95	Inconsistent procedure arguments

Language specific errors

-96	Illegal Opcode (*corrupt program file -translate it again*)
-97	Wrong number of arguments
-98	Undefined externals (*a variable has been encountered which hasn't been declared: this usually means a typing error has been made in entering the variable's name*)
-99	Procedure not found (*either it hasn't been entered, or it has been misspelled*)
-100	Field not found
-101	File already open
-102	File not open
-103	Record too big (*data file contains a record too large for OPL*)
-104	Module already loaded (*trying to load an already loaded file with* LOADM)
-105	Maximum modules loaded (*only four can be loaded at a time with* LOADM)
-106	Module does not exist (LOADM *specifies a file that cannot be found*)
-107	Incompatible translator version (*an OPL file needs to be translated again*)
-108	Module not loaded (*using* UNLOADM *to unload a file that hasn't been loaded*)
-109	Bad file type (*the data file header is wrong or has been corrupted*)
-110	Type violation (*for example, passing an integer to a function which expects a string*)
-111	Subscript or dimension error (*specifying an array element higher than the number declared for the array*)

-112	String too long
-113	Device already open (*when using* LOPEN)
-114	Escape key pressed
-115	Incompatible runtime version
-116	ODB file(s) not closed
-117	Maximum drawables open (*you can't have more than eight windows and/or bitmaps opened at a time*)
-118	Drawable not open
-119	Invalid Window (*an attempt has been made to perform a window-type operation on a bitmap*)
-120	Screen access denied (*when running a program from the calculator*)

Glossary of terms

For those unfamiliar with some of the words used in computing, here is a glossary.

Address
A reference to a location in memory, usually written as a hexadecimal number.

Alpha-numeric
Alphabetical and numerical characters, a-z, A-Z and 0-9 inclusive

Application
An application on the Series 3a is a program specially prepared so that it can be installed with an icon on the system screen display.

Argument
A value needed by a *function* in order to complete a calculation. For example, in LOG(x), 'x' is the argument for the LOGarithm function.

Array
A particular type of variable that can have a number of 'elements', each identified by a number, and each storing different data of the same type. For example nop%(3) is an *integer* array variable with three elements, each of which can store an integer value. The three elements can be selected by referring to them as nop%(1), nop%(2) and nop%(3).

Arrow keys
The four keyboard keys, marked with arrows to denote direction, used to move the cursor on the screen.

ASCII
American Standard Code for Information Interchange. ASCII characters are defined as the first 128 (0-127) in a character set, and are reasonably consistent amongst all computers. Extended ASCII characters range from 128-255, and a number of

different sets are used by computers. An ASCII file (otherwise often known as a 'text file', generally uses only characters with codes 32 - 126.

Assign

This is the action of giving a variable a value. For example, m$="great" assigns the word *great* to the string variable m$.

Binary

The numbering system used in computers. It uses only two digits - a zero, and a one. Any number can be represented in binary.

Bit

A binary digit. In computers, numbers are stored in memory blocks of 8, 16 or 32 binary digits or *bits.*

Bitmap

A 'window' that is stored in memory, rather than being displayed on the screen. Each memory location stores information for 8 pixels: '1' representing a set pixel, and '0' an unset pixel.

Buffer

A special memory area for the temporary storage of data. For example, the keyboard has a 'buffer' memory, where a character is stored until examined by an application or program: once examined, the buffer memory is cleared.

Call

When program flow is directed from one procedure to another procedure (or function), the second procedure is *called..* Once the second procedure has completed its task, program flow returns to the first procedure, to a point immediately following the *call..*

Character

A letter or number or symbol *shape.* Each character can be identified by a code number: for example the letter 'A' has the code number 65, and the letter 'a' has the code number 97.

Command   An instruction to perform an action.

Concatenate   To join two or more *strings* together.

Current   Psion Series 3a actions have to be directed to one window, one file or one record at a time - known as the *current* window, file or record. Similarly, there are various 'modes' for printing and so on: the latest mode selected is the *current* mode.

Cursor   The screen marker or pointer, used mainly for text inputs, which shows where the next 'action' on the screen will be.

Database   Data stored as a collection of records, so that it can be easily retrieved.

Declare   Psion Series 3a needs to be informed of the names of *variables* that will be used in a program, so that the appropriate amount of memory can be reserved for saving data assigned to them. The variables are *declared*.

Device   A piece of hardware, such as a Solid State Disk or printer.

Dialog box   A displayed box in which specific information is imparted, requested, or both, allowing the user to communicate and interact with the application.

Directory   A named group of files or sub-directories in a hierarchical system.

Expression   A calculation that can be evaluated to a single value. $(2*(d+w)*h)+(w*d)$, for example is an expression: provided each of the variables has been assigned a value, it can be resolved to a single value.

Extension   In keeping with the file naming system used on desktop PCs, Psion Series 3a file names comprise two parts. The first part is up to eight letters and numbers (and one or two other accepted characters) long, without a space. This is separated from the second part - the *extension* - by a full point. The second part is up to three characters long, and is usually three letters which indicate the *type* of the file. For example, a *source* code file saved when you name a program has the extension '.OPL', whilst the *running* code file has an extension of '.OPD'.

False

To help control program flow, conditions are tested to see whether they are true or false. For example, IF c=4 is a test on the value of c. If c *doesn't* equal 4, the result is said to be *false* (the result is represented in the computer by a zero) and the ensuing set of instructions is ignored. If, in this example, c *does* equal 4, then the result is *true* (represented in the computer by a -1), and the ensuing set of instructions will be performed. When *testing* for a *true* or *non-zero* condition, however, *any* value other than zero results in 'true'. Thus, whether c had a value of 4, 9 or -34, an IF c test would result in *true*. If the value of c is zero, then the result of the test would be *false*.

Field

In a database file, each *part* or *item* of a record is known as a field.

File

A file is *data* stored in memory and given a name so that it can be recalled. The data can be for a program source code or its running code, a database, a document, spreadsheet, and so on.

File name

The exclusive name given to a computer file. The Psion Series 3a uses the file name format of eight characters, a full point, and three characters.

Floating point

Any number or value that has or is allowed to have a decimal point.

Function

A programming word or procedure that acts on *arguments* to return a calculated value. For example, LOG(x) is a function that calculates the logarithm of 'x'. When named in a program line, the function is *called* to effectively replace the 'LOG(x)' with the actual value of the logarithm of 'x' ('x' must, of course, have a value).

Hexa-decimal

A system of counting used in computers: whereas in the decimal system numbers range from 0 to 9 (10 in all), in *hexadecimal* numbers range from 0 to 15 (16 in all), with the letters A to F used to represent the numbers 10 to 15. This system is far more convenient for computer calculations than the decimal system.

Increment

To increase the value of a number, usually by one.

Integer

Any whole number *without* a decimal point in it anywhere. In the Psion Series 3a integers are limited to whole numbers between -32768 and +32767. Integer variables are identified by a '%' sign after their name.

Logical file

When a file is opened from within a program, it is given an identifying letter - a, b, c or d (only four are allowed). This identifying letter is the file's *logical* name, and can be used to select the file for subsequent actions.

Long integer

Like integers, a long integer is any number *without* a decimal point in it. The difference is, in the Psion Series 3a, long integers can have whole number values between -2147483648 and +2147483647.

	Long integer variables are identified by a '&' sign after their name.
Machine code	The instructions which *directly* control the computer.
Nesting	Certain types of programming constructions - such as DO...UNTIL, and IF...ENDIF - can be placed within other similar constructions. They are said to be *nested* . Each nested construction must be properly terminated.
Parameter	A value passed from one procedure to another when it is *called*.
Procedure	A set of instructions to perform one (or more) tasks within a program. In the Psion Series 3a the first line of a procedure is *always* the word PROC followed by the procedure's name, a colon, and then arguments or parameters (if any) within brackets, and the last line is always ENDP.
Program	A complete set of instructions to a computer, to perform a specific task or set of tasks. In the Psion Series 3a programs are constructed using one or more *procedures.*
Source code	The instructions written in a programming language, such as OPL, which are easier to understand, but which have to be translated into the machine code that the computer understands.
SSD	Solid State Disk - a memory storage device - as used by the Series 3a.
Statement	A complete programming instruction involving one of the language words and its arguments.
String	A series of *characters*.
True	*See 'False'*

Variable   A named area in memory where specific types of (changing) data can be stored. By *naming* the area, the memory can be accessed simply by reference to the *name*. There are several types of variable - catering for the different types of data to be stored: each type requires a different amount of memory. The variable type is defined by a suffix identifier. Thus:

x   The variable's name is 'x', and the lack of an identifier means it is *floating-point* variable.

y%   The variable's name is 'y', and the '%' sign identifies it as an *integer* type.

g&   The variable's name is 'g', and the '&' sign identifies it as a *long integer* type: it can hold larger numbers than ordinary *integers*..

s$ the variable's name is 's', and the '$' sign identifies it as a *string* variable.

Note that the identifier is a part of the variable's name, so a, a%, a& and a$ are all *different* variables, each requiring a different amount of storage space in memory.

Window   A rectangular area of the screen, usually but not always outlined by a box. Graphic and text displays always take place within a window, and up to 9 graphic windows can be defined at any one time, though not all of them need be visible. One full screen window is always 'open'.

INDEX

OPL words are shown in capital letters.
Programs are listed under 'PROGRAMS'.

INDEX

INDEX

INDEX

Y